Ad or Media Agency Agree

Legally Binding

Business Agreement, Legal Forms Book

Copyright ® 2017 Julien Coallier

An Archetype Publishing Production

License Notes

This book is licensed for your personal enjoyment and usage. This book / ebook may not be re-sold or given away to other people unless additional copies are purchased. If you enjoy this book / ebook and have not yet purchased, please buy this book at an authorized book store.

Ad or Media Agency Agreement
Review List

This review list is provided to inform you about the document in question and to assist you in completing it.

1. This Agreement is primarily of benefit to the Agency. As a result, you as the Media User should be able to exact substantially better terms for your company in return for making this medium or long-term agreement. Favorable terms should apply to getting as many extra services at no or minimal charges, as well as negotiating a favorable hourly or percentage rate. You should review this exercise as no different than in negotiating terms with any outside vendor when predictability, volume, and a long-term agreement are of substantial value to them with all of their customers.

2. If you can not obtain favorable terms, you should consider tabling the Agreement other than to assure that all materials involving them are out rightly owned by your company with no further payments due them. This Agreement has provisions that apply to this concern and can be extracted from it for your firm's benefit.

3. Each party should review the terms of the Agency Agreement to make sure you are both comfortable with all of the provisions, particularly concerning:

    Agency's dealings with other companies
    Media User's dealings with other agencies
    Ownership of advertisements and other materials

4. As a practical matter, print at least two copies and have them signed in the original so both parties have an original for their records.

5. Laws do vary somewhat from state to stat and are modified by both statute and legal precedent over time. This is always a good reason to have a lawyer review any agreement, including this one, for hidden problems.

Ad or other Media Agency Agreement

This Agency Agreement ("Agreement") is made and effective this _____ (Date), by and between ("Agency") and _____ (Your Firm) ("Media User").

Agency is in the business of providing media agency services for a fee.

Media User desires to engage Agency to render, and Agency desires to render to Media User, certain Agency services, all as set forth.

NOW, THEREFORE, in consideration of the mutual agreements and covenants herein contained, the parties hereto agree as follows:

1. Engagement.

Media User engages Agency to render, and Agency agrees to render to Media User, services in connection with Media User's planning, preparing and placing of advertising and other media services for certain of Media User's products as follows:

_____

A. Analyze Media User's current and proposed products and services and presentations and potential markets.

B. Create, prepare and submit to Media User for its prior approval advertising ideas, media suggestions, and other such related programs.

C. Prepare and submit to Media User for its prior approval estimates of costs and expenses associated with proposed advertising ideas and programs prior to any such implementation or financial commitment.

D. Design and prepare, or arrange for the design and preparation of advertisements, public relations, and other such materials.

E. Perform such other services as Media User may request from time to time such as, but not limited to, direct mail ad preparations, speech writing, publicity and public relations work, market research and analysis, and other similar and related activities.

F. Order advertising space, time or other means to be used for publication of Media User's advertisements, at all times endeavoring to secure the most efficient and advantageous rates available. All such activities to be approved in advance by the Media User unless otherwise written and stipulated.

G. Proof for accuracy and completeness of insertions, displays, broadcasts, or other forms of advertisements.

H. Audit invoices for proper and agreed upon space, time, material preparation and charges.

2. Products.

Agency's engagement shall relate to the following products and services of Media User:

_____.

3. Exclusivity.

Agency shall be the Agency in the United States and worldwide for Media User with respect to the products described in Section 2 above, unless otherwise specified in this section:

_____.

4. Compensation.

A. Agency shall receive an amount equal to ___ percentage of the gross charges levied by media for advertising placed by Agency pursuant to this Agreement; and   after volume discount, of the charges of suppliers of services or properties, such as finished art, comprehensive layouts, type composition, photostats, engravings, printing, radio and television programs, talent, literary, dramatic and musical works, records and exhibits, purchased by Agency on Media User's authorization during the term of this Agreement; provided that: No percentage will be added to Agency charges for packing, shipping, express, postage, telephone, telex, fax, travel expenses and other out of pocket expenses of Agency personnel.

B. For those items where Agency is not compensated on a commission basis, Media User shall pay Agency on an hourly basis for services provided hereunder. The rate will be determined by the type of services provided and the person or persons providing such services, but in no event shall the rate exceed _____ per hour. Media User may elect in advance to be charged on this hourly rate basis. If Media User fails to notify Agency of its choice, it shall be presumed that Media User elected to be charged on a percentage basis.

C. In the event that Agency undertakes, at Media User's request subject to Media User's prior approval, special projects such as those described in Section I.F above, Agency shall prepare an estimate of total charges for any such special project in advance, including any charges for materials or services purchased from outside vendors. In the event that Media User elects to proceed with the special project based upon Agency's estimated cost, Agency shall perform the services with respect to such special project at its estimated cost, subject to modification as mutually agreed by the parties.

D. For any special project or other services provided by Agency pursuant to this Agreement upon which the parties have not agreed as to charges, Media User shall pay
Agency at its regular percentage rates, as stated in Section 4.A above.

E. Media User shall not be obligated to reimburse Agency for any travel or other out-of-pocket expenses incurred in the performance of services pursuant to this Agreement unless expressly agreed by Media User in advance.

5. Billing.

A. Agency shall invoice Media User for all media costs where possible in advance of Agency's payment date to allow for prepayment by the Media User so that Media User may receive the benefit of any available prepayment or similar discount. For any media purchase or service for which Agency is not entitled to a commission, Agency shall ensure that the charges to Media User are net of all agency commissions and discounts.

B. Charges for production materials and services shall be billed by Agency upon completion of the production job or, if cash discounts are available, upon receipt of the supplier's invoice.

C. On all outside purchases other than for media, Agency shall attach to the invoice evidence of the supplier's charges.

D. All cash discounts on Agency's purchases including, but not limited to, media, art, printing and mechanical work, shall be available to Media User, provided that Media User meets Agency's requisite billing terms and there is no outstanding undisputed indebtedness of Media User to Agency at the time of the payment to the supplier.

E. Rate or billing adjustments shall be credited or charged to Media User on the next regular invoice date or as soon thereafter as otherwise practical.

F. Invoices shall be submitted in an itemized format and shall be paid by Media User within sixty (60) days of the invoice date.

6. Competitors.

During the term of this Agreement, Agency shall not accept employment from, render services to, represent or otherwise be affiliated with any person, firm, corporation or entity in connection with any product or service directly or indirectly competitive with or similar to any product or service of Media User with respect to which the Agency is providing any service pursuant to this Agreement, without the advance approval of the Media User. Media User shall not unreasonably withhold this approval.

7. Cost Estimates.

Agency shall not initiate billable work on any project pursuant to this Agreement without first estimating costs for preparation, including copy, service, layout, art, engraving, typography, processing, paste up and production. After determining the estimated cost, completion of the work shall be subject to Media User's prior approval.

8. Audit Rights.

Agency agrees that following reasonable prior notice any and all contracts, agreements, correspondence, books, accounts and other information relating to Media User's business or this Agreement shall be available for inspection by Media User and Media User's outside accountants, at Media User's expense and during the normal business hours of the Agency.

9. Ownership and Use.

A. Agency shall insure, to the fullest extent possible under law, that Media User shall own all right, title and interest in and to, including copyrights, trade secret, patent and other intellectual property rights, with respect to any copy, photograph, advertisement, music, lyrics, video, or other work or thing created by Agency or at Agency's direction for Media User pursuant to this Agreement and utilized by Media User.

B. Upon termination, Media User agrees that any advertising, merchandising, package, plan or idea prepared by Agency and submitted to Media User (whether submitted separately or in conjunction with or as a part of other material) which Media User has elected not to utilize, shall remain the property of Agency, unless Media User has paid Agency for its services in preparing such item. Media User agrees to return to Agency any copy, artwork, plates or other physical embodiment of such creative work relating to any such idea or plan which may be in Media User's possession at termination or expiration of this Agreement. Notwithstanding this, Media User has the unconditional right to pay for any of these materials or activities at the rate agreed upon in this Agreement and thereby these materials and activities would fall under the Section 9.A ownership and use rights accruing to Media User.

C. Materials and advertisements created by Agency pursuant to this Agreement may be used by Media User outside the United States without additional compensation, provided that Media User shall

be responsible for any additional expense associated with such use, such as charges for translation and amounts due talent.

10. Indemnification and Insurance.

A. Agency shall indemnify and hold Media User harmless with respect to any claims, loss, suit, liability or judgment suffered by Media User, including reasonable attorney's fees and costs, based upon or related to any item prepared by Agency or at Agency's direction, including, but not limited to, any claim of libel, slander, piracy, plagiarism, invasion of privacy, or infringement of copyright or other intellectual property interest, except where any such claim arises out of material supplied by Media User and incorporated into any materials or advertisement prepared by Agency. Agency agrees to procure and maintain in force during the term of this Agreement, at Agency's expense, an Agency liability policy or policies having a minimum limit of at least _____, naming Media User as an additional insured and loss payee under such policy or policies.

B. Media User agrees to indemnify and hold Agency harmless with respect to any claims, loss, liability, damage or judgment suffered by Agency, including reasonable attorney's fees and court costs, which results from the use by Agency of any material furnished by Media User or where material created by Agency or at the direction of Agency subject to the indemnification in subsection A. above is materially changed by Media User. Information or data obtained by Agency from Media User to substantiate claims made in advertising shall be deemed to be "material furnished by Media User to Agency."

C. In the event of any proceeding, litigation or suit against Media User by any regulatory agency or in the event of any court action or other proceeding challenging any advertising prepared by Agency, Agency shall assist in the preparation of the defense of such action or proceeding and cooperate with Media User and Media User's attorneys.

11. Term.

The term of this Agreement shall commence on _____ and shall continue in full force and effect until terminated by either party upon at least sixty (60) days prior written notice, provided that in no event (except breach) may this Agreement be terminated prior to _____. The rights, duties and obligations of the parties shall continue in full force during or following the period of the termination notice until termination, including the ordering and billing of advertising in media whose closing dates follow then such period.

12. Rights Upon Termination.

A. Upon termination of the Agreement, Agency shall transfer, assign and make available to Media User all property and materials in Agency's possession or subject to Agency's control that are the property of Media User, subject to payment in full of amounts due pursuant to this Agreement.

B. Upon termination, Agency agrees to provide reasonable cooperation in arranging for the transfer or approval of third party's interest in all contracts, agreements and other arrangements with advertising media, suppliers, talent and others not then utilized, and all rights and claims thereto and therein, following appropriate release from the obligations therein.

13. Default.

In the event of any default of any material obligation by or owed by a party pursuant to this Agreement, then the other party may provide written notice of such default and if such default is not cured within ten (10) days of the written notice, then the nondefaulting party may terminate this Agreement. In addition, the only damages collectible by Agency shall be the exact amounts due; no other damages,

for any reason whatsoever, may be assessed against Media User including, but limited to, punitive damages and unreasonable termination charges, and any other such claim. This provision shall be broadly interpreted in the favor of the Media User by any Court of competent jurisdiction.

14. <u>Notices</u>.

Any notice required by this Agreement or given in connection with it, shall be in writing and shall be given to the appropriate party by personal delivery or by postage prepaid, or recognized overnight delivery services such as Federal Express.

If to Media User: _____

_____

If to Agency: _____

_____

15. <u>Headings in this Agreement</u>.

The headings in this Agreement are for convenience only, confirm no rights or obligations in either party, and do not alter any terms of this Agreement.

16. <u>Entirety of Agreement</u>.

The terms and conditions set forth herein constitute the entire agreement between the parties and supersede any communications or previous agreements with respect to the subject matter of this Agreement. There are no written or oral understandings directly or indirectly related to this Agreement that are not set forth herein. No change can be made to this Agreement other than in writing and signed by both parties.

17. <u>Governing Law</u>.

This Agreement shall be construed and enforced according to the laws of the State of _____ and any dispute under this Agreement must be brought in this venue and in no other.

In Witness whereof, the parties have executed this Agreement as of the date first written above.

_____   _____
Agency   Media User

Ad or other Media Agency Agreement

This Agency Agreement ("Agreement") is made and effective this _____ (Date), by and between ("Agency") and _____ (Your Firm) ("Media User").

Agency is in the business of providing media agency services for a fee.

Media User desires to engage Agency to render, and Agency desires to render to Media User, certain Agency services, all as set forth.

NOW, THEREFORE, in consideration of the mutual agreements and covenants herein contained, the parties hereto agree as follows:

1. <u>Engagement</u>.

Media User engages Agency to render, and Agency agrees to render to Media User, services in connection with Media User's planning, preparing and placing of advertising and other media services for certain of Media User's products as follows:

_____

A. Analyze Media User's current and proposed products and services and presentations and potential markets.

B. Create, prepare and submit to Media User for its prior approval advertising ideas, media suggestions, and other such related programs.

C. Prepare and submit to Media User for its prior approval estimates of costs and expenses associated with proposed advertising ideas and programs prior to any such implementation or financial commitment.

D. Design and prepare, or arrange for the design and preparation of advertisements, public relations, and other such materials.

E. Perform such other services as Media User may request from time to time such as, but not limited to, direct mail ad preparations, speech writing, publicity and public relations work, market research and analysis, and other similar and related activities.

F. Order advertising space, time or other means to be used for publication of Media User's advertisements, at all times endeavoring to secure the most efficient and advantageous rates available. All such activities to be approved in advance by the Media User unless otherwise written and stipulated.

G. Proof for accuracy and completeness of insertions, displays, broadcasts, or other forms of advertisements.

H. Audit invoices for proper and agreed upon space, time, material preparation and charges.

2. <u>Products</u>.

Agency's engagement shall relate to the following products and services of Media User:

_____.

3. Exclusivity.

Agency shall be the Agency in the United States and worldwide for Media User with respect to the products described in Section 2 above, unless otherwise specified in this section:

_____.

4.   Compensation.

A.   Agency shall receive an amount equal to ___ percentage of the gross charges levied by media for advertising placed by Agency pursuant to this Agreement; and   after volume discount, of the charges of suppliers of services or properties, such as finished art, comprehensive layouts, type composition, photostats, engravings, printing, radio and television programs, talent, literary, dramatic and musical works, records and exhibits, purchased by Agency on Media User's authorization during the term of this Agreement; provided that: No percentage will be added to Agency charges for packing, shipping, express, postage, telephone, telex, fax, travel expenses and other out of pocket expenses of Agency personnel.

B.   For those items where Agency is not compensated on a commission basis, Media User shall pay Agency on an hourly basis for services provided hereunder. The rate will be determined by the type of services provided and the person or persons providing such services, but in no event shall the rate exceed _____ per hour. Media User may elect in advance to be charged on this hourly rate basis. If Media User fails to notify Agency of its choice, it shall be presumed that Media User elected to be charged on a percentage basis.

C.   In the event that Agency undertakes, at Media User's request subject to Media User's prior approval, special projects such as those described in Section I.F above, Agency shall prepare an estimate of total charges for any such special project in advance, including any charges for materials or services purchased from outside vendors. In the event that Media User elects to proceed with the special project based upon Agency's estimated cost, Agency shall perform the services with respect to such special project at its estimated cost, subject to modification as mutually agreed by the parties.

D. For any special project or other services provided by Agency pursuant to this Agreement upon which the parties have not agreed as to charges, Media User shall pay
Agency at its regular percentage rates, as stated in Section 4.A above.

E.   Media User shall not be obligated to reimburse Agency for any travel or other out-of-pocket expenses incurred in the performance of services pursuant to this Agreement unless expressly agreed by Media User in advance.

5. Billing.

A.   Agency shall invoice Media User for all media costs where possible in advance of Agency's payment date to allow for prepayment by the Media User so that Media User may receive the benefit of any available prepayment or similar discount. For any media purchase or service for which Agency is not entitled to a commission, Agency shall ensure that the charges to Media User are net of all agency commissions and discounts.

B.   Charges for production materials and services shall be billed by Agency upon completion of the production job or, if cash discounts are available, upon receipt of the supplier's invoice.

C. On all outside purchases other than for media, Agency shall attach to the invoice evidence of the supplier's charges.

D. All cash discounts on Agency's purchases including, but not limited to, media, art, printing and mechanical work, shall be available to Media User, provided that Media User meets Agency's requisite billing terms and there is no outstanding undisputed indebtedness of Media User to Agency at the time of the payment to the supplier.

E. Rate or billing adjustments shall be credited or charged to Media User on the next regular invoice date or as soon thereafter as otherwise practical.

F. Invoices shall be submitted in an itemized format and shall be paid by Media User within sixty (60) days of the invoice date.

6. Competitors.

During the term of this Agreement, Agency shall not accept employment from, render services to, represent or otherwise be affiliated with any person, firm, corporation or entity in connection with any product or service directly or indirectly competitive with or similar to any product or service of Media User with respect to which the Agency is providing any service pursuant to this Agreement, without the advance approval of the Media User. Media User shall not unreasonably withhold this approval.

7. Cost Estimates.

Agency shall not initiate billable work on any project pursuant to this Agreement without first estimating costs for preparation, including copy, service, layout, art, engraving, typography, processing, paste up and production. After determining the estimated cost, completion of the work shall be subject to Media User's prior approval.

8. Audit Rights.

Agency agrees that following reasonable prior notice any and all contracts, agreements, correspondence, books, accounts and other information relating to Media User's business or this Agreement shall be available for inspection by Media User and Media User's outside accountants, at Media User's expense and during the normal business hours of the Agency.

9. Ownership and Use.

A. Agency shall insure, to the fullest extent possible under law, that Media User shall own all right, title and interest in and to, including copyrights, trade secret, patent and other intellectual property rights, with respect to any copy, photograph, advertisement, music, lyrics, video, or other work or thing created by Agency or at Agency's direction for Media User pursuant to this Agreement and utilized by Media User.

B. Upon termination, Media User agrees that any advertising, merchandising, package, plan or idea prepared by Agency and submitted to Media User (whether submitted separately or in conjunction with or as a part of other material) which Media User has elected not to utilize, shall remain the property of Agency, unless Media User has paid Agency for its services in preparing such item. Media User agrees to return to Agency any copy, artwork, plates or other physical embodiment of such creative work relating to any such idea or plan which may be in Media User's possession at termination or expiration of this Agreement. Notwithstanding this, Media User has the unconditional right to pay for any of these materials or activities at the rate agreed upon in this Agreement and thereby these materials and activities would fall under the Section 9.A ownership and use rights accruing to Media User.

C. Materials and advertisements created by Agency pursuant to this Agreement may be used by Media User outside the United States without additional compensation, provided that Media User shall

be responsible for any additional expense associated with such use, such as charges for translation and amounts due talent.

10. Indemnification and Insurance.

A. Agency shall indemnify and hold Media User harmless with respect to any claims, loss, suit, liability or judgment suffered by Media User, including reasonable attorney's fees and costs, based upon or related to any item prepared by Agency or at Agency's direction, including, but not limited to, any claim of libel, slander, piracy, plagiarism, invasion of privacy, or infringement of copyright or other intellectual property interest, except where any such claim arises out of material supplied by Media User and incorporated into any materials or advertisement prepared by Agency. Agency agrees to procure and maintain in force during the term of this Agreement, at Agency's expense, an Agency liability policy or policies having a minimum limit of at least _____, naming Media User as an additional insured and loss payee under such policy or policies.

B. Media User agrees to indemnify and hold Agency harmless with respect to any claims, loss, liability, damage or judgment suffered by Agency, including reasonable attorney's fees and court costs, which results from the use by Agency of any material furnished by Media User or where material created by Agency or at the direction of Agency subject to the indemnification in subsection A. above is materially changed by Media User. Information or data obtained by Agency from Media User to substantiate claims made in advertising shall be deemed to be "material furnished by Media User to Agency."

C. In the event of any proceeding, litigation or suit against Media User by any regulatory agency or in the event of any court action or other proceeding challenging any advertising prepared by Agency, Agency shall assist in the preparation of the defense of such action or proceeding and cooperate with Media User and Media User's attorneys.

11. Term.

The term of this Agreement shall commence on _____ and shall continue in full force and effect until terminated by either party upon at least sixty (60) days prior written notice, provided that in no event (except breach) may this Agreement be terminated prior to _____. The rights, duties and obligations of the parties shall continue in full force during or following the period of the termination notice until termination, including the ordering and billing of advertising in media whose closing dates follow then such period.

12. Rights Upon Termination.

A. Upon termination of the Agreement, Agency shall transfer, assign and make available to Media User all property and materials in Agency's possession or subject to Agency's control that are the property of Media User, subject to payment in full of amounts due pursuant to this Agreement.

B. Upon termination, Agency agrees to provide reasonable cooperation in arranging for the transfer or approval of third party's interest in all contracts, agreements and other arrangements with advertising media, suppliers, talent and others not then utilized, and all rights and claims thereto and therein, following appropriate release from the obligations therein.

13. Default.

In the event of any default of any material obligation by or owed by a party pursuant to this Agreement, then the other party may provide written notice of such default and if such default is not cured within ten (10) days of the written notice, then the nondefaulting party may terminate this Agreement. In addition, the only damages collectible by Agency shall be the exact amounts due; no other damages,

for any reason whatsoever, may be assessed against Media User including, but limited to, punitive damages and unreasonable termination charges, and any other such claim. This provision shall be broadly interpreted in the favor of the Media User by any Court of competent jurisdiction.

14. Notices.

Any notice required by this Agreement or given in connection with it, shall be in writing and shall be given to the appropriate party by personal delivery or by postage prepaid, or recognized overnight delivery services such as Federal Express.

If to Media User: _____

_____

If to Agency: _____

_____

15. Headings in this Agreement.

The headings in this Agreement are for convenience only, confirm no rights or obligations in either party, and do not alter any terms of this Agreement.

16. Entirety of Agreement.

The terms and conditions set forth herein constitute the entire agreement between the parties and supersede any communications or previous agreements with respect to the subject matter of this Agreement. There are no written or oral understandings directly or indirectly related to this Agreement that are not set forth herein. No change can be made to this Agreement other than in writing and signed by both parties.

17. Governing Law.

This Agreement shall be construed and enforced according to the laws of the State of _____ and any dispute under this Agreement must be brought in this venue and in no other.

In Witness whereof, the parties have executed this Agreement as of the date first written above.

_____ _____
Agency   Media User

Ad or other Media Agency Agreement

This Agency Agreement ("Agreement") is made and effective this _____ (Date), by and between ("Agency") and _____ (Your Firm) ("Media User").

Agency is in the business of providing media agency services for a fee.

Media User desires to engage Agency to render, and Agency desires to render to Media User, certain Agency services, all as set forth.

NOW, THEREFORE, in consideration of the mutual agreements and covenants herein contained, the parties hereto agree as follows:

1. <u>Engagement</u>.

Media User engages Agency to render, and Agency agrees to render to Media User, services in connection with Media User's planning, preparing and placing of advertising and other media services for certain of Media User's products as follows:

_____

A. Analyze Media User's current and proposed products and services and presentations and potential markets.

B. Create, prepare and submit to Media User for its prior approval advertising ideas, media suggestions, and other such related programs.

C. Prepare and submit to Media User for its prior approval estimates of costs and expenses associated with proposed advertising ideas and programs prior to any such implementation or financial commitment.

D. Design and prepare, or arrange for the design and preparation of advertisements, public relations, and other such materials.

E. Perform such other services as Media User may request from time to time such as, but not limited to, direct mail ad preparations, speech writing, publicity and public relations work, market research and analysis, and other similar and related activities.

F. Order advertising space, time or other means to be used for publication of Media User's advertisements, at all times endeavoring to secure the most efficient and advantageous rates available. All such activities to be approved in advance by the Media User unless otherwise written and stipulated.

G. Proof for accuracy and completeness of insertions, displays, broadcasts, or other forms of advertisements.

H. Audit invoices for proper and agreed upon space, time, material preparation and charges.

2. <u>Products</u>.

Agency's engagement shall relate to the following products and services of Media User:

_____.

3. Exclusivity.

Agency shall be the Agency in the United States and worldwide for Media User with respect to the products described in Section 2 above, unless otherwise specified in this section:

_____.

4. Compensation.

A. Agency shall receive an amount equal to ___ percentage of the gross charges levied by media for advertising placed by Agency pursuant to this Agreement; and after volume discount, of the charges of suppliers of services or properties, such as finished art, comprehensive layouts, type composition, photostats, engravings, printing, radio and television programs, talent, literary, dramatic and musical works, records and exhibits, purchased by Agency on Media User's authorization during the term of this Agreement; provided that: No percentage will be added to Agency charges for packing, shipping, express, postage, telephone, telex, fax, travel expenses and other out of pocket expenses of Agency personnel.

B. For those items where Agency is not compensated on a commission basis, Media User shall pay Agency on an hourly basis for services provided hereunder. The rate will be determined by the type of services provided and the person or persons providing such services, but in no event shall the rate exceed _____ per hour. Media User may elect in advance to be charged on this hourly rate basis. If Media User fails to notify Agency of its choice, it shall be presumed that Media User elected to be charged on a percentage basis.

C. In the event that Agency undertakes, at Media User's request subject to Media User's prior approval, special projects such as those described in Section I.F above, Agency shall prepare an estimate of total charges for any such special project in advance, including any charges for materials or services purchased from outside vendors. In the event that Media User elects to proceed with the special project based upon Agency's estimated cost, Agency shall perform the services with respect to such special project at its estimated cost, subject to modification as mutually agreed by the parties.

D. For any special project or other services provided by Agency pursuant to this Agreement upon which the parties have not agreed as to charges, Media User shall pay
Agency at its regular percentage rates, as stated in Section 4.A above.

E. Media User shall not be obligated to reimburse Agency for any travel or other out-of-pocket expenses incurred in the performance of services pursuant to this Agreement unless expressly agreed by Media User in advance.

5. Billing.

A. Agency shall invoice Media User for all media costs where possible in advance of Agency's payment date to allow for prepayment by the Media User so that Media User may receive the benefit of any available prepayment or similar discount. For any media purchase or service for which Agency is not entitled to a commission, Agency shall ensure that the charges to Media User are net of all agency commissions and discounts.

B. Charges for production materials and services shall be billed by Agency upon completion of the production job or, if cash discounts are available, upon receipt of the supplier's invoice.

C. On all outside purchases other than for media, Agency shall attach to the invoice evidence of the supplier's charges.

D. All cash discounts on Agency's purchases including, but not limited to, media, art, printing and mechanical work, shall be available to Media User, provided that Media User meets Agency's requisite billing terms and there is no outstanding undisputed indebtedness of Media User to Agency at the time of the payment to the supplier.

E. Rate or billing adjustments shall be credited or charged to Media User on the next regular invoice date or as soon thereafter as otherwise practical.

F. Invoices shall be submitted in an itemized format and shall be paid by Media User within sixty (60) days of the invoice date.

6. Competitors.

During the term of this Agreement, Agency shall not accept employment from, render services to, represent or otherwise be affiliated with any person, firm, corporation or entity in connection with any product or service directly or indirectly competitive with or similar to any product or service of Media User with respect to which the Agency is providing any service pursuant to this Agreement, without the advance approval of the Media User. Media User shall not unreasonably withhold this approval.

7. Cost Estimates.

Agency shall not initiate billable work on any project pursuant to this Agreement without first estimating costs for preparation, including copy, service, layout, art, engraving, typography, processing, paste up and production. After determining the estimated cost, completion of the work shall be subject to Media User's prior approval.

8. Audit Rights.

Agency agrees that following reasonable prior notice any and all contracts, agreements, correspondence, books, accounts and other information relating to Media User's business or this Agreement shall be available for inspection by Media User and Media User's outside accountants, at Media User's expense and during the normal business hours of the Agency.

9. Ownership and Use.

A. Agency shall insure, to the fullest extent possible under law, that Media User shall own all right, title and interest in and to, including copyrights, trade secret, patent and other intellectual property rights, with respect to any copy, photograph, advertisement, music, lyrics, video, or other work or thing created by Agency or at Agency's direction for Media User pursuant to this Agreement and utilized by Media User.

B. Upon termination, Media User agrees that any advertising, merchandising, package, plan or idea prepared by Agency and submitted to Media User (whether submitted separately or in conjunction with or as a part of other material) which Media User has elected not to utilize, shall remain the property of Agency, unless Media User has paid Agency for its services in preparing such item. Media User agrees to return to Agency any copy, artwork, plates or other physical embodiment of such creative work relating to any such idea or plan which may be in Media User's possession at termination or expiration of this Agreement. Notwithstanding this, Media User has the unconditional right to pay for any of these materials or activities at the rate agreed upon in this Agreement and thereby these materials and activities would fall under the Section 9.A ownership and use rights accruing to Media User.

C. Materials and advertisements created by Agency pursuant to this Agreement may be used by Media User outside the United States without additional compensation, provided that Media User shall

be responsible for any additional expense associated with such use, such as charges for translation and amounts due talent.

10. Indemnification and Insurance.

A.   Agency shall indemnify and hold Media User harmless with respect to any claims, loss, suit, liability or judgment suffered by Media User, including reasonable attorney's fees and costs, based upon or related to any item prepared by Agency or at Agency's direction, including, but not limited to, any claim of libel, slander, piracy, plagiarism, invasion of privacy, or infringement of copyright or other intellectual property interest, except where any such claim arises out of material supplied by Media User and incorporated into any materials or advertisement prepared by Agency. Agency agrees to procure and maintain in force during the term of this Agreement, at Agency's expense, an Agency liability policy or policies having a minimum limit of at least _____, naming Media User as an additional insured and loss payee under such policy or policies.

B.   Media User agrees to indemnify and hold Agency harmless with respect to any claims, loss, liability, damage or judgment suffered by Agency, including reasonable attorney's fees and court costs, which results from the use by Agency of any material furnished by Media User or where material created by Agency or at the direction of Agency subject to the indemnification in subsection A. above is materially changed by Media User. Information or data obtained by Agency from Media User to substantiate claims made in advertising shall be deemed to be "material furnished by Media User to Agency."

C.   In the event of any proceeding, litigation or suit against Media User by any regulatory agency or in the event of any court action or other proceeding challenging any advertising prepared by Agency, Agency shall assist in the preparation of the defense of such action or proceeding and cooperate with Media User and Media User's attorneys.

11. Term.

The term of this Agreement shall commence on _____ and shall continue in full force and effect until terminated by either party upon at least sixty (60) days prior written notice, provided that in no event (except breach) may this Agreement be terminated prior to _____. The rights, duties and obligations of the parties shall continue in full force during or following the period of the termination notice until termination, including the ordering and billing of advertising in media whose closing dates follow then such period.

12. Rights Upon Termination.

A.   Upon termination of the Agreement, Agency shall transfer, assign and make available to Media User all property and materials in Agency's possession or subject to Agency's control that are the property of Media User, subject to payment in full of amounts due pursuant to this Agreement.

B.   Upon termination, Agency agrees to provide reasonable cooperation in arranging for the transfer or approval of third party's interest in all contracts, agreements and other arrangements with advertising media, suppliers, talent and others not then utilized, and all rights and claims thereto and therein, following appropriate release from the obligations therein.

13. Default.

In the event of any default of any material obligation by or owed by a party pursuant to this Agreement, then the other party may provide written notice of such default and if such default is not cured within ten (10) days of the written notice, then the nondefaulting party may terminate this Agreement. In addition, the only damages collectible by Agency shall be the exact amounts due; no other damages,

for any reason whatsoever, may be assessed against Media User including, but limited to, punitive damages and unreasonable termination charges, and any other such claim. This provision shall be broadly interpreted in the favor of the Media User by any Court of competent jurisdiction.

14. <u>Notices</u>.

Any notice required by this Agreement or given in connection with it, shall be in writing and shall be given to the appropriate party by personal delivery or by postage prepaid, or recognized overnight delivery services such as Federal Express.

If to Media User: _____

_____

If to Agency: _____

_____

15. <u>Headings in this Agreement</u>.

The headings in this Agreement are for convenience only, confirm no rights or obligations in either party, and do not alter any terms of this Agreement.

16. <u>Entirety of Agreement</u>.

The terms and conditions set forth herein constitute the entire agreement between the parties and supersede any communications or previous agreements with respect to the subject matter of this Agreement. There are no written or oral understandings directly or indirectly related to this Agreement that are not set forth herein. No change can be made to this Agreement other than in writing and signed by both parties.

17. <u>Governing Law</u>.

This Agreement shall be construed and enforced according to the laws of the State of _____ and any dispute under this Agreement must be brought in this venue and in no other.

In Witness whereof, the parties have executed this Agreement as of the date first written above.

_____ _____
Agency Media User

Ad or other Media Agency Agreement

This Agency Agreement ("Agreement") is made and effective this _____ (Date), by and between ("Agency") and _____ (Your Firm) ("Media User").

Agency is in the business of providing media agency services for a fee.

Media User desires to engage Agency to render, and Agency desires to render to Media User, certain Agency services, all as set forth.

NOW, THEREFORE, in consideration of the mutual agreements and covenants herein contained, the parties hereto agree as follows:

1. <u>Engagement</u>.

Media User engages Agency to render, and Agency agrees to render to Media User, services in connection with Media User's planning, preparing and placing of advertising and other media services for certain of Media User's products as follows:

_____

A. Analyze Media User's current and proposed products and services and presentations and potential markets.

B. Create, prepare and submit to Media User for its prior approval advertising ideas, media suggestions, and other such related programs.

C. Prepare and submit to Media User for its prior approval estimates of costs and expenses associated with proposed advertising ideas and programs prior to any such implementation or financial commitment.

D. Design and prepare, or arrange for the design and preparation of advertisements, public relations, and other such materials.

E. Perform such other services as Media User may request from time to time such as, but not limited to, direct mail ad preparations, speech writing, publicity and public relations work, market research and analysis, and other similar and related activities.

F. Order advertising space, time or other means to be used for publication of Media User's advertisements, at all times endeavoring to secure the most efficient and advantageous rates available. All such activities to be approved in advance by the Media User unless otherwise written and stipulated.

G. Proof for accuracy and completeness of insertions, displays, broadcasts, or other forms of advertisements.

H. Audit invoices for proper and agreed upon space, time, material preparation and charges.

2. <u>Products</u>.

Agency's engagement shall relate to the following products and services of Media User:

_____.

3. <u>Exclusivity</u>.

Agency shall be the Agency in the United States and worldwide for Media User with respect to the products described in Section 2 above, unless otherwise specified in this section:

_____.

4. <u>Compensation</u>.

A. Agency shall receive an amount equal to ___ percentage of the gross charges levied by media for advertising placed by Agency pursuant to this Agreement; and   after volume discount, of the charges of suppliers of services or properties, such as finished art, comprehensive layouts, type composition, photostats, engravings, printing, radio and television programs, talent, literary, dramatic and musical works, records and exhibits, purchased by Agency on Media User's authorization during the term of this Agreement; provided that: No percentage will be added to Agency charges for packing, shipping, express, postage, telephone, telex, fax, travel expenses and other out of pocket expenses of Agency personnel.

B. For those items where Agency is not compensated on a commission basis, Media User shall pay Agency on an hourly basis for services provided hereunder. The rate will be determined by the type of services provided and the person or persons providing such services, but in no event shall the rate exceed _____ per hour. Media User may elect in advance to be charged on this hourly rate basis. If Media User fails to notify Agency of its choice, it shall be presumed that Media User elected to be charged on a percentage basis.

C. In the event that Agency undertakes, at Media User's request subject to Media User's prior approval, special projects such as those described in Section I.F above, Agency shall prepare an estimate of total charges for any such special project in advance, including any charges for materials or services purchased from outside vendors. In the event that Media User elects to proceed with the special project based upon Agency's estimated cost, Agency shall perform the services with respect to such special project at its estimated cost, subject to modification as mutually agreed by the parties.

D. For any special project or other services provided by Agency pursuant to this Agreement upon which the parties have not agreed as to charges, Media User shall pay
Agency at its regular percentage rates, as stated in Section 4.A above.

E. Media User shall not be obligated to reimburse Agency for any travel or other out-of-pocket expenses incurred in the performance of services pursuant to this Agreement unless expressly agreed by Media User in advance.

5. <u>Billing</u>.

A. Agency shall invoice Media User for all media costs where possible in advance of Agency's payment date to allow for prepayment by the Media User so that Media User may receive the benefit of any available prepayment or similar discount. For any media purchase or service for which Agency is not entitled to a commission, Agency shall ensure that the charges to Media User are net of all agency commissions and discounts.

B. Charges for production materials and services shall be billed by Agency upon completion of the production job or, if cash discounts are available, upon receipt of the supplier's invoice.

C. On all outside purchases other than for media, Agency shall attach to the invoice evidence of the supplier's charges.

D.   All cash discounts on Agency's purchases including, but not limited to, media, art, printing and mechanical work, shall be available to Media User, provided that Media User meets Agency's requisite billing terms and there is no outstanding undisputed indebtedness of Media User to Agency at the time of the payment to the supplier.

E. Rate or billing adjustments shall be credited or charged to Media User on the next regular invoice date or as soon thereafter as otherwise practical.

F. Invoices shall be submitted in an itemized format and shall be paid by Media User within sixty (60) days of the invoice date.

6. Competitors.

During the term of this Agreement, Agency shall not accept employment from, render services to, represent or otherwise be affiliated with any person, firm, corporation or entity in connection with any product or service directly or indirectly competitive with or similar to any product or service of Media User with respect to which the Agency is providing any service pursuant to this Agreement, without the advance approval of the Media User. Media User shall not unreasonably withhold this approval.

7. Cost Estimates.

Agency shall not initiate billable work on any project pursuant to this Agreement without first estimating costs for preparation, including copy, service, layout, art, engraving, typography, processing, paste up and production. After determining the estimated cost, completion of the work shall be subject to Media User's prior approval.

8. Audit Rights.

Agency agrees that following reasonable prior notice any and all contracts, agreements, correspondence, books, accounts and other information relating to Media User's business or this Agreement shall be available for inspection by Media User and Media User's outside accountants, at Media User's expense and during the normal business hours of the Agency.

9. Ownership and Use.

A.   Agency shall insure, to the fullest extent possible under law, that Media User shall own all right, title and interest in and to, including copyrights, trade secret, patent and other intellectual property rights, with respect to any copy, photograph, advertisement, music, lyrics, video, or other work or thing created by Agency or at Agency's direction for Media User pursuant to this Agreement and utilized by Media User.

B.   Upon termination, Media User agrees that any advertising, merchandising, package, plan or idea prepared by Agency and submitted to Media User (whether submitted separately or in conjunction with or as a part of other material) which Media User has elected not to utilize, shall remain the property of Agency, unless Media User has paid Agency for its services in preparing such item. Media User agrees to return to Agency any copy, artwork, plates or other physical embodiment of such creative work relating to any such idea or plan which may be in Media User's possession at termination or expiration of this Agreement. Notwithstanding this, Media User has the unconditional right to pay for any of these materials or activities at the rate agreed upon in this Agreement and thereby these materials and activities would fall under the Section 9.A ownership and use rights accruing to Media User.

C.   Materials and advertisements created by Agency pursuant to this Agreement may be used by Media User outside the United States without additional compensation, provided that Media User shall

be responsible for any additional expense associated with such use, such as charges for translation and amounts due talent.

10. Indemnification and Insurance.

A.   Agency shall indemnify and hold Media User harmless with respect to any claims, loss, suit, liability or judgment suffered by Media User, including reasonable attorney's fees and costs, based upon or related to any item prepared by Agency or at Agency's direction, including, but not limited to, any claim of libel, slander, piracy, plagiarism, invasion of privacy, or infringement of copyright or other intellectual property interest, except where any such claim arises out of material supplied by Media User and incorporated into any materials or advertisement prepared by Agency. Agency agrees to procure and maintain in force during the term of this Agreement, at Agency's expense, an Agency liability policy or policies having a minimum limit of at least _____, naming Media User as an additional insured and loss payee under such policy or policies.

B.   Media User agrees to indemnify and hold Agency harmless with respect to any claims, loss, liability, damage or judgment suffered by Agency, including reasonable attorney's fees and court costs, which results from the use by Agency of any material furnished by Media User or where material created by Agency or at the direction of Agency subject to the indemnification in subsection A. above is materially changed by Media User. Information or data obtained by Agency from Media User to substantiate claims made in advertising shall be deemed to be "material furnished by Media User to Agency."

C.   In the event of any proceeding, litigation or suit against Media User by any regulatory agency or in the event of any court action or other proceeding challenging any advertising prepared by Agency, Agency shall assist in the preparation of the defense of such action or proceeding and cooperate with Media User and Media User's attorneys.

11. Term.

The term of this Agreement shall commence on _____ and shall continue in full force and effect until terminated by either party upon at least sixty (60) days prior written notice, provided that in no event (except breach) may this Agreement be terminated prior to _____. The rights, duties and obligations of the parties shall continue in full force during or following the period of the termination notice until termination, including the ordering and billing of advertising in media whose closing dates follow then such period.

12. Rights Upon Termination.

A.   Upon termination of the Agreement, Agency shall transfer, assign and make available to Media User all property and materials in Agency's possession or subject to Agency's control that are the property of Media User, subject to payment in full of amounts due pursuant to this Agreement.

B.   Upon termination, Agency agrees to provide reasonable cooperation in arranging for the transfer or approval of third party's interest in all contracts, agreements and other arrangements with advertising media, suppliers, talent and others not then utilized, and all rights and claims thereto and therein, following appropriate release from the obligations therein.

13. Default.

In the event of any default of any material obligation by or owed by a party pursuant to this Agreement, then the other party may provide written notice of such default and if such default is not cured within ten (10) days of the written notice, then the nondefaulting party may terminate this Agreement. In addition, the only damages collectible by Agency shall be the exact amounts due; no other damages,

for any reason whatsoever, may be assessed against Media User including, but limited to, punitive damages and unreasonable termination charges, and any other such claim. This provision shall be broadly interpreted in the favor of the Media User by any Court of competent jurisdiction.

14. <u>Notices</u>.

Any notice required by this Agreement or given in connection with it, shall be in writing and shall be given to the appropriate party by personal delivery or by postage prepaid, or recognized overnight delivery services such as Federal Express.

If to Media User: _____

_____

If to Agency: _____

_____

15. <u>Headings in this Agreement</u>.

The headings in this Agreement are for convenience only, confirm no rights or obligations in either party, and do not alter any terms of this Agreement.

16. <u>Entirety of Agreement</u>.

The terms and conditions set forth herein constitute the entire agreement between the parties and supersede any communications or previous agreements with respect to the subject matter of this Agreement. There are no written or oral understandings directly or indirectly related to this Agreement that are not set forth herein. No change can be made to this Agreement other than in writing and signed by both parties.

17. <u>Governing Law</u>.

This Agreement shall be construed and enforced according to the laws of the State of _____ and any dispute under this Agreement must be brought in this venue and in no other.

In Witness whereof, the parties have executed this Agreement as of the date first written above.

_____ _____
Agency   Media User

Ad or other Media Agency Agreement

This Agency Agreement ("Agreement") is made and effective this _____ (Date), by and between ("Agency") and _____ (Your Firm) ("Media User").

Agency is in the business of providing media agency services for a fee.

Media User desires to engage Agency to render, and Agency desires to render to Media User, certain Agency services, all as set forth.

NOW, THEREFORE, in consideration of the mutual agreements and covenants herein contained, the parties hereto agree as follows:

1. Engagement.

Media User engages Agency to render, and Agency agrees to render to Media User, services in connection with Media User's planning, preparing and placing of advertising and other media services for certain of Media User's products as follows:

_____

A. Analyze Media User's current and proposed products and services and presentations and potential markets.

B. Create, prepare and submit to Media User for its prior approval advertising ideas, media suggestions, and other such related programs.

C. Prepare and submit to Media User for its prior approval estimates of costs and expenses associated with proposed advertising ideas and programs prior to any such implementation or financial commitment.

D. Design and prepare, or arrange for the design and preparation of advertisements, public relations, and other such materials.

E. Perform such other services as Media User may request from time to time such as, but not limited to, direct mail ad preparations, speech writing, publicity and public relations work, market research and analysis, and other similar and related activities.

F. Order advertising space, time or other means to be used for publication of Media User's advertisements, at all times endeavoring to secure the most efficient and advantageous rates available. All such activities to be approved in advance by the Media User unless otherwise written and stipulated.

G. Proof for accuracy and completeness of insertions, displays, broadcasts, or other forms of advertisements.

H. Audit invoices for proper and agreed upon space, time, material preparation and charges.

2. Products.

Agency's engagement shall relate to the following products and services of Media User:

_____.

3. Exclusivity.

Agency shall be the Agency in the United States and worldwide for Media User with respect to the products described in Section 2 above, unless otherwise specified in this section:

_____.

4. Compensation.

A. Agency shall receive an amount equal to ___ percentage of the gross charges levied by media for advertising placed by Agency pursuant to this Agreement; and   after volume discount, of the charges of suppliers of services or properties, such as finished art, comprehensive layouts, type composition, photostats, engravings, printing, radio and television programs, talent, literary, dramatic and musical works, records and exhibits, purchased by Agency on Media User's authorization during the term of this Agreement; provided that: No percentage will be added to Agency charges for packing, shipping, express, postage, telephone, telex, fax, travel expenses and other out of pocket expenses of Agency personnel.

B. For those items where Agency is not compensated on a commission basis, Media User shall pay Agency on an hourly basis for services provided hereunder. The rate will be determined by the type of services provided and the person or persons providing such services, but in no event shall the rate exceed _____ per hour. Media User may elect in advance to be charged on this hourly rate basis. If Media User fails to notify Agency of its choice, it shall be presumed that Media User elected to be charged on a percentage basis.

C. In the event that Agency undertakes, at Media User's request subject to Media User's prior approval, special projects such as those described in Section I.F above, Agency shall prepare an estimate of total charges for any such special project in advance, including any charges for materials or services purchased from outside vendors. In the event that Media User elects to proceed with the special project based upon Agency's estimated cost, Agency shall perform the services with respect to such special project at its estimated cost, subject to modification as mutually agreed by the parties.

D. For any special project or other services provided by Agency pursuant to this Agreement upon which the parties have not agreed as to charges, Media User shall pay
Agency at its regular percentage rates, as stated in Section 4.A above.

E. Media User shall not be obligated to reimburse Agency for any travel or other out-of-pocket expenses incurred in the performance of services pursuant to this Agreement unless expressly agreed by Media User in advance.

5. Billing.

A. Agency shall invoice Media User for all media costs where possible in advance of Agency's payment date to allow for prepayment by the Media User so that Media User may receive the benefit of any available prepayment or similar discount. For any media purchase or service for which Agency is not entitled to a commission, Agency shall ensure that the charges to Media User are net of all agency commissions and discounts.

B. Charges for production materials and services shall be billed by Agency upon completion of the production job or, if cash discounts are available, upon receipt of the supplier's invoice.

C. On all outside purchases other than for media, Agency shall attach to the invoice evidence of the supplier's charges.

D.   All cash discounts on Agency's purchases including, but not limited to, media, art, printing and mechanical work, shall be available to Media User, provided that Media User meets Agency's requisite billing terms and there is no outstanding undisputed indebtedness of Media User to Agency at the time of the payment to the supplier.

E. Rate or billing adjustments shall be credited or charged to Media User on the next regular invoice date or as soon thereafter as otherwise practical.

F. Invoices shall be submitted in an itemized format and shall be paid by Media User within sixty (60) days of the invoice date.

6. Competitors.

During the term of this Agreement, Agency shall not accept employment from, render services to, represent or otherwise be affiliated with any person, firm, corporation or entity in connection with any product or service directly or indirectly competitive with or similar to any product or service of Media User with respect to which the Agency is providing any service pursuant to this Agreement, without the advance approval of the Media User. Media User shall not unreasonably withhold this approval.

7. Cost Estimates.

Agency shall not initiate billable work on any project pursuant to this Agreement without first estimating costs for preparation, including copy, service, layout, art, engraving, typography, processing, paste up and production. After determining the estimated cost, completion of the work shall be subject to Media User's prior approval.

8. Audit Rights.

Agency agrees that following reasonable prior notice any and all contracts, agreements, correspondence, books, accounts and other information relating to Media User's business or this Agreement shall be available for inspection by Media User and Media User's outside accountants, at Media User's expense and during the normal business hours of the Agency.

9. Ownership and Use.

A.   Agency shall insure, to the fullest extent possible under law, that Media User shall own all right, title and interest in and to, including copyrights, trade secret, patent and other intellectual property rights, with respect to any copy, photograph, advertisement, music, lyrics, video, or other work or thing created by Agency or at Agency's direction for Media User pursuant to this Agreement and utilized by Media User.

B.   Upon termination, Media User agrees that any advertising, merchandising, package, plan or idea prepared by Agency and submitted to Media User (whether submitted separately or in conjunction with or as a part of other material) which Media User has elected not to utilize, shall remain the property of Agency, unless Media User has paid Agency for its services in preparing such item. Media User agrees to return to Agency any copy, artwork, plates or other physical embodiment of such creative work relating to any such idea or plan which may be in Media User's possession at termination or expiration of this Agreement. Notwithstanding this, Media User has the unconditional right to pay for any of these materials or activities at the rate agreed upon in this Agreement and thereby these materials and activities would fall under the Section 9.A ownership and use rights accruing to Media User.

C.   Materials and advertisements created by Agency pursuant to this Agreement may be used by Media User outside the United States without additional compensation, provided that Media User shall

be responsible for any additional expense associated with such use, such as charges for translation and amounts due talent.

10. Indemnification and Insurance.

A.   Agency shall indemnify and hold Media User harmless with respect to any claims, loss, suit, liability or judgment suffered by Media User, including reasonable attorney's fees and costs, based upon or related to any item prepared by Agency or at Agency's direction, including, but not limited to, any claim of libel, slander, piracy, plagiarism, invasion of privacy, or infringement of copyright or other intellectual property interest, except where any such claim arises out of material supplied by Media User and incorporated into any materials or advertisement prepared by Agency. Agency agrees to procure and maintain in force during the term of this Agreement, at Agency's expense, an Agency liability policy or policies having a minimum limit of at least _____, naming Media User as an additional insured and loss payee under such policy or policies.

B.   Media User agrees to indemnify and hold Agency harmless with respect to any claims, loss, liability, damage or judgment suffered by Agency, including reasonable attorney's fees and court costs, which results from the use by Agency of any material furnished by Media User or where material created by Agency or at the direction of Agency subject to the indemnification in subsection A. above is materially changed by Media User. Information or data obtained by Agency from Media User to substantiate claims made in advertising shall be deemed to be "material furnished by Media User to Agency."

C.   In the event of any proceeding, litigation or suit against Media User by any regulatory agency or in the event of any court action or other proceeding challenging any advertising prepared by Agency, Agency shall assist in the preparation of the defense of such action or proceeding and cooperate with Media User and Media User's attorneys.

11. Term.

The term of this Agreement shall commence on _____ and shall continue in full force and effect until terminated by either party upon at least sixty (60) days prior written notice, provided that in no event (except breach) may this Agreement be terminated prior to _____. The rights, duties and obligations of the parties shall continue in full force during or following the period of the termination notice until termination, including the ordering and billing of advertising in media whose closing dates follow then such period.

12. Rights Upon Termination.

A.   Upon termination of the Agreement, Agency shall transfer, assign and make available to Media User all property and materials in Agency's possession or subject to Agency's control that are the property of Media User, subject to payment in full of amounts due pursuant to this Agreement.

B.   Upon termination, Agency agrees to provide reasonable cooperation in arranging for the transfer or approval of third party's interest in all contracts, agreements and other arrangements with advertising media, suppliers, talent and others not then utilized, and all rights and claims thereto and therein, following appropriate release from the obligations therein.

13. Default.

In the event of any default of any material obligation by or owed by a party pursuant to this Agreement, then the other party may provide written notice of such default and if such default is not cured within ten (10) days of the written notice, then the nondefaulting party may terminate this Agreement. In addition, the only damages collectible by Agency shall be the exact amounts due; no other damages,

for any reason whatsoever, may be assessed against Media User including, but limited to, punitive damages and unreasonable termination charges, and any other such claim. This provision shall be broadly interpreted in the favor of the Media User by any Court of competent jurisdiction.

14. Notices.

Any notice required by this Agreement or given in connection with it, shall be in writing and shall be given to the appropriate party by personal delivery or by postage prepaid, or recognized overnight delivery services such as Federal Express.

If to Media User: _____

_____

If to Agency: _____

_____

15. Headings in this Agreement.

The headings in this Agreement are for convenience only, confirm no rights or obligations in either party, and do not alter any terms of this Agreement.

16. Entirety of Agreement.

The terms and conditions set forth herein constitute the entire agreement between the parties and supersede any communications or previous agreements with respect to the subject matter of this Agreement. There are no written or oral understandings directly or indirectly related to this Agreement that are not set forth herein. No change can be made to this Agreement other than in writing and signed by both parties.

17. Governing Law.

This Agreement shall be construed and enforced according to the laws of the State of _____ and any dispute under this Agreement must be brought in this venue and in no other.

In Witness whereof, the parties have executed this Agreement as of the date first written above.

_____ _____
Agency   Media User

Ad or other Media Agency Agreement

This Agency Agreement ("Agreement") is made and effective this _____ (Date), by and between ("Agency") and _____ (Your Firm) ("Media User").

Agency is in the business of providing media agency services for a fee.

Media User desires to engage Agency to render, and Agency desires to render to Media User, certain Agency services, all as set forth.

NOW, THEREFORE, in consideration of the mutual agreements and covenants herein contained, the parties hereto agree as follows:

1. <u>Engagement</u>.

Media User engages Agency to render, and Agency agrees to render to Media User, services in connection with Media User's planning, preparing and placing of advertising and other media services for certain of Media User's products as follows:

_____

A. Analyze Media User's current and proposed products and services and presentations and potential markets.

B. Create, prepare and submit to Media User for its prior approval advertising ideas, media suggestions, and other such related programs.

C. Prepare and submit to Media User for its prior approval estimates of costs and expenses associated with proposed advertising ideas and programs prior to any such implementation or financial commitment.

D. Design and prepare, or arrange for the design and preparation of advertisements, public relations, and other such materials.

E. Perform such other services as Media User may request from time to time such as, but not limited to, direct mail ad preparations, speech writing, publicity and public relations work, market research and analysis, and other similar and related activities.

F. Order advertising space, time or other means to be used for publication of Media User's advertisements, at all times endeavoring to secure the most efficient and advantageous rates available. All such activities to be approved in advance by the Media User unless otherwise written and stipulated.

G. Proof for accuracy and completeness of insertions, displays, broadcasts, or other forms of advertisements.

H. Audit invoices for proper and agreed upon space, time, material preparation and charges.

2. <u>Products</u>.

Agency's engagement shall relate to the following products and services of Media User:

_____.

3. Exclusivity.

Agency shall be the Agency in the United States and worldwide for Media User with respect to the products described in Section 2 above, unless otherwise specified in this section:

_____.

4. Compensation.

A. Agency shall receive an amount equal to ___ percentage of the gross charges levied by media for advertising placed by Agency pursuant to this Agreement; and   after volume discount, of the charges of suppliers of services or properties, such as finished art, comprehensive layouts, type composition, photostats, engravings, printing, radio and television programs, talent, literary, dramatic and musical works, records and exhibits, purchased by Agency on Media User's authorization during the term of this Agreement; provided that: No percentage will be added to Agency charges for packing, shipping, express, postage, telephone, telex, fax, travel expenses and other out of pocket expenses of Agency personnel.

B. For those items where Agency is not compensated on a commission basis, Media User shall pay Agency on an hourly basis for services provided hereunder. The rate will be determined by the type of services provided and the person or persons providing such services, but in no event shall the rate exceed _____ per hour. Media User may elect in advance to be charged on this hourly rate basis. If Media User fails to notify Agency of its choice, it shall be presumed that Media User elected to be charged on a percentage basis.

C. In the event that Agency undertakes, at Media User's request subject to Media User's prior approval, special projects such as those described in Section I.F above, Agency shall prepare an estimate of total charges for any such special project in advance, including any charges for materials or services purchased from outside vendors. In the event that Media User elects to proceed with the special project based upon Agency's estimated cost, Agency shall perform the services with respect to such special project at its estimated cost, subject to modification as mutually agreed by the parties.

D. For any special project or other services provided by Agency pursuant to this Agreement upon which the parties have not agreed as to charges, Media User shall pay
Agency at its regular percentage rates, as stated in Section 4.A above.

E. Media User shall not be obligated to reimburse Agency for any travel or other out-of-pocket expenses incurred in the performance of services pursuant to this Agreement unless expressly agreed by Media User in advance.

5. Billing.

A. Agency shall invoice Media User for all media costs where possible in advance of Agency's payment date to allow for prepayment by the Media User so that Media User may receive the benefit of any available prepayment or similar discount. For any media purchase or service for which Agency is not entitled to a commission, Agency shall ensure that the charges to Media User are net of all agency commissions and discounts.

B. Charges for production materials and services shall be billed by Agency upon completion of the production job or, if cash discounts are available, upon receipt of the supplier's invoice.

C. On all outside purchases other than for media, Agency shall attach to the invoice evidence of the supplier's charges.

D. All cash discounts on Agency's purchases including, but not limited to, media, art, printing and mechanical work, shall be available to Media User, provided that Media User meets Agency's requisite billing terms and there is no outstanding undisputed indebtedness of Media User to Agency at the time of the payment to the supplier.

E. Rate or billing adjustments shall be credited or charged to Media User on the next regular invoice date or as soon thereafter as otherwise practical.

F. Invoices shall be submitted in an itemized format and shall be paid by Media User within sixty (60) days of the invoice date.

6. Competitors.

During the term of this Agreement, Agency shall not accept employment from, render services to, represent or otherwise be affiliated with any person, firm, corporation or entity in connection with any product or service directly or indirectly competitive with or similar to any product or service of Media User with respect to which the Agency is providing any service pursuant to this Agreement, without the advance approval of the Media User. Media User shall not unreasonably withhold this approval.

7. Cost Estimates.

Agency shall not initiate billable work on any project pursuant to this Agreement without first estimating costs for preparation, including copy, service, layout, art, engraving, typography, processing, paste up and production. After determining the estimated cost, completion of the work shall be subject to Media User's prior approval.

8. Audit Rights.

Agency agrees that following reasonable prior notice any and all contracts, agreements, correspondence, books, accounts and other information relating to Media User's business or this Agreement shall be available for inspection by Media User and Media User's outside accountants, at Media User's expense and during the normal business hours of the Agency.

9. Ownership and Use.

A. Agency shall insure, to the fullest extent possible under law, that Media User shall own all right, title and interest in and to, including copyrights, trade secret, patent and other intellectual property rights, with respect to any copy, photograph, advertisement, music, lyrics, video, or other work or thing created by Agency or at Agency's direction for Media User pursuant to this Agreement and utilized by Media User.

B. Upon termination, Media User agrees that any advertising, merchandising, package, plan or idea prepared by Agency and submitted to Media User (whether submitted separately or in conjunction with or as a part of other material) which Media User has elected not to utilize, shall remain the property of Agency, unless Media User has paid Agency for its services in preparing such item. Media User agrees to return to Agency any copy, artwork, plates or other physical embodiment of such creative work relating to any such idea or plan which may be in Media User's possession at termination or expiration of this Agreement. Notwithstanding this, Media User has the unconditional right to pay for any of these materials or activities at the rate agreed upon in this Agreement and thereby these materials and activities would fall under the Section 9.A ownership and use rights accruing to Media User.

C. Materials and advertisements created by Agency pursuant to this Agreement may be used by Media User outside the United States without additional compensation, provided that Media User shall

be responsible for any additional expense associated with such use, such as charges for translation and amounts due talent.

10. Indemnification and Insurance.

A. Agency shall indemnify and hold Media User harmless with respect to any claims, loss, suit, liability or judgment suffered by Media User, including reasonable attorney's fees and costs, based upon or related to any item prepared by Agency or at Agency's direction, including, but not limited to, any claim of libel, slander, piracy, plagiarism, invasion of privacy, or infringement of copyright or other intellectual property interest, except where any such claim arises out of material supplied by Media User and incorporated into any materials or advertisement prepared by Agency. Agency agrees to procure and maintain in force during the term of this Agreement, at Agency's expense, an Agency liability policy or policies having a minimum limit of at least _____, naming Media User as an additional insured and loss payee under such policy or policies.

B. Media User agrees to indemnify and hold Agency harmless with respect to any claims, loss, liability, damage or judgment suffered by Agency, including reasonable attorney's fees and court costs, which results from the use by Agency of any material furnished by Media User or where material created by Agency or at the direction of Agency subject to the indemnification in subsection A. above is materially changed by Media User. Information or data obtained by Agency from Media User to substantiate claims made in advertising shall be deemed to be "material furnished by Media User to Agency."

C. In the event of any proceeding, litigation or suit against Media User by any regulatory agency or in the event of any court action or other proceeding challenging any advertising prepared by Agency, Agency shall assist in the preparation of the defense of such action or proceeding and cooperate with Media User and Media User's attorneys.

11. Term.

The term of this Agreement shall commence on _____ and shall continue in full force and effect until terminated by either party upon at least sixty (60) days prior written notice, provided that in no event (except breach) may this Agreement be terminated prior to _____. The rights, duties and obligations of the parties shall continue in full force during or following the period of the termination notice until termination, including the ordering and billing of advertising in media whose closing dates follow then such period.

12. Rights Upon Termination.

A. Upon termination of the Agreement, Agency shall transfer, assign and make available to Media User all property and materials in Agency's possession or subject to Agency's control that are the property of Media User, subject to payment in full of amounts due pursuant to this Agreement.

B. Upon termination, Agency agrees to provide reasonable cooperation in arranging for the transfer or approval of third party's interest in all contracts, agreements and other arrangements with advertising media, suppliers, talent and others not then utilized, and all rights and claims thereto and therein, following appropriate release from the obligations therein.

13. Default.

In the event of any default of any material obligation by or owed by a party pursuant to this Agreement, then the other party may provide written notice of such default and if such default is not cured within ten (10) days of the written notice, then the nondefaulting party may terminate this Agreement. In addition, the only damages collectible by Agency shall be the exact amounts due; no other damages,

for any reason whatsoever, may be assessed against Media User including, but limited to, punitive damages and unreasonable termination charges, and any other such claim. This provision shall be broadly interpreted in the favor of the Media User by any Court of competent jurisdiction.

14. Notices.

Any notice required by this Agreement or given in connection with it, shall be in writing and shall be given to the appropriate party by personal delivery or by postage prepaid, or recognized overnight delivery services such as Federal Express.

If to Media User: _____

_____

If to Agency: _____

_____

15. Headings in this Agreement.

The headings in this Agreement are for convenience only, confirm no rights or obligations in either party, and do not alter any terms of this Agreement.

16. Entirety of Agreement.

The terms and conditions set forth herein constitute the entire agreement between the parties and supersede any communications or previous agreements with respect to the subject matter of this Agreement. There are no written or oral understandings directly or indirectly related to this Agreement that are not set forth herein. No change can be made to this Agreement other than in writing and signed by both parties.

17. Governing Law.

This Agreement shall be construed and enforced according to the laws of the State of _____ and any dispute under this Agreement must be brought in this venue and in no other.

In Witness whereof, the parties have executed this Agreement as of the date first written above.

_____ _____
Agency   Media User

Ad or other Media Agency Agreement

This Agency Agreement ("Agreement") is made and effective this _____ (Date), by and between ("Agency") and _____ (Your Firm) ("Media User").

Agency is in the business of providing media agency services for a fee.

Media User desires to engage Agency to render, and Agency desires to render to Media User, certain Agency services, all as set forth.

NOW, THEREFORE, in consideration of the mutual agreements and covenants herein contained, the parties hereto agree as follows:

1. Engagement.

Media User engages Agency to render, and Agency agrees to render to Media User, services in connection with Media User's planning, preparing and placing of advertising and other media services for certain of Media User's products as follows:

_____

A. Analyze Media User's current and proposed products and services and presentations and potential markets.

B. Create, prepare and submit to Media User for its prior approval advertising ideas, media suggestions, and other such related programs.

C. Prepare and submit to Media User for its prior approval estimates of costs and expenses associated with proposed advertising ideas and programs prior to any such implementation or financial commitment.

D. Design and prepare, or arrange for the design and preparation of advertisements, public relations, and other such materials.

E. Perform such other services as Media User may request from time to time such as, but not limited to, direct mail ad preparations, speech writing, publicity and public relations work, market research and analysis, and other similar and related activities.

F. Order advertising space, time or other means to be used for publication of Media User's advertisements, at all times endeavoring to secure the most efficient and advantageous rates available. All such activities to be approved in advance by the Media User unless otherwise written and stipulated.

G. Proof for accuracy and completeness of insertions, displays, broadcasts, or other forms of advertisements.

H. Audit invoices for proper and agreed upon space, time, material preparation and charges.

2. Products.

Agency's engagement shall relate to the following products and services of Media User:

_____.

3. Exclusivity.

Agency shall be the Agency in the United States and worldwide for Media User with respect to the products described in Section 2 above, unless otherwise specified in this section:

_____.

4.   Compensation.

A.   Agency shall receive an amount equal to ___ percentage of the gross charges levied by media for advertising placed by Agency pursuant to this Agreement; and   after volume discount, of the charges of suppliers of services or properties, such as finished art, comprehensive layouts, type composition, photostats, engravings, printing, radio and television programs, talent, literary, dramatic and musical works, records and exhibits, purchased by Agency on Media User's authorization during the term of this Agreement; provided that: No percentage will be added to Agency charges for packing, shipping, express, postage, telephone, telex, fax, travel expenses and other out of pocket expenses of Agency personnel.

B.   For those items where Agency is not compensated on a commission basis, Media User shall pay Agency on an hourly basis for services provided hereunder. The rate will be determined by the type of services provided and the person or persons providing such services, but in no event shall the rate exceed _____ per hour. Media User may elect in advance to be charged on this hourly rate basis. If Media User fails to notify Agency of its choice, it shall be presumed that Media User elected to be charged on a percentage basis.

C.   In the event that Agency undertakes, at Media User's request subject to Media User's prior approval, special projects such as those described in Section I.F above, Agency shall prepare an estimate of total charges for any such special project in advance, including any charges for materials or services purchased from outside vendors. In the event that Media User elects to proceed with the special project based upon Agency's estimated cost, Agency shall perform the services with respect to such special project at its estimated cost, subject to modification as mutually agreed by the parties.

D. For any special project or other services provided by Agency pursuant to this Agreement upon which the parties have not agreed as to charges, Media User shall pay
Agency at its regular percentage rates, as stated in Section 4.A above.

E.   Media User shall not be obligated to reimburse Agency for any travel or other out-of-pocket expenses incurred in the performance of services pursuant to this Agreement unless expressly agreed by Media User in advance.

5. Billing.

A.   Agency shall invoice Media User for all media costs where possible in advance of Agency's payment date to allow for prepayment by the Media User so that Media User may receive the benefit of any available prepayment or similar discount. For any media purchase or service for which Agency is not entitled to a commission, Agency shall ensure that the charges to Media User are net of all agency commissions and discounts.

B.   Charges for production materials and services shall be billed by Agency upon completion of the production job or, if cash discounts are available, upon receipt of the supplier's invoice.

C. On all outside purchases other than for media, Agency shall attach to the invoice evidence of the supplier's charges.

D. All cash discounts on Agency's purchases including, but not limited to, media, art, printing and mechanical work, shall be available to Media User, provided that Media User meets Agency's requisite billing terms and there is no outstanding undisputed indebtedness of Media User to Agency at the time of the payment to the supplier.

E. Rate or billing adjustments shall be credited or charged to Media User on the next regular invoice date or as soon thereafter as otherwise practical.

F. Invoices shall be submitted in an itemized format and shall be paid by Media User within sixty (60) days of the invoice date.

6. Competitors.

During the term of this Agreement, Agency shall not accept employment from, render services to, represent or otherwise be affiliated with any person, firm, corporation or entity in connection with any product or service directly or indirectly competitive with or similar to any product or service of Media User with respect to which the Agency is providing any service pursuant to this Agreement, without the advance approval of the Media User. Media User shall not unreasonably withhold this approval.

7. Cost Estimates.

Agency shall not initiate billable work on any project pursuant to this Agreement without first estimating costs for preparation, including copy, service, layout, art, engraving, typography, processing, paste up and production. After determining the estimated cost, completion of the work shall be subject to Media User's prior approval.

8. Audit Rights.

Agency agrees that following reasonable prior notice any and all contracts, agreements, correspondence, books, accounts and other information relating to Media User's business or this Agreement shall be available for inspection by Media User and Media User's outside accountants, at Media User's expense and during the normal business hours of the Agency.

9. Ownership and Use.

A. Agency shall insure, to the fullest extent possible under law, that Media User shall own all right, title and interest in and to, including copyrights, trade secret, patent and other intellectual property rights, with respect to any copy, photograph, advertisement, music, lyrics, video, or other work or thing created by Agency or at Agency's direction for Media User pursuant to this Agreement and utilized by Media User.

B. Upon termination, Media User agrees that any advertising, merchandising, package, plan or idea prepared by Agency and submitted to Media User (whether submitted separately or in conjunction with or as a part of other material) which Media User has elected not to utilize, shall remain the property of Agency, unless Media User has paid Agency for its services in preparing such item. Media User agrees to return to Agency any copy, artwork, plates or other physical embodiment of such creative work relating to any such idea or plan which may be in Media User's possession at termination or expiration of this Agreement. Notwithstanding this, Media User has the unconditional right to pay for any of these materials or activities at the rate agreed upon in this Agreement and thereby these materials and activities would fall under the Section 9.A ownership and use rights accruing to Media User.

C. Materials and advertisements created by Agency pursuant to this Agreement may be used by Media User outside the United States without additional compensation, provided that Media User shall

be responsible for any additional expense associated with such use, such as charges for translation and amounts due talent.

10. Indemnification and Insurance.

A.   Agency shall indemnify and hold Media User harmless with respect to any claims, loss, suit, liability or judgment suffered by Media User, including reasonable attorney's fees and costs, based upon or related to any item prepared by Agency or at Agency's direction, including, but not limited to, any claim of libel, slander, piracy, plagiarism, invasion of privacy, or infringement of copyright or other intellectual property interest, except where any such claim arises out of material supplied by Media User and incorporated into any materials or advertisement prepared by Agency. Agency agrees to procure and maintain in force during the term of this Agreement, at Agency's expense, an Agency liability policy or policies having a minimum limit of at least _____, naming Media User as an additional insured and loss payee under such policy or policies.

B.   Media User agrees to indemnify and hold Agency harmless with respect to any claims, loss, liability, damage or judgment suffered by Agency, including reasonable attorney's fees and court costs, which results from the use by Agency of any material furnished by Media User or where material created by Agency or at the direction of Agency subject to the indemnification in subsection A. above is materially changed by Media User. Information or data obtained by Agency from Media User to substantiate claims made in advertising shall be deemed to be "material furnished by Media User to Agency."

C.   In the event of any proceeding, litigation or suit against Media User by any regulatory agency or in the event of any court action or other proceeding challenging any advertising prepared by Agency, Agency shall assist in the preparation of the defense of such action or proceeding and cooperate with Media User and Media User's attorneys.

11. Term.

The term of this Agreement shall commence on _____ and shall continue in full force and effect until terminated by either party upon at least sixty (60) days prior written notice, provided that in no event (except breach) may this Agreement be terminated prior to _____. The rights, duties and obligations of the parties shall continue in full force during or following the period of the termination notice until termination, including the ordering and billing of advertising in media whose closing dates follow then such period.

12. Rights Upon Termination.

A.   Upon termination of the Agreement, Agency shall transfer, assign and make available to Media User all property and materials in Agency's possession or subject to Agency's control that are the property of Media User, subject to payment in full of amounts due pursuant to this Agreement.

B.   Upon termination, Agency agrees to provide reasonable cooperation in arranging for the transfer or approval of third party's interest in all contracts, agreements and other arrangements with advertising media, suppliers, talent and others not then utilized, and all rights and claims thereto and therein, following appropriate release from the obligations therein.

13. Default.

In the event of any default of any material obligation by or owed by a party pursuant to this Agreement, then the other party may provide written notice of such default and if such default is not cured within ten (10) days of the written notice, then the nondefaulting party may terminate this Agreement. In addition, the only damages collectible by Agency shall be the exact amounts due; no other damages,

for any reason whatsoever, may be assessed against Media User including, but limited to, punitive damages and unreasonable termination charges, and any other such claim. This provision shall be broadly interpreted in the favor of the Media User by any Court of competent jurisdiction.

14. Notices.

Any notice required by this Agreement or given in connection with it, shall be in writing and shall be given to the appropriate party by personal delivery or by postage prepaid, or recognized overnight delivery services such as Federal Express.

If to Media User: _____

_____

If to Agency: _____

_____

15. Headings in this Agreement.

The headings in this Agreement are for convenience only, confirm no rights or obligations in either party, and do not alter any terms of this Agreement.

16. Entirety of Agreement.

The terms and conditions set forth herein constitute the entire agreement between the parties and supersede any communications or previous agreements with respect to the subject matter of this Agreement. There are no written or oral understandings directly or indirectly related to this Agreement that are not set forth herein. No change can be made to this Agreement other than in writing and signed by both parties.

17. Governing Law.

This Agreement shall be construed and enforced according to the laws of the State of _____ and any dispute under this Agreement must be brought in this venue and in no other.

In Witness whereof, the parties have executed this Agreement as of the date first written above.

_____   _____
Agency   Media User

Ad or other Media Agency Agreement

This Agency Agreement ("Agreement") is made and effective this _____ (Date), by and between ("Agency") and _____ (Your Firm) ("Media User").

Agency is in the business of providing media agency services for a fee.

Media User desires to engage Agency to render, and Agency desires to render to Media User, certain Agency services, all as set forth.

NOW, THEREFORE, in consideration of the mutual agreements and covenants herein contained, the parties hereto agree as follows:

1. <u>Engagement</u>.

Media User engages Agency to render, and Agency agrees to render to Media User, services in connection with Media User's planning, preparing and placing of advertising and other media services for certain of Media User's products as follows:

_____

A. Analyze Media User's current and proposed products and services and presentations and potential markets.

B. Create, prepare and submit to Media User for its prior approval advertising ideas, media suggestions, and other such related programs.

C. Prepare and submit to Media User for its prior approval estimates of costs and expenses associated with proposed advertising ideas and programs prior to any such implementation or financial commitment.

D. Design and prepare, or arrange for the design and preparation of advertisements, public relations, and other such materials.

E. Perform such other services as Media User may request from time to time such as, but not limited to, direct mail ad preparations, speech writing, publicity and public relations work, market research and analysis, and other similar and related activities.

F. Order advertising space, time or other means to be used for publication of Media User's advertisements, at all times endeavoring to secure the most efficient and advantageous rates available. All such activities to be approved in advance by the Media User unless otherwise written and stipulated.

G. Proof for accuracy and completeness of insertions, displays, broadcasts, or other forms of advertisements.

H. Audit invoices for proper and agreed upon space, time, material preparation and charges.

2. <u>Products</u>.

Agency's engagement shall relate to the following products and services of Media User:

_____

3. <u>Exclusivity</u>.

Agency shall be the Agency in the United States and worldwide for Media User with respect to the products described in Section 2 above, unless otherwise specified in this section:

_____.

4.   <u>Compensation</u>.

A.   Agency shall receive an amount equal to ___ percentage of the gross charges levied by media for advertising placed by Agency pursuant to this Agreement; and after volume discount, of the charges of suppliers of services or properties, such as finished art, comprehensive layouts, type composition, photostats, engravings, printing, radio and television programs, talent, literary, dramatic and musical works, records and exhibits, purchased by Agency on Media User's authorization during the term of this Agreement; provided that: No percentage will be added to Agency charges for packing, shipping, express, postage, telephone, telex, fax, travel expenses and other out of pocket expenses of Agency personnel.

B.   For those items where Agency is not compensated on a commission basis, Media User shall pay Agency on an hourly basis for services provided hereunder. The rate will be determined by the type of services provided and the person or persons providing such services, but in no event shall the rate exceed _____ per hour. Media User may elect in advance to be charged on this hourly rate basis. If Media User fails to notify Agency of its choice, it shall be presumed that Media User elected to be charged on a percentage basis.

C.   In the event that Agency undertakes, at Media User's request subject to Media User's prior approval, special projects such as those described in Section I.F above, Agency shall prepare an estimate of total charges for any such special project in advance, including any charges for materials or services purchased from outside vendors. In the event that Media User elects to proceed with the special project based upon Agency's estimated cost, Agency shall perform the services with respect to such special project at its estimated cost, subject to modification as mutually agreed by the parties.

D. For any special project or other services provided by Agency pursuant to this Agreement upon which the parties have not agreed as to charges, Media User shall pay
Agency at its regular percentage rates, as stated in Section 4.A above.

E.   Media User shall not be obligated to reimburse Agency for any travel or other out-of-pocket expenses incurred in the performance of services pursuant to this Agreement unless expressly agreed by Media User in advance.

5. <u>Billing</u>.

A.   Agency shall invoice Media User for all media costs where possible in advance of Agency's payment date to allow for prepayment by the Media User so that Media User may receive the benefit of any available prepayment or similar discount. For any media purchase or service for which Agency is not entitled to a commission, Agency shall ensure that the charges to Media User are net of all agency commissions and discounts.

B.   Charges for production materials and services shall be billed by Agency upon completion of the production job or, if cash discounts are available, upon receipt of the supplier's invoice.

C. On all outside purchases other than for media, Agency shall attach to the invoice evidence of the supplier's charges.

D.   All cash discounts on Agency's purchases including, but not limited to, media, art, printing and mechanical work, shall be available to Media User, provided that Media User meets Agency's requisite billing terms and there is no outstanding undisputed indebtedness of Media User to Agency at the time of the payment to the supplier.

E. Rate or billing adjustments shall be credited or charged to Media User on the next regular invoice date or as soon thereafter as otherwise practical.

F. Invoices shall be submitted in an itemized format and shall be paid by Media User within sixty (60) days of the invoice date.

6. Competitors.

During the term of this Agreement, Agency shall not accept employment from, render services to, represent or otherwise be affiliated with any person, firm, corporation or entity in connection with any product or service directly or indirectly competitive with or similar to any product or service of Media User with respect to which the Agency is providing any service pursuant to this Agreement, without the advance approval of the Media User. Media User shall not unreasonably withhold this approval.

7. Cost Estimates.

Agency shall not initiate billable work on any project pursuant to this Agreement without first estimating costs for preparation, including copy, service, layout, art, engraving, typography, processing, paste up and production. After determining the estimated cost, completion of the work shall be subject to Media User's prior approval.

8. Audit Rights.

Agency agrees that following reasonable prior notice any and all contracts, agreements, correspondence, books, accounts and other information relating to Media User's business or this Agreement shall be available for inspection by Media User and Media User's outside accountants, at Media User's expense and during the normal business hours of the Agency.

9.Ownership and Use.

A.   Agency shall insure, to the fullest extent possible under law, that Media User shall own all right, title and interest in and to, including copyrights, trade secret, patent and other intellectual property rights, with respect to any copy, photograph, advertisement, music, lyrics, video, or other work or thing created by Agency or at Agency's direction for Media User pursuant to this Agreement and utilized by Media User.

B.   Upon termination, Media User agrees that any advertising, merchandising, package, plan or idea prepared by Agency and submitted to Media User (whether submitted separately or in conjunction with or as a part of other material) which Media User has elected not to utilize, shall remain the property of Agency, unless Media User has paid Agency for its services in preparing such item. Media User agrees to return to Agency any copy, artwork, plates or other physical embodiment of such creative work relating to any such idea or plan which may be in Media User's possession at termination or expiration of this Agreement. Notwithstanding this, Media User has the unconditional right to pay for any of these materials or activities at the rate agreed upon in this Agreement and thereby these materials and activities would fall under the Section 9.A ownership and use rights accruing to Media User.

C.   Materials and advertisements created by Agency pursuant to this Agreement may be used by Media User outside the United States without additional compensation, provided that Media User shall

be responsible for any additional expense associated with such use, such as charges for translation and amounts due talent.

10. Indemnification and Insurance.

A. Agency shall indemnify and hold Media User harmless with respect to any claims, loss, suit, liability or judgment suffered by Media User, including reasonable attorney's fees and costs, based upon or related to any item prepared by Agency or at Agency's direction, including, but not limited to, any claim of libel, slander, piracy, plagiarism, invasion of privacy, or infringement of copyright or other intellectual property interest, except where any such claim arises out of material supplied by Media User and incorporated into any materials or advertisement prepared by Agency. Agency agrees to procure and maintain in force during the term of this Agreement, at Agency's expense, an Agency liability policy or policies having a minimum limit of at least _____, naming Media User as an additional insured and loss payee under such policy or policies.

B. Media User agrees to indemnify and hold Agency harmless with respect to any claims, loss, liability, damage or judgment suffered by Agency, including reasonable attorney's fees and court costs, which results from the use by Agency of any material furnished by Media User or where material created by Agency or at the direction of Agency subject to the indemnification in subsection A. above is materially changed by Media User. Information or data obtained by Agency from Media User to substantiate claims made in advertising shall be deemed to be "material furnished by Media User to Agency."

C. In the event of any proceeding, litigation or suit against Media User by any regulatory agency or in the event of any court action or other proceeding challenging any advertising prepared by Agency, Agency shall assist in the preparation of the defense of such action or proceeding and cooperate with Media User and Media User's attorneys.

11. Term.

The term of this Agreement shall commence on _____ and shall continue in full force and effect until terminated by either party upon at least sixty (60) days prior written notice, provided that in no event (except breach) may this Agreement be terminated prior to _____. The rights, duties and obligations of the parties shall continue in full force during or following the period of the termination notice until termination, including the ordering and billing of advertising in media whose closing dates follow then such period.

12. Rights Upon Termination.

A. Upon termination of the Agreement, Agency shall transfer, assign and make available to Media User all property and materials in Agency's possession or subject to Agency's control that are the property of Media User, subject to payment in full of amounts due pursuant to this Agreement.

B. Upon termination, Agency agrees to provide reasonable cooperation in arranging for the transfer or approval of third party's interest in all contracts, agreements and other arrangements with advertising media, suppliers, talent and others not then utilized, and all rights and claims thereto and therein, following appropriate release from the obligations therein.

13. Default.

In the event of any default of any material obligation by or owed by a party pursuant to this Agreement, then the other party may provide written notice of such default and if such default is not cured within ten (10) days of the written notice, then the nondefaulting party may terminate this Agreement. In addition, the only damages collectible by Agency shall be the exact amounts due; no other damages,

for any reason whatsoever, may be assessed against Media User including, but limited to, punitive damages and unreasonable termination charges, and any other such claim. This provision shall be broadly interpreted in the favor of the Media User by any Court of competent jurisdiction.

14. Notices.

Any notice required by this Agreement or given in connection with it, shall be in writing and shall be given to the appropriate party by personal delivery or by postage prepaid, or recognized overnight delivery services such as Federal Express.

If to Media User: _____

                          _____

If to Agency: _____

                          _____

15. Headings in this Agreement.

The headings in this Agreement are for convenience only, confirm no rights or obligations in either party, and do not alter any terms of this Agreement.

16. Entirety of Agreement.

The terms and conditions set forth herein constitute the entire agreement between the parties and supersede any communications or previous agreements with respect to the subject matter of this Agreement. There are no written or oral understandings directly or indirectly related to this Agreement that are not set forth herein. No change can be made to this Agreement other than in writing and signed by both parties.

17. Governing Law.

This Agreement shall be construed and enforced according to the laws of the State of _____ and any dispute under this Agreement must be brought in this venue and in no other.

In Witness whereof, the parties have executed this Agreement as of the date first written above.

_____   _____
Agency   Media User

Ad or other Media Agency Agreement

This Agency Agreement ("Agreement") is made and effective this _____ (Date), by and between ("Agency") and _____ (Your Firm) ("Media User").

Agency is in the business of providing media agency services for a fee.

Media User desires to engage Agency to render, and Agency desires to render to Media User, certain Agency services, all as set forth.

NOW, THEREFORE, in consideration of the mutual agreements and covenants herein contained, the parties hereto agree as follows:

1. Engagement.

Media User engages Agency to render, and Agency agrees to render to Media User, services in connection with Media User's planning, preparing and placing of advertising and other media services for certain of Media User's products as follows:

_____

A. Analyze Media User's current and proposed products and services and presentations and potential markets.

B. Create, prepare and submit to Media User for its prior approval advertising ideas, media suggestions, and other such related programs.

C. Prepare and submit to Media User for its prior approval estimates of costs and expenses associated with proposed advertising ideas and programs prior to any such implementation or financial commitment.

D. Design and prepare, or arrange for the design and preparation of advertisements, public relations, and other such materials.

E. Perform such other services as Media User may request from time to time such as, but not limited to, direct mail ad preparations, speech writing, publicity and public relations work, market research and analysis, and other similar and related activities.

F. Order advertising space, time or other means to be used for publication of Media User's advertisements, at all times endeavoring to secure the most efficient and advantageous rates available. All such activities to be approved in advance by the Media User unless otherwise written and stipulated.

G. Proof for accuracy and completeness of insertions, displays, broadcasts, or other forms of advertisements.

H. Audit invoices for proper and agreed upon space, time, material preparation and charges.

2. Products.

Agency's engagement shall relate to the following products and services of Media User:

_____ .

3. Exclusivity.

Agency shall be the Agency in the United States and worldwide for Media User with respect to the products described in Section 2 above, unless otherwise specified in this section:

_____.

4.   Compensation.

A.   Agency shall receive an amount equal to ___ percentage of the gross charges levied by media for advertising placed by Agency pursuant to this Agreement; and   after volume discount, of the charges of suppliers of services or properties, such as finished art, comprehensive layouts, type composition, photostats, engravings, printing, radio and television programs, talent, literary, dramatic and musical works, records and exhibits, purchased by Agency on Media User's authorization during the term of this Agreement; provided that: No percentage will be added to Agency charges for packing, shipping, express, postage, telephone, telex, fax, travel expenses and other out of pocket expenses of Agency personnel.

B.   For those items where Agency is not compensated on a commission basis, Media User shall pay Agency on an hourly basis for services provided hereunder. The rate will be determined by the type of services provided and the person or persons providing such services, but in no event shall the rate exceed _____ per hour. Media User may elect in advance to be charged on this hourly rate basis. If Media User fails to notify Agency of its choice, it shall be presumed that Media User elected to be charged on a percentage basis.

C.   In the event that Agency undertakes, at Media User's request subject to Media User's prior approval, special projects such as those described in Section I.F above, Agency shall prepare an estimate of total charges for any such special project in advance, including any charges for materials or services purchased from outside vendors. In the event that Media User elects to proceed with the special project based upon Agency's estimated cost, Agency shall perform the services with respect to such special project at its estimated cost, subject to modification as mutually agreed by the parties.

D. For any special project or other services provided by Agency pursuant to this Agreement upon which the parties have not agreed as to charges, Media User shall pay
Agency at its regular percentage rates, as stated in Section 4.A above.

E.   Media User shall not be obligated to reimburse Agency for any travel or other out-of-pocket expenses incurred in the performance of services pursuant to this Agreement unless expressly agreed by Media User in advance.

5. Billing.

A.   Agency shall invoice Media User for all media costs where possible in advance of Agency's payment date to allow for prepayment by the Media User so that Media User may receive the benefit of any available prepayment or similar discount. For any media purchase or service for which Agency is not entitled to a commission, Agency shall ensure that the charges to Media User are net of all agency commissions and discounts.

B.   Charges for production materials and services shall be billed by Agency upon completion of the production job or, if cash discounts are available, upon receipt of the supplier's invoice.

C. On all outside purchases other than for media, Agency shall attach to the invoice evidence of the supplier's charges.

D.   All cash discounts on Agency's purchases including, but not limited to, media, art, printing and mechanical work, shall be available to Media User, provided that Media User meets Agency's requisite billing terms and there is no outstanding undisputed indebtedness of Media User to Agency at the time of the payment to the supplier.

E. Rate or billing adjustments shall be credited or charged to Media User on the next regular invoice date or as soon thereafter as otherwise practical.

F. Invoices shall be submitted in an itemized format and shall be paid by Media User within sixty (60) days of the invoice date.

6. Competitors.

During the term of this Agreement, Agency shall not accept employment from, render services to, represent or otherwise be affiliated with any person, firm, corporation or entity in connection with any product or service directly or indirectly competitive with or similar to any product or service of Media User with respect to which the Agency is providing any service pursuant to this Agreement, without the advance approval of the Media User. Media User shall not unreasonably withhold this approval.

7. Cost Estimates.

Agency shall not initiate billable work on any project pursuant to this Agreement without first estimating costs for preparation, including copy, service, layout, art, engraving, typography, processing, paste up and production. After determining the estimated cost, completion of the work shall be subject to Media User's prior approval.

8. Audit Rights.

Agency agrees that following reasonable prior notice any and all contracts, agreements, correspondence, books, accounts and other information relating to Media User's business or this Agreement shall be available for inspection by Media User and Media User's outside accountants, at Media User's expense and during the normal business hours of the Agency.

9. Ownership and Use.

A.   Agency shall insure, to the fullest extent possible under law, that Media User shall own all right, title and interest in and to, including copyrights, trade secret, patent and other intellectual property rights, with respect to any copy, photograph, advertisement, music, lyrics, video, or other work or thing created by Agency or at Agency's direction for Media User pursuant to this Agreement and utilized by Media User.

B.   Upon termination, Media User agrees that any advertising, merchandising, package, plan or idea prepared by Agency and submitted to Media User (whether submitted separately or in conjunction with or as a part of other material) which Media User has elected not to utilize, shall remain the property of Agency, unless Media User has paid Agency for its services in preparing such item. Media User agrees to return to Agency any copy, artwork, plates or other physical embodiment of such creative work relating to any such idea or plan which may be in Media User's possession at termination or expiration of this Agreement. Notwithstanding this, Media User has the unconditional right to pay for any of these materials or activities at the rate agreed upon in this Agreement and thereby these materials and activities would fall under the Section 9.A ownership and use rights accruing to Media User.

C.   Materials and advertisements created by Agency pursuant to this Agreement may be used by Media User outside the United States without additional compensation, provided that Media User shall

be responsible for any additional expense associated with such use, such as charges for translation and amounts due talent.

10. <u>Indemnification and Insurance</u>.

A. Agency shall indemnify and hold Media User harmless with respect to any claims, loss, suit, liability or judgment suffered by Media User, including reasonable attorney's fees and costs, based upon or related to any item prepared by Agency or at Agency's direction, including, but not limited to, any claim of libel, slander, piracy, plagiarism, invasion of privacy, or infringement of copyright or other intellectual property interest, except where any such claim arises out of material supplied by Media User and incorporated into any materials or advertisement prepared by Agency. Agency agrees to procure and maintain in force during the term of this Agreement, at Agency's expense, an Agency liability policy or policies having a minimum limit of at least _____, naming Media User as an additional insured and loss payee under such policy or policies.

B. Media User agrees to indemnify and hold Agency harmless with respect to any claims, loss, liability, damage or judgment suffered by Agency, including reasonable attorney's fees and court costs, which results from the use by Agency of any material furnished by Media User or where material created by Agency or at the direction of Agency subject to the indemnification in subsection A. above is materially changed by Media User. Information or data obtained by Agency from Media User to substantiate claims made in advertising shall be deemed to be "material furnished by Media User to Agency."

C. In the event of any proceeding, litigation or suit against Media User by any regulatory agency or in the event of any court action or other proceeding challenging any advertising prepared by Agency, Agency shall assist in the preparation of the defense of such action or proceeding and cooperate with Media User and Media User's attorneys.

11. <u>Term</u>.

The term of this Agreement shall commence on _____ and shall continue in full force and effect until terminated by either party upon at least sixty (60) days prior written notice, provided that in no event (except breach) may this Agreement be terminated prior to _____. The rights, duties and obligations of the parties shall continue in full force during or following the period of the termination notice until termination, including the ordering and billing of advertising in media whose closing dates follow then such period.

12. <u>Rights Upon Termination</u>.

A. Upon termination of the Agreement, Agency shall transfer, assign and make available to Media User all property and materials in Agency's possession or subject to Agency's control that are the property of Media User, subject to payment in full of amounts due pursuant to this Agreement.

B. Upon termination, Agency agrees to provide reasonable cooperation in arranging for the transfer or approval of third party's interest in all contracts, agreements and other arrangements with advertising media, suppliers, talent and others not then utilized, and all rights and claims thereto and therein, following appropriate release from the obligations therein.

13. <u>Default</u>.

In the event of any default of any material obligation by or owed by a party pursuant to this Agreement, then the other party may provide written notice of such default and if such default is not cured within ten (10) days of the written notice, then the nondefaulting party may terminate this Agreement. In addition, the only damages collectible by Agency shall be the exact amounts due; no other damages,

for any reason whatsoever, may be assessed against Media User including, but limited to, punitive damages and unreasonable termination charges, and any other such claim. This provision shall be broadly interpreted in the favor of the Media User by any Court of competent jurisdiction.

14. Notices.

Any notice required by this Agreement or given in connection with it, shall be in writing and shall be given to the appropriate party by personal delivery or by postage prepaid, or recognized overnight delivery services such as Federal Express.

If to Media User: _____

_____

If to Agency: _____

_____

15. Headings in this Agreement.

The headings in this Agreement are for convenience only, confirm no rights or obligations in either party, and do not alter any terms of this Agreement.

16. Entirety of Agreement.

The terms and conditions set forth herein constitute the entire agreement between the parties and supersede any communications or previous agreements with respect to the subject matter of this Agreement. There are no written or oral understandings directly or indirectly related to this Agreement that are not set forth herein. No change can be made to this Agreement other than in writing and signed by both parties.

17. Governing Law.

This Agreement shall be construed and enforced according to the laws of the State of _____ and any dispute under this Agreement must be brought in this venue and in no other.

In Witness whereof, the parties have executed this Agreement as of the date first written above.

_____   _____
Agency   Media User

Ad or other Media Agency Agreement

This Agency Agreement ("Agreement") is made and effective this _____ (Date), by and between ("Agency") and _____ (Your Firm) ("Media User").

Agency is in the business of providing media agency services for a fee.

Media User desires to engage Agency to render, and Agency desires to render to Media User, certain Agency services, all as set forth.

NOW, THEREFORE, in consideration of the mutual agreements and covenants herein contained, the parties hereto agree as follows:

1. Engagement.

Media User engages Agency to render, and Agency agrees to render to Media User, services in connection with Media User's planning, preparing and placing of advertising and other media services for certain of Media User's products as follows:

_____

A. Analyze Media User's current and proposed products and services and presentations and potential markets.

B. Create, prepare and submit to Media User for its prior approval advertising ideas, media suggestions, and other such related programs.

C. Prepare and submit to Media User for its prior approval estimates of costs and expenses associated with proposed advertising ideas and programs prior to any such implementation or financial commitment.

D. Design and prepare, or arrange for the design and preparation of advertisements, public relations, and other such materials.

E. Perform such other services as Media User may request from time to time such as, but not limited to, direct mail ad preparations, speech writing, publicity and public relations work, market research and analysis, and other similar and related activities.

F. Order advertising space, time or other means to be used for publication of Media User's advertisements, at all times endeavoring to secure the most efficient and advantageous rates available. All such activities to be approved in advance by the Media User unless otherwise written and stipulated.

G. Proof for accuracy and completeness of insertions, displays, broadcasts, or other forms of advertisements.

H. Audit invoices for proper and agreed upon space, time, material preparation and charges.

2. Products.

Agency's engagement shall relate to the following products and services of Media User:

_____.

3. Exclusivity.

Agency shall be the Agency in the United States and worldwide for Media User with respect to the products described in Section 2 above, unless otherwise specified in this section:

_____.

4. Compensation.

A. Agency shall receive an amount equal to ___ percentage of the gross charges levied by media for advertising placed by Agency pursuant to this Agreement; and   after volume discount, of the charges of suppliers of services or properties, such as finished art, comprehensive layouts, type composition, photostats, engravings, printing, radio and television programs, talent, literary, dramatic and musical works, records and exhibits, purchased by Agency on Media User's authorization during the term of this Agreement; provided that: No percentage will be added to Agency charges for packing, shipping, express, postage, telephone, telex, fax, travel expenses and other out of pocket expenses of Agency personnel.

B. For those items where Agency is not compensated on a commission basis, Media User shall pay Agency on an hourly basis for services provided hereunder. The rate will be determined by the type of services provided and the person or persons providing such services, but in no event shall the rate exceed _____ per hour. Media User may elect in advance to be charged on this hourly rate basis. If Media User fails to notify Agency of its choice, it shall be presumed that Media User elected to be charged on a percentage basis.

C. In the event that Agency undertakes, at Media User's request subject to Media User's prior approval, special projects such as those described in Section I.F above, Agency shall prepare an estimate of total charges for any such special project in advance, including any charges for materials or services purchased from outside vendors. In the event that Media User elects to proceed with the special project based upon Agency's estimated cost, Agency shall perform the services with respect to such special project at its estimated cost, subject to modification as mutually agreed by the parties.

D. For any special project or other services provided by Agency pursuant to this Agreement upon which the parties have not agreed as to charges, Media User shall pay
Agency at its regular percentage rates, as stated in Section 4.A above.

E. Media User shall not be obligated to reimburse Agency for any travel or other out-of-pocket expenses incurred in the performance of services pursuant to this Agreement unless expressly agreed by Media User in advance.

5. Billing.

A. Agency shall invoice Media User for all media costs where possible in advance of Agency's payment date to allow for prepayment by the Media User so that Media User may receive the benefit of any available prepayment or similar discount. For any media purchase or service for which Agency is not entitled to a commission, Agency shall ensure that the charges to Media User are net of all agency commissions and discounts.

B. Charges for production materials and services shall be billed by Agency upon completion of the production job or, if cash discounts are available, upon receipt of the supplier's invoice.

C. On all outside purchases other than for media, Agency shall attach to the invoice evidence of the supplier's charges.

D.	All cash discounts on Agency's purchases including, but not limited to, media, art, printing and mechanical work, shall be available to Media User, provided that Media User meets Agency's requisite billing terms and there is no outstanding undisputed indebtedness of Media User to Agency at the time of the payment to the supplier.

E. Rate or billing adjustments shall be credited or charged to Media User on the next regular invoice date or as soon thereafter as otherwise practical.

F. Invoices shall be submitted in an itemized format and shall be paid by Media User within sixty (60) days of the invoice date.

6. Competitors.

During the term of this Agreement, Agency shall not accept employment from, render services to, represent or otherwise be affiliated with any person, firm, corporation or entity in connection with any product or service directly or indirectly competitive with or similar to any product or service of Media User with respect to which the Agency is providing any service pursuant to this Agreement, without the advance approval of the Media User. Media User shall not unreasonably withhold this approval.

7. Cost Estimates.

Agency shall not initiate billable work on any project pursuant to this Agreement without first estimating costs for preparation, including copy, service, layout, art, engraving, typography, processing, paste up and production. After determining the estimated cost, completion of the work shall be subject to Media User's prior approval.

8. Audit Rights.

Agency agrees that following reasonable prior notice any and all contracts, agreements, correspondence, books, accounts and other information relating to Media User's business or this Agreement shall be available for inspection by Media User and Media User's outside accountants, at Media User's expense and during the normal business hours of the Agency.

9.Ownership and Use.

A.	Agency shall insure, to the fullest extent possible under law, that Media User shall own all right, title and interest in and to, including copyrights, trade secret, patent and other intellectual property rights, with respect to any copy, photograph, advertisement, music, lyrics, video, or other work or thing created by Agency or at Agency's direction for Media User pursuant to this Agreement and utilized by Media User.

B.	Upon termination, Media User agrees that any advertising, merchandising, package, plan or idea prepared by Agency and submitted to Media User (whether submitted separately or in conjunction with or as a part of other material) which Media User has elected not to utilize, shall remain the property of Agency, unless Media User has paid Agency for its services in preparing such item. Media User agrees to return to Agency any copy, artwork, plates or other physical embodiment of such creative work relating to any such idea or plan which may be in Media User's possession at termination or expiration of this Agreement. Notwithstanding this, Media User has the unconditional right to pay for any of these materials or activities at the rate agreed upon in this Agreement and thereby these materials and activities would fall under the Section 9.A ownership and use rights accruing to Media User.

C.	Materials and advertisements created by Agency pursuant to this Agreement may be used by Media User outside the United States without additional compensation, provided that Media User shall

be responsible for any additional expense associated with such use, such as charges for translation and amounts due talent.

10. Indemnification and Insurance.

A. Agency shall indemnify and hold Media User harmless with respect to any claims, loss, suit, liability or judgment suffered by Media User, including reasonable attorney's fees and costs, based upon or related to any item prepared by Agency or at Agency's direction, including, but not limited to, any claim of libel, slander, piracy, plagiarism, invasion of privacy, or infringement of copyright or other intellectual property interest, except where any such claim arises out of material supplied by Media User and incorporated into any materials or advertisement prepared by Agency. Agency agrees to procure and maintain in force during the term of this Agreement, at Agency's expense, an Agency liability policy or policies having a minimum limit of at least _____, naming Media User as an additional insured and loss payee under such policy or policies.

B. Media User agrees to indemnify and hold Agency harmless with respect to any claims, loss, liability, damage or judgment suffered by Agency, including reasonable attorney's fees and court costs, which results from the use by Agency of any material furnished by Media User or where material created by Agency or at the direction of Agency subject to the indemnification in subsection A. above is materially changed by Media User. Information or data obtained by Agency from Media User to substantiate claims made in advertising shall be deemed to be "material furnished by Media User to Agency."

C. In the event of any proceeding, litigation or suit against Media User by any regulatory agency or in the event of any court action or other proceeding challenging any advertising prepared by Agency, Agency shall assist in the preparation of the defense of such action or proceeding and cooperate with Media User and Media User's attorneys.

11. Term.

The term of this Agreement shall commence on _____ and shall continue in full force and effect until terminated by either party upon at least sixty (60) days prior written notice, provided that in no event (except breach) may this Agreement be terminated prior to _____. The rights, duties and obligations of the parties shall continue in full force during or following the period of the termination notice until termination, including the ordering and billing of advertising in media whose closing dates follow then such period.

12. Rights Upon Termination.

A. Upon termination of the Agreement, Agency shall transfer, assign and make available to Media User all property and materials in Agency's possession or subject to Agency's control that are the property of Media User, subject to payment in full of amounts due pursuant to this Agreement.

B. Upon termination, Agency agrees to provide reasonable cooperation in arranging for the transfer or approval of third party's interest in all contracts, agreements and other arrangements with advertising media, suppliers, talent and others not then utilized, and all rights and claims thereto and therein, following appropriate release from the obligations therein.

13. Default.

In the event of any default of any material obligation by or owed by a party pursuant to this Agreement, then the other party may provide written notice of such default and if such default is not cured within ten (10) days of the written notice, then the nondefaulting party may terminate this Agreement. In addition, the only damages collectible by Agency shall be the exact amounts due; no other damages,

for any reason whatsoever, may be assessed against Media User including, but limited to, punitive damages and unreasonable termination charges, and any other such claim. This provision shall be broadly interpreted in the favor of the Media User by any Court of competent jurisdiction.

14. Notices.

Any notice required by this Agreement or given in connection with it, shall be in writing and shall be given to the appropriate party by personal delivery or by postage prepaid, or recognized overnight delivery services such as Federal Express.

If to Media User: _____

_____

If to Agency: _____

_____

15. Headings in this Agreement.

The headings in this Agreement are for convenience only, confirm no rights or obligations in either party, and do not alter any terms of this Agreement.

16. Entirety of Agreement.

The terms and conditions set forth herein constitute the entire agreement between the parties and supersede any communications or previous agreements with respect to the subject matter of this Agreement. There are no written or oral understandings directly or indirectly related to this Agreement that are not set forth herein. No change can be made to this Agreement other than in writing and signed by both parties.

17. Governing Law.

This Agreement shall be construed and enforced according to the laws of the State of _____ and any dispute under this Agreement must be brought in this venue and in no other.

In Witness whereof, the parties have executed this Agreement as of the date first written above.

_____ _____
Agency   Media User

Ad or other Media Agency Agreement

This Agency Agreement ("Agreement") is made and effective this _____ (Date), by and between ("Agency") and _____ (Your Firm) ("Media User").

Agency is in the business of providing media agency services for a fee.

Media User desires to engage Agency to render, and Agency desires to render to Media User, certain Agency services, all as set forth.

NOW, THEREFORE, in consideration of the mutual agreements and covenants herein contained, the parties hereto agree as follows:

1. <u>Engagement</u>.

Media User engages Agency to render, and Agency agrees to render to Media User, services in connection with Media User's planning, preparing and placing of advertising and other media services for certain of Media User's products as follows:

_____

A. Analyze Media User's current and proposed products and services and presentations and potential markets.

B. Create, prepare and submit to Media User for its prior approval advertising ideas, media suggestions, and other such related programs.

C. Prepare and submit to Media User for its prior approval estimates of costs and expenses associated with proposed advertising ideas and programs prior to any such implementation or financial commitment.

D. Design and prepare, or arrange for the design and preparation of advertisements, public relations, and other such materials.

E. Perform such other services as Media User may request from time to time such as, but not limited to, direct mail ad preparations, speech writing, publicity and public relations work, market research and analysis, and other similar and related activities.

F. Order advertising space, time or other means to be used for publication of Media User's advertisements, at all times endeavoring to secure the most efficient and advantageous rates available. All such activities to be approved in advance by the Media User unless otherwise written and stipulated.

G. Proof for accuracy and completeness of insertions, displays, broadcasts, or other forms of advertisements.

H. Audit invoices for proper and agreed upon space, time, material preparation and charges.

2. <u>Products</u>.

Agency's engagement shall relate to the following products and services of Media User:

_____

3. Exclusivity.

Agency shall be the Agency in the United States and worldwide for Media User with respect to the products described in Section 2 above, unless otherwise specified in this section:

_____.

4.　　Compensation.

A.　　Agency shall receive an amount equal to ___ percentage of the gross charges levied by media for advertising placed by Agency pursuant to this Agreement; and _____ after volume discount, of the charges of suppliers of services or properties, such as finished art, comprehensive layouts, type composition, photostats, engravings, printing, radio and television programs, talent, literary, dramatic and musical works, records and exhibits, purchased by Agency on Media User's authorization during the term of this Agreement; provided that: No percentage will be added to Agency charges for packing, shipping, express, postage, telephone, telex, fax, travel expenses and other out of pocket expenses of Agency personnel.

B.　　For those items where Agency is not compensated on a commission basis, Media User shall pay Agency on an hourly basis for services provided hereunder. The rate will be determined by the type of services provided and the person or persons providing such services, but in no event shall the rate exceed _____ per hour. Media User may elect in advance to be charged on this hourly rate basis. If Media User fails to notify Agency of its choice, it shall be presumed that Media User elected to be charged on a percentage basis.

C.　　In the event that Agency undertakes, at Media User's request subject to Media User's prior approval, special projects such as those described in Section I.F above, Agency shall prepare an estimate of total charges for any such special project in advance, including any charges for materials or services purchased from outside vendors. In the event that Media User elects to proceed with the special project based upon Agency's estimated cost, Agency shall perform the services with respect to such special project at its estimated cost, subject to modification as mutually agreed by the parties.

D. For any special project or other services provided by Agency pursuant to this Agreement upon which the parties have not agreed as to charges, Media User shall pay
Agency at its regular percentage rates, as stated in Section 4.A above.

E.　　Media User shall not be obligated to reimburse Agency for any travel or other out-of-pocket expenses incurred in the performance of services pursuant to this Agreement unless expressly agreed by Media User in advance.

5. Billing.

A.　　Agency shall invoice Media User for all media costs where possible in advance of Agency's payment date to allow for prepayment by the Media User so that Media User may receive the benefit of any available prepayment or similar discount. For any media purchase or service for which Agency is not entitled to a commission, Agency shall ensure that the charges to Media User are net of all agency commissions and discounts.

B.　　Charges for production materials and services shall be billed by Agency upon completion of the production job or, if cash discounts are available, upon receipt of the supplier's invoice.

C. On all outside purchases other than for media, Agency shall attach to the invoice evidence of the supplier's charges.

D. All cash discounts on Agency's purchases including, but not limited to, media, art, printing and mechanical work, shall be available to Media User, provided that Media User meets Agency's requisite billing terms and there is no outstanding undisputed indebtedness of Media User to Agency at the time of the payment to the supplier.

E. Rate or billing adjustments shall be credited or charged to Media User on the next regular invoice date or as soon thereafter as otherwise practical.

F. Invoices shall be submitted in an itemized format and shall be paid by Media User within sixty (60) days of the invoice date.

6. Competitors.

During the term of this Agreement, Agency shall not accept employment from, render services to, represent or otherwise be affiliated with any person, firm, corporation or entity in connection with any product or service directly or indirectly competitive with or similar to any product or service of Media User with respect to which the Agency is providing any service pursuant to this Agreement, without the advance approval of the Media User. Media User shall not unreasonably withhold this approval.

7. Cost Estimates.

Agency shall not initiate billable work on any project pursuant to this Agreement without first estimating costs for preparation, including copy, service, layout, art, engraving, typography, processing, paste up and production. After determining the estimated cost, completion of the work shall be subject to Media User's prior approval.

8. Audit Rights.

Agency agrees that following reasonable prior notice any and all contracts, agreements, correspondence, books, accounts and other information relating to Media User's business or this Agreement shall be available for inspection by Media User and Media User's outside accountants, at Media User's expense and during the normal business hours of the Agency.

9. Ownership and Use.

A. Agency shall insure, to the fullest extent possible under law, that Media User shall own all right, title and interest in and to, including copyrights, trade secret, patent and other intellectual property rights, with respect to any copy, photograph, advertisement, music, lyrics, video, or other work or thing created by Agency or at Agency's direction for Media User pursuant to this Agreement and utilized by Media User.

B. Upon termination, Media User agrees that any advertising, merchandising, package, plan or idea prepared by Agency and submitted to Media User (whether submitted separately or in conjunction with or as a part of other material) which Media User has elected not to utilize, shall remain the property of Agency, unless Media User has paid Agency for its services in preparing such item. Media User agrees to return to Agency any copy, artwork, plates or other physical embodiment of such creative work relating to any such idea or plan which may be in Media User's possession at termination or expiration of this Agreement. Notwithstanding this, Media User has the unconditional right to pay for any of these materials or activities at the rate agreed upon in this Agreement and thereby these materials and activities would fall under the Section 9.A ownership and use rights accruing to Media User.

C. Materials and advertisements created by Agency pursuant to this Agreement may be used by Media User outside the United States without additional compensation, provided that Media User shall

be responsible for any additional expense associated with such use, such as charges for translation and amounts due talent.

10. Indemnification and Insurance.

A.   Agency shall indemnify and hold Media User harmless with respect to any claims, loss, suit, liability or judgment suffered by Media User, including reasonable attorney's fees and costs, based upon or related to any item prepared by Agency or at Agency's direction, including, but not limited to, any claim of libel, slander, piracy, plagiarism, invasion of privacy, or infringement of copyright or other intellectual property interest, except where any such claim arises out of material supplied by Media User and incorporated into any materials or advertisement prepared by Agency. Agency agrees to procure and maintain in force during the term of this Agreement, at Agency's expense, an Agency liability policy or policies having a minimum limit of at least _____, naming Media User as an additional insured and loss payee under such policy or policies.

B.   Media User agrees to indemnify and hold Agency harmless with respect to any claims, loss, liability, damage or judgment suffered by Agency, including reasonable attorney's fees and court costs, which results from the use by Agency of any material furnished by Media User or where material created by Agency or at the direction of Agency subject to the indemnification in subsection A. above is materially changed by Media User. Information or data obtained by Agency from Media User to substantiate claims made in advertising shall be deemed to be "material furnished by Media User to Agency."

C.   In the event of any proceeding, litigation or suit against Media User by any regulatory agency or in the event of any court action or other proceeding challenging any advertising prepared by Agency, Agency shall assist in the preparation of the defense of such action or proceeding and cooperate with Media User and Media User's attorneys.

11. Term.

The term of this Agreement shall commence on _____ and shall continue in full force and effect until terminated by either party upon at least sixty (60) days prior written notice, provided that in no event (except breach) may this Agreement be terminated prior to _____. The rights, duties and obligations of the parties shall continue in full force during or following the period of the termination notice until termination, including the ordering and billing of advertising in media whose closing dates follow then such period.

12. Rights Upon Termination.

A.   Upon termination of the Agreement, Agency shall transfer, assign and make available to Media User all property and materials in Agency's possession or subject to Agency's control that are the property of Media User, subject to payment in full of amounts due pursuant to this Agreement.

B.   Upon termination, Agency agrees to provide reasonable cooperation in arranging for the transfer or approval of third party's interest in all contracts, agreements and other arrangements with advertising media, suppliers, talent and others not then utilized, and all rights and claims thereto and therein, following appropriate release from the obligations therein.

13. Default.

In the event of any default of any material obligation by or owed by a party pursuant to this Agreement, then the other party may provide written notice of such default and if such default is not cured within ten (10) days of the written notice, then the nondefaulting party may terminate this Agreement. In addition, the only damages collectible by Agency shall be the exact amounts due; no other damages,

for any reason whatsoever, may be assessed against Media User including, but limited to, punitive damages and unreasonable termination charges, and any other such claim. This provision shall be broadly interpreted in the favor of the Media User by any Court of competent jurisdiction.

14. <u>Notices</u>.

Any notice required by this Agreement or given in connection with it, shall be in writing and shall be given to the appropriate party by personal delivery or by postage prepaid, or recognized overnight delivery services such as Federal Express.

If to Media User: _____

_____

If to Agency: _____

_____

15. <u>Headings in this Agreement</u>.

The headings in this Agreement are for convenience only, confirm no rights or obligations in either party, and do not alter any terms of this Agreement.

16. <u>Entirety of Agreement</u>.

The terms and conditions set forth herein constitute the entire agreement between the parties and supersede any communications or previous agreements with respect to the subject matter of this Agreement. There are no written or oral understandings directly or indirectly related to this Agreement that are not set forth herein. No change can be made to this Agreement other than in writing and signed by both parties.

17. <u>Governing Law</u>.

This Agreement shall be construed and enforced according to the laws of the State of _____ and any dispute under this Agreement must be brought in this venue and in no other.

In Witness whereof, the parties have executed this Agreement as of the date first written above.

_____   _____
Agency   Media User

Ad or other Media Agency Agreement

This Agency Agreement ("Agreement") is made and effective this _____ (Date), by and between ("Agency") and _____ (Your Firm) ("Media User").

Agency is in the business of providing media agency services for a fee.

Media User desires to engage Agency to render, and Agency desires to render to Media User, certain Agency services, all as set forth.

NOW, THEREFORE, in consideration of the mutual agreements and covenants herein contained, the parties hereto agree as follows:

1. <u>Engagement</u>.

Media User engages Agency to render, and Agency agrees to render to Media User, services in connection with Media User's planning, preparing and placing of advertising and other media services for certain of Media User's products as follows:

_____

A. Analyze Media User's current and proposed products and services and presentations and potential markets.

B. Create, prepare and submit to Media User for its prior approval advertising ideas, media suggestions, and other such related programs.

C. Prepare and submit to Media User for its prior approval estimates of costs and expenses associated with proposed advertising ideas and programs prior to any such implementation or financial commitment.

D. Design and prepare, or arrange for the design and preparation of advertisements, public relations, and other such materials.

E. Perform such other services as Media User may request from time to time such as, but not limited to, direct mail ad preparations, speech writing, publicity and public relations work, market research and analysis, and other similar and related activities.

F. Order advertising space, time or other means to be used for publication of Media User's advertisements, at all times endeavoring to secure the most efficient and advantageous rates available. All such activities to be approved in advance by the Media User unless otherwise written and stipulated.

G. Proof for accuracy and completeness of insertions, displays, broadcasts, or other forms of advertisements.

H. Audit invoices for proper and agreed upon space, time, material preparation and charges.

2. <u>Products</u>.

Agency's engagement shall relate to the following products and services of Media User:

_____.

3. <u>Exclusivity</u>.

Agency shall be the Agency in the United States and worldwide for Media User with respect to the products described in Section 2 above, unless otherwise specified in this section:

_____.

4.   <u>Compensation</u>.

A.   Agency shall receive an amount equal to ___ percentage of the gross charges levied by media for advertising placed by Agency pursuant to this Agreement; and   after volume discount, of the charges of suppliers of services or properties, such as finished art, comprehensive layouts, type composition, photostats, engravings, printing, radio and television programs, talent, literary, dramatic and musical works, records and exhibits, purchased by Agency on Media User's authorization during the term of this Agreement; provided that: No percentage will be added to Agency charges for packing, shipping, express, postage, telephone, telex, fax, travel expenses and other out of pocket expenses of Agency personnel.

B.   For those items where Agency is not compensated on a commission basis, Media User shall pay Agency on an hourly basis for services provided hereunder. The rate will be determined by the type of services provided and the person or persons providing such services, but in no event shall the rate exceed _____ per hour. Media User may elect in advance to be charged on this hourly rate basis. If Media User fails to notify Agency of its choice, it shall be presumed that Media User elected to be charged on a percentage basis.

C.   In the event that Agency undertakes, at Media User's request subject to Media User's prior approval, special projects such as those described in Section I.F above, Agency shall prepare an estimate of total charges for any such special project in advance, including any charges for materials or services purchased from outside vendors. In the event that Media User elects to proceed with the special project based upon Agency's estimated cost, Agency shall perform the services with respect to such special project at its estimated cost, subject to modification as mutually agreed by the parties.

D. For any special project or other services provided by Agency pursuant to this Agreement upon which the parties have not agreed as to charges, Media User shall pay
Agency at its regular percentage rates, as stated in Section 4.A above.

E.   Media User shall not be obligated to reimburse Agency for any travel or other out-of-pocket expenses incurred in the performance of services pursuant to this Agreement unless expressly agreed by Media User in advance.

5. <u>Billing</u>.

A.   Agency shall invoice Media User for all media costs where possible in advance of Agency's payment date to allow for prepayment by the Media User so that Media User may receive the benefit of any available prepayment or similar discount. For any media purchase or service for which Agency is not entitled to a commission, Agency shall ensure that the charges to Media User are net of all agency commissions and discounts.

B.   Charges for production materials and services shall be billed by Agency upon completion of the production job or, if cash discounts are available, upon receipt of the supplier's invoice.

C. On all outside purchases other than for media, Agency shall attach to the invoice evidence of the supplier's charges.

D. All cash discounts on Agency's purchases including, but not limited to, media, art, printing and mechanical work, shall be available to Media User, provided that Media User meets Agency's requisite billing terms and there is no outstanding undisputed indebtedness of Media User to Agency at the time of the payment to the supplier.

E. Rate or billing adjustments shall be credited or charged to Media User on the next regular invoice date or as soon thereafter as otherwise practical.

F. Invoices shall be submitted in an itemized format and shall be paid by Media User within sixty (60) days of the invoice date.

6. Competitors.

During the term of this Agreement, Agency shall not accept employment from, render services to, represent or otherwise be affiliated with any person, firm, corporation or entity in connection with any product or service directly or indirectly competitive with or similar to any product or service of Media User with respect to which the Agency is providing any service pursuant to this Agreement, without the advance approval of the Media User. Media User shall not unreasonably withhold this approval.

7. Cost Estimates.

Agency shall not initiate billable work on any project pursuant to this Agreement without first estimating costs for preparation, including copy, service, layout, art, engraving, typography, processing, paste up and production. After determining the estimated cost, completion of the work shall be subject to Media User's prior approval.

8. Audit Rights.

Agency agrees that following reasonable prior notice any and all contracts, agreements, correspondence, books, accounts and other information relating to Media User's business or this Agreement shall be available for inspection by Media User and Media User's outside accountants, at Media User's expense and during the normal business hours of the Agency.

9. Ownership and Use.

A. Agency shall insure, to the fullest extent possible under law, that Media User shall own all right, title and interest in and to, including copyrights, trade secret, patent and other intellectual property rights, with respect to any copy, photograph, advertisement, music, lyrics, video, or other work or thing created by Agency or at Agency's direction for Media User pursuant to this Agreement and utilized by Media User.

B. Upon termination, Media User agrees that any advertising, merchandising, package, plan or idea prepared by Agency and submitted to Media User (whether submitted separately or in conjunction with or as a part of other material) which Media User has elected not to utilize, shall remain the property of Agency, unless Media User has paid Agency for its services in preparing such item. Media User agrees to return to Agency any copy, artwork, plates or other physical embodiment of such creative work relating to any such idea or plan which may be in Media User's possession at termination or expiration of this Agreement. Notwithstanding this, Media User has the unconditional right to pay for any of these materials or activities at the rate agreed upon in this Agreement and thereby these materials and activities would fall under the Section 9.A ownership and use rights accruing to Media User.

C. Materials and advertisements created by Agency pursuant to this Agreement may be used by Media User outside the United States without additional compensation, provided that Media User shall

be responsible for any additional expense associated with such use, such as charges for translation and amounts due talent.

10. Indemnification and Insurance.

A. Agency shall indemnify and hold Media User harmless with respect to any claims, loss, suit, liability or judgment suffered by Media User, including reasonable attorney's fees and costs, based upon or related to any item prepared by Agency or at Agency's direction, including, but not limited to, any claim of libel, slander, piracy, plagiarism, invasion of privacy, or infringement of copyright or other intellectual property interest, except where any such claim arises out of material supplied by Media User and incorporated into any materials or advertisement prepared by Agency. Agency agrees to procure and maintain in force during the term of this Agreement, at Agency's expense, an Agency liability policy or policies having a minimum limit of at least _____, naming Media User as an additional insured and loss payee under such policy or policies.

B. Media User agrees to indemnify and hold Agency harmless with respect to any claims, loss, liability, damage or judgment suffered by Agency, including reasonable attorney's fees and court costs, which results from the use by Agency of any material furnished by Media User or where material created by Agency or at the direction of Agency subject to the indemnification in subsection A. above is materially changed by Media User. Information or data obtained by Agency from Media User to substantiate claims made in advertising shall be deemed to be "material furnished by Media User to Agency."

C. In the event of any proceeding, litigation or suit against Media User by any regulatory agency or in the event of any court action or other proceeding challenging any advertising prepared by Agency, Agency shall assist in the preparation of the defense of such action or proceeding and cooperate with Media User and Media User's attorneys.

11. Term.

The term of this Agreement shall commence on _____ and shall continue in full force and effect until terminated by either party upon at least sixty (60) days prior written notice, provided that in no event (except breach) may this Agreement be terminated prior to _____. The rights, duties and obligations of the parties shall continue in full force during or following the period of the termination notice until termination, including the ordering and billing of advertising in media whose closing dates follow then such period.

12. Rights Upon Termination.

A. Upon termination of the Agreement, Agency shall transfer, assign and make available to Media User all property and materials in Agency's possession or subject to Agency's control that are the property of Media User, subject to payment in full of amounts due pursuant to this Agreement.

B. Upon termination, Agency agrees to provide reasonable cooperation in arranging for the transfer or approval of third party's interest in all contracts, agreements and other arrangements with advertising media, suppliers, talent and others not then utilized, and all rights and claims thereto and therein, following appropriate release from the obligations therein.

13. Default.

In the event of any default of any material obligation by or owed by a party pursuant to this Agreement, then the other party may provide written notice of such default and if such default is not cured within ten (10) days of the written notice, then the nondefaulting party may terminate this Agreement. In addition, the only damages collectible by Agency shall be the exact amounts due; no other damages,

for any reason whatsoever, may be assessed against Media User including, but limited to, punitive damages and unreasonable termination charges, and any other such claim. This provision shall be broadly interpreted in the favor of the Media User by any Court of competent jurisdiction.

14. Notices.

Any notice required by this Agreement or given in connection with it, shall be in writing and shall be given to the appropriate party by personal delivery or by postage prepaid, or recognized overnight delivery services such as Federal Express.

If to Media User: _____

_____

If to Agency: _____

_____

15. Headings in this Agreement.

The headings in this Agreement are for convenience only, confirm no rights or obligations in either party, and do not alter any terms of this Agreement.

16. Entirety of Agreement.

The terms and conditions set forth herein constitute the entire agreement between the parties and supersede any communications or previous agreements with respect to the subject matter of this Agreement. There are no written or oral understandings directly or indirectly related to this Agreement that are not set forth herein. No change can be made to this Agreement other than in writing and signed by both parties.

17. Governing Law.

This Agreement shall be construed and enforced according to the laws of the State of _____ and any dispute under this Agreement must be brought in this venue and in no other.

In Witness whereof, the parties have executed this Agreement as of the date first written above.

_____ _____
Agency   Media User

Ad or other Media Agency Agreement

This Agency Agreement ("Agreement") is made and effective this _____ (Date), by and between ("Agency") and _____ (Your Firm) ("Media User").

Agency is in the business of providing media agency services for a fee.

Media User desires to engage Agency to render, and Agency desires to render to Media User, certain Agency services, all as set forth.

NOW, THEREFORE, in consideration of the mutual agreements and covenants herein contained, the parties hereto agree as follows:

1. Engagement.

Media User engages Agency to render, and Agency agrees to render to Media User, services in connection with Media User's planning, preparing and placing of advertising and other media services for certain of Media User's products as follows:

_____

A. Analyze Media User's current and proposed products and services and presentations and potential markets.

B. Create, prepare and submit to Media User for its prior approval advertising ideas, media suggestions, and other such related programs.

C. Prepare and submit to Media User for its prior approval estimates of costs and expenses associated with proposed advertising ideas and programs prior to any such implementation or financial commitment.

D. Design and prepare, or arrange for the design and preparation of advertisements, public relations, and other such materials.

E. Perform such other services as Media User may request from time to time such as, but not limited to, direct mail ad preparations, speech writing, publicity and public relations work, market research and analysis, and other similar and related activities.

F. Order advertising space, time or other means to be used for publication of Media User's advertisements, at all times endeavoring to secure the most efficient and advantageous rates available. All such activities to be approved in advance by the Media User unless otherwise written and stipulated.

G. Proof for accuracy and completeness of insertions, displays, broadcasts, or other forms of advertisements.

H. Audit invoices for proper and agreed upon space, time, material preparation and charges.

2. Products.

Agency's engagement shall relate to the following products and services of Media User:

_____.

3. Exclusivity.

Agency shall be the Agency in the United States and worldwide for Media User with respect to the products described in Section 2 above, unless otherwise specified in this section:

_____.

4.   Compensation.

A.   Agency shall receive an amount equal to ___ percentage of the gross charges levied by media for advertising placed by Agency pursuant to this Agreement; and   after volume discount, of the charges of suppliers of services or properties, such as finished art, comprehensive layouts, type composition, photostats, engravings, printing, radio and television programs, talent, literary, dramatic and musical works, records and exhibits, purchased by Agency on Media User's authorization during the term of this Agreement; provided that: No percentage will be added to Agency charges for packing, shipping, express, postage, telephone, telex, fax, travel expenses and other out of pocket expenses of Agency personnel.

B.   For those items where Agency is not compensated on a commission basis, Media User shall pay Agency on an hourly basis for services provided hereunder. The rate will be determined by the type of services provided and the person or persons providing such services, but in no event shall the rate exceed _____ per hour. Media User may elect in advance to be charged on this hourly rate basis. If Media User fails to notify Agency of its choice, it shall be presumed that Media User elected to be charged on a percentage basis.

C.   In the event that Agency undertakes, at Media User's request subject to Media User's prior approval, special projects such as those described in Section I.F above, Agency shall prepare an estimate of total charges for any such special project in advance, including any charges for materials or services purchased from outside vendors. In the event that Media User elects to proceed with the special project based upon Agency's estimated cost, Agency shall perform the services with respect to such special project at its estimated cost, subject to modification as mutually agreed by the parties.

D. For any special project or other services provided by Agency pursuant to this Agreement upon which the parties have not agreed as to charges, Media User shall pay
Agency at its regular percentage rates, as stated in Section 4.A above.

E.   Media User shall not be obligated to reimburse Agency for any travel or other out-of-pocket expenses incurred in the performance of services pursuant to this Agreement unless expressly agreed by Media User in advance.

5. Billing.

A.   Agency shall invoice Media User for all media costs where possible in advance of Agency's payment date to allow for prepayment by the Media User so that Media User may receive the benefit of any available prepayment or similar discount. For any media purchase or service for which Agency is not entitled to a commission, Agency shall ensure that the charges to Media User are net of all agency commissions and discounts.

B.   Charges for production materials and services shall be billed by Agency upon completion of the production job or, if cash discounts are available, upon receipt of the supplier's invoice.

C. On all outside purchases other than for media, Agency shall attach to the invoice evidence of the supplier's charges.

D.   All cash discounts on Agency's purchases including, but not limited to, media, art, printing and mechanical work, shall be available to Media User, provided that Media User meets Agency's requisite billing terms and there is no outstanding undisputed indebtedness of Media User to Agency at the time of the payment to the supplier.

E. Rate or billing adjustments shall be credited or charged to Media User on the next regular invoice date or as soon thereafter as otherwise practical.

F. Invoices shall be submitted in an itemized format and shall be paid by Media User within sixty (60) days of the invoice date.

6. Competitors.

During the term of this Agreement, Agency shall not accept employment from, render services to, represent or otherwise be affiliated with any person, firm, corporation or entity in connection with any product or service directly or indirectly competitive with or similar to any product or service of Media User with respect to which the Agency is providing any service pursuant to this Agreement, without the advance approval of the Media User. Media User shall not unreasonably withhold this approval.

7. Cost Estimates.

Agency shall not initiate billable work on any project pursuant to this Agreement without first estimating costs for preparation, including copy, service, layout, art, engraving, typography, processing, paste up and production. After determining the estimated cost, completion of the work shall be subject to Media User's prior approval.

8. Audit Rights.

Agency agrees that following reasonable prior notice any and all contracts, agreements, correspondence, books, accounts and other information relating to Media User's business or this Agreement shall be available for inspection by Media User and Media User's outside accountants, at Media User's expense and during the normal business hours of the Agency.

9. Ownership and Use.

A.   Agency shall insure, to the fullest extent possible under law, that Media User shall own all right, title and interest in and to, including copyrights, trade secret, patent and other intellectual property rights, with respect to any copy, photograph, advertisement, music, lyrics, video, or other work or thing created by Agency or at Agency's direction for Media User pursuant to this Agreement and utilized by Media User.

B.   Upon termination, Media User agrees that any advertising, merchandising, package, plan or idea prepared by Agency and submitted to Media User (whether submitted separately or in conjunction with or as a part of other material) which Media User has elected not to utilize, shall remain the property of Agency, unless Media User has paid Agency for its services in preparing such item. Media User agrees to return to Agency any copy, artwork, plates or other physical embodiment of such creative work relating to any such idea or plan which may be in Media User's possession at termination or expiration of this Agreement. Notwithstanding this, Media User has the unconditional right to pay for any of these materials or activities at the rate agreed upon in this Agreement and thereby these materials and activities would fall under the Section 9.A ownership and use rights accruing to Media User.

C.   Materials and advertisements created by Agency pursuant to this Agreement may be used by Media User outside the United States without additional compensation, provided that Media User shall

be responsible for any additional expense associated with such use, such as charges for translation and amounts due talent.

10. Indemnification and Insurance.

A.   Agency shall indemnify and hold Media User harmless with respect to any claims, loss, suit, liability or judgment suffered by Media User, including reasonable attorney's fees and costs, based upon or related to any item prepared by Agency or at Agency's direction, including, but not limited to, any claim of libel, slander, piracy, plagiarism, invasion of privacy, or infringement of copyright or other intellectual property interest, except where any such claim arises out of material supplied by Media User and incorporated into any materials or advertisement prepared by Agency. Agency agrees to procure and maintain in force during the term of this Agreement, at Agency's expense, an Agency liability policy or policies having a minimum limit of at least _____, naming Media User as an additional insured and loss payee under such policy or policies.

B.   Media User agrees to indemnify and hold Agency harmless with respect to any claims, loss, liability, damage or judgment suffered by Agency, including reasonable attorney's fees and court costs, which results from the use by Agency of any material furnished by Media User or where material created by Agency or at the direction of Agency subject to the indemnification in subsection A. above is materially changed by Media User. Information or data obtained by Agency from Media User to substantiate claims made in advertising shall be deemed to be "material furnished by Media User to Agency."

C.   In the event of any proceeding, litigation or suit against Media User by any regulatory agency or in the event of any court action or other proceeding challenging any advertising prepared by Agency, Agency shall assist in the preparation of the defense of such action or proceeding and cooperate with Media User and Media User's attorneys.

11. Term.

The term of this Agreement shall commence on _____ and shall continue in full force and effect until terminated by either party upon at least sixty (60) days prior written notice, provided that in no event (except breach) may this Agreement be terminated prior to _____. The rights, duties and obligations of the parties shall continue in full force during or following the period of the termination notice until termination, including the ordering and billing of advertising in media whose closing dates follow then such period.

12. Rights Upon Termination.

A.   Upon termination of the Agreement, Agency shall transfer, assign and make available to Media User all property and materials in Agency's possession or subject to Agency's control that are the property of Media User, subject to payment in full of amounts due pursuant to this Agreement.

B.   Upon termination, Agency agrees to provide reasonable cooperation in arranging for the transfer or approval of third party's interest in all contracts, agreements and other arrangements with advertising media, suppliers, talent and others not then utilized, and all rights and claims thereto and therein, following appropriate release from the obligations therein.

13. Default.

In the event of any default of any material obligation by or owed by a party pursuant to this Agreement, then the other party may provide written notice of such default and if such default is not cured within ten (10) days of the written notice, then the nondefaulting party may terminate this Agreement. In addition, the only damages collectible by Agency shall be the exact amounts due; no other damages,

for any reason whatsoever, may be assessed against Media User including, but limited to, punitive damages and unreasonable termination charges, and any other such claim. This provision shall be broadly interpreted in the favor of the Media User by any Court of competent jurisdiction.

14. Notices.

Any notice required by this Agreement or given in connection with it, shall be in writing and shall be given to the appropriate party by personal delivery or by postage prepaid, or recognized overnight delivery services such as Federal Express.

If to Media User: _____

_____

If to Agency: _____

_____

15. Headings in this Agreement.

The headings in this Agreement are for convenience only, confirm no rights or obligations in either party, and do not alter any terms of this Agreement.

16. Entirety of Agreement.

The terms and conditions set forth herein constitute the entire agreement between the parties and supersede any communications or previous agreements with respect to the subject matter of this Agreement. There are no written or oral understandings directly or indirectly related to this Agreement that are not set forth herein. No change can be made to this Agreement other than in writing and signed by both parties.

17. Governing Law.

This Agreement shall be construed and enforced according to the laws of the State of _____ and any dispute under this Agreement must be brought in this venue and in no other.

In Witness whereof, the parties have executed this Agreement as of the date first written above.

_____   _____
Agency   Media User

Ad or other Media Agency Agreement

This Agency Agreement ("Agreement") is made and effective this _____ (Date), by and between ("Agency") and _____ (Your Firm) ("Media User").

Agency is in the business of providing media agency services for a fee.

Media User desires to engage Agency to render, and Agency desires to render to Media User, certain Agency services, all as set forth.

NOW, THEREFORE, in consideration of the mutual agreements and covenants herein contained, the parties hereto agree as follows:

1. <u>Engagement</u>.

Media User engages Agency to render, and Agency agrees to render to Media User, services in connection with Media User's planning, preparing and placing of advertising and other media services for certain of Media User's products as follows:

_____

A. Analyze Media User's current and proposed products and services and presentations and potential markets.

B. Create, prepare and submit to Media User for its prior approval advertising ideas, media suggestions, and other such related programs.

C. Prepare and submit to Media User for its prior approval estimates of costs and expenses associated with proposed advertising ideas and programs prior to any such implementation or financial commitment.

D. Design and prepare, or arrange for the design and preparation of advertisements, public relations, and other such materials.

E. Perform such other services as Media User may request from time to time such as, but not limited to, direct mail ad preparations, speech writing, publicity and public relations work, market research and analysis, and other similar and related activities.

F. Order advertising space, time or other means to be used for publication of Media User's advertisements, at all times endeavoring to secure the most efficient and advantageous rates available. All such activities to be approved in advance by the Media User unless otherwise written and stipulated.

G. Proof for accuracy and completeness of insertions, displays, broadcasts, or other forms of advertisements.

H. Audit invoices for proper and agreed upon space, time, material preparation and charges.

2. <u>Products</u>.

Agency's engagement shall relate to the following products and services of Media User:

_____

3. Exclusivity.

Agency shall be the Agency in the United States and worldwide for Media User with respect to the products described in Section 2 above, unless otherwise specified in this section:

_____.

4.   Compensation.

A.   Agency shall receive an amount equal to ___ percentage of the gross charges levied by media for advertising placed by Agency pursuant to this Agreement; and _____ after volume discount, of the charges of suppliers of services or properties, such as finished art, comprehensive layouts, type composition, photostats, engravings, printing, radio and television programs, talent, literary, dramatic and musical works, records and exhibits, purchased by Agency on Media User's authorization during the term of this Agreement; provided that: No percentage will be added to Agency charges for packing, shipping, express, postage, telephone, telex, fax, travel expenses and other out of pocket expenses of Agency personnel.

B.   For those items where Agency is not compensated on a commission basis, Media User shall pay Agency on an hourly basis for services provided hereunder. The rate will be determined by the type of services provided and the person or persons providing such services, but in no event shall the rate exceed _____ per hour. Media User may elect in advance to be charged on this hourly rate basis. If Media User fails to notify Agency of its choice, it shall be presumed that Media User elected to be charged on a percentage basis.

C.   In the event that Agency undertakes, at Media User's request subject to Media User's prior approval, special projects such as those described in Section I.F above, Agency shall prepare an estimate of total charges for any such special project in advance, including any charges for materials or services purchased from outside vendors. In the event that Media User elects to proceed with the special project based upon Agency's estimated cost, Agency shall perform the services with respect to such special project at its estimated cost, subject to modification as mutually agreed by the parties.

D. For any special project or other services provided by Agency pursuant to this Agreement upon which the parties have not agreed as to charges, Media User shall pay
Agency at its regular percentage rates, as stated in Section 4.A above.

E.   Media User shall not be obligated to reimburse Agency for any travel or other out-of-pocket expenses incurred in the performance of services pursuant to this Agreement unless expressly agreed by Media User in advance.

5. Billing.

A.   Agency shall invoice Media User for all media costs where possible in advance of Agency's payment date to allow for prepayment by the Media User so that Media User may receive the benefit of any available prepayment or similar discount. For any media purchase or service for which Agency is not entitled to a commission, Agency shall ensure that the charges to Media User are net of all agency commissions and discounts.

B.   Charges for production materials and services shall be billed by Agency upon completion of the production job or, if cash discounts are available, upon receipt of the supplier's invoice.

C. On all outside purchases other than for media, Agency shall attach to the invoice evidence of the supplier's charges.

D.   All cash discounts on Agency's purchases including, but not limited to, media, art, printing and mechanical work, shall be available to Media User, provided that Media User meets Agency's requisite billing terms and there is no outstanding undisputed indebtedness of Media User to Agency at the time of the payment to the supplier.

E. Rate or billing adjustments shall be credited or charged to Media User on the next regular invoice date or as soon thereafter as otherwise practical.

F. Invoices shall be submitted in an itemized format and shall be paid by Media User within sixty (60) days of the invoice date.

6. Competitors.

During the term of this Agreement, Agency shall not accept employment from, render services to, represent or otherwise be affiliated with any person, firm, corporation or entity in connection with any product or service directly or indirectly competitive with or similar to any product or service of Media User with respect to which the Agency is providing any service pursuant to this Agreement, without the advance approval of the Media User. Media User shall not unreasonably withhold this approval.

7. Cost Estimates.

Agency shall not initiate billable work on any project pursuant to this Agreement without first estimating costs for preparation, including copy, service, layout, art, engraving, typography, processing, paste up and production. After determining the estimated cost, completion of the work shall be subject to Media User's prior approval.

8. Audit Rights.

Agency agrees that following reasonable prior notice any and all contracts, agreements, correspondence, books, accounts and other information relating to Media User's business or this Agreement shall be available for inspection by Media User and Media User's outside accountants, at Media User's expense and during the normal business hours of the Agency.

9. Ownership and Use.

A.   Agency shall insure, to the fullest extent possible under law, that Media User shall own all right, title and interest in and to, including copyrights, trade secret, patent and other intellectual property rights, with respect to any copy, photograph, advertisement, music, lyrics, video, or other work or thing created by Agency or at Agency's direction for Media User pursuant to this Agreement and utilized by Media User.

B.   Upon termination, Media User agrees that any advertising, merchandising, package, plan or idea prepared by Agency and submitted to Media User (whether submitted separately or in conjunction with or as a part of other material) which Media User has elected not to utilize, shall remain the property of Agency, unless Media User has paid Agency for its services in preparing such item. Media User agrees to return to Agency any copy, artwork, plates or other physical embodiment of such creative work relating to any such idea or plan which may be in Media User's possession at termination or expiration of this Agreement. Notwithstanding this, Media User has the unconditional right to pay for any of these materials or activities at the rate agreed upon in this Agreement and thereby these materials and activities would fall under the Section 9.A ownership and use rights accruing to Media User.

C.   Materials and advertisements created by Agency pursuant to this Agreement may be used by Media User outside the United States without additional compensation, provided that Media User shall

be responsible for any additional expense associated with such use, such as charges for translation and amounts due talent.

10. Indemnification and Insurance.

A. Agency shall indemnify and hold Media User harmless with respect to any claims, loss, suit, liability or judgment suffered by Media User, including reasonable attorney's fees and costs, based upon or related to any item prepared by Agency or at Agency's direction, including, but not limited to, any claim of libel, slander, piracy, plagiarism, invasion of privacy, or infringement of copyright or other intellectual property interest, except where any such claim arises out of material supplied by Media User and incorporated into any materials or advertisement prepared by Agency. Agency agrees to procure and maintain in force during the term of this Agreement, at Agency's expense, an Agency liability policy or policies having a minimum limit of at least _____, naming Media User as an additional insured and loss payee under such policy or policies.

B. Media User agrees to indemnify and hold Agency harmless with respect to any claims, loss, liability, damage or judgment suffered by Agency, including reasonable attorney's fees and court costs, which results from the use by Agency of any material furnished by Media User or where material created by Agency or at the direction of Agency subject to the indemnification in subsection A. above is materially changed by Media User. Information or data obtained by Agency from Media User to substantiate claims made in advertising shall be deemed to be "material furnished by Media User to Agency."

C. In the event of any proceeding, litigation or suit against Media User by any regulatory agency or in the event of any court action or other proceeding challenging any advertising prepared by Agency, Agency shall assist in the preparation of the defense of such action or proceeding and cooperate with Media User and Media User's attorneys.

11. Term.

The term of this Agreement shall commence on _____ and shall continue in full force and effect until terminated by either party upon at least sixty (60) days prior written notice, provided that in no event (except breach) may this Agreement be terminated prior to _____. The rights, duties and obligations of the parties shall continue in full force during or following the period of the termination notice until termination, including the ordering and billing of advertising in media whose closing dates follow then such period.

12. Rights Upon Termination.

A. Upon termination of the Agreement, Agency shall transfer, assign and make available to Media User all property and materials in Agency's possession or subject to Agency's control that are the property of Media User, subject to payment in full of amounts due pursuant to this Agreement.

B. Upon termination, Agency agrees to provide reasonable cooperation in arranging for the transfer or approval of third party's interest in all contracts, agreements and other arrangements with advertising media, suppliers, talent and others not then utilized, and all rights and claims thereto and therein, following appropriate release from the obligations therein.

13. Default.

In the event of any default of any material obligation by or owed by a party pursuant to this Agreement, then the other party may provide written notice of such default and if such default is not cured within ten (10) days of the written notice, then the nondefaulting party may terminate this Agreement. In addition, the only damages collectible by Agency shall be the exact amounts due; no other damages,

for any reason whatsoever, may be assessed against Media User including, but limited to, punitive damages and unreasonable termination charges, and any other such claim. This provision shall be broadly interpreted in the favor of the Media User by any Court of competent jurisdiction.

14. <u>Notices</u>.

Any notice required by this Agreement or given in connection with it, shall be in writing and shall be given to the appropriate party by personal delivery or by postage prepaid, or recognized overnight delivery services such as Federal Express.

If to Media User: _____

                                                   _____

If to Agency: _____

                                                   _____

15. <u>Headings in this Agreement</u>.

The headings in this Agreement are for convenience only, confirm no rights or obligations in either party, and do not alter any terms of this Agreement.

16. <u>Entirety of Agreement</u>.

The terms and conditions set forth herein constitute the entire agreement between the parties and supersede any communications or previous agreements with respect to the subject matter of this Agreement. There are no written or oral understandings directly or indirectly related to this Agreement that are not set forth herein. No change can be made to this Agreement other than in writing and signed by both parties.

17. <u>Governing Law</u>.

This Agreement shall be construed and enforced according to the laws of the State of _____ and any dispute under this Agreement must be brought in this venue and in no other.

In Witness whereof, the parties have executed this Agreement as of the date first written above.

_____   _____
Agency   Media User

Ad or other Media Agency Agreement

This Agency Agreement ("Agreement") is made and effective this _____ (Date), by and between ("Agency") and _____ (Your Firm) ("Media User").

Agency is in the business of providing media agency services for a fee.

Media User desires to engage Agency to render, and Agency desires to render to Media User, certain Agency services, all as set forth.

NOW, THEREFORE, in consideration of the mutual agreements and covenants herein contained, the parties hereto agree as follows:

1. Engagement.

Media User engages Agency to render, and Agency agrees to render to Media User, services in connection with Media User's planning, preparing and placing of advertising and other media services for certain of Media User's products as follows:

_____

A. Analyze Media User's current and proposed products and services and presentations and potential markets.

B. Create, prepare and submit to Media User for its prior approval advertising ideas, media suggestions, and other such related programs.

C. Prepare and submit to Media User for its prior approval estimates of costs and expenses associated with proposed advertising ideas and programs prior to any such implementation or financial commitment.

D. Design and prepare, or arrange for the design and preparation of advertisements, public relations, and other such materials.

E. Perform such other services as Media User may request from time to time such as, but not limited to, direct mail ad preparations, speech writing, publicity and public relations work, market research and analysis, and other similar and related activities.

F. Order advertising space, time or other means to be used for publication of Media User's advertisements, at all times endeavoring to secure the most efficient and advantageous rates available. All such activities to be approved in advance by the Media User unless otherwise written and stipulated.

G. Proof for accuracy and completeness of insertions, displays, broadcasts, or other forms of advertisements.

H. Audit invoices for proper and agreed upon space, time, material preparation and charges.

2. Products.

Agency's engagement shall relate to the following products and services of Media User:

_____.

3. Exclusivity.

Agency shall be the Agency in the United States and worldwide for Media User with respect to the products described in Section 2 above, unless otherwise specified in this section:

_____.

4. Compensation.

A. Agency shall receive an amount equal to ___ percentage of the gross charges levied by media for advertising placed by Agency pursuant to this Agreement; and after volume discount, of the charges of suppliers of services or properties, such as finished art, comprehensive layouts, type composition, photostats, engravings, printing, radio and television programs, talent, literary, dramatic and musical works, records and exhibits, purchased by Agency on Media User's authorization during the term of this Agreement; provided that: No percentage will be added to Agency charges for packing, shipping, express, postage, telephone, telex, fax, travel expenses and other out of pocket expenses of Agency personnel.

B. For those items where Agency is not compensated on a commission basis, Media User shall pay Agency on an hourly basis for services provided hereunder. The rate will be determined by the type of services provided and the person or persons providing such services, but in no event shall the rate exceed _____ per hour. Media User may elect in advance to be charged on this hourly rate basis. If Media User fails to notify Agency of its choice, it shall be presumed that Media User elected to be charged on a percentage basis.

C. In the event that Agency undertakes, at Media User's request subject to Media User's prior approval, special projects such as those described in Section I.F above, Agency shall prepare an estimate of total charges for any such special project in advance, including any charges for materials or services purchased from outside vendors. In the event that Media User elects to proceed with the special project based upon Agency's estimated cost, Agency shall perform the services with respect to such special project at its estimated cost, subject to modification as mutually agreed by the parties.

D. For any special project or other services provided by Agency pursuant to this Agreement upon which the parties have not agreed as to charges, Media User shall pay
Agency at its regular percentage rates, as stated in Section 4.A above.

E. Media User shall not be obligated to reimburse Agency for any travel or other out-of-pocket expenses incurred in the performance of services pursuant to this Agreement unless expressly agreed by Media User in advance.

5. Billing.

A. Agency shall invoice Media User for all media costs where possible in advance of Agency's payment date to allow for prepayment by the Media User so that Media User may receive the benefit of any available prepayment or similar discount. For any media purchase or service for which Agency is not entitled to a commission, Agency shall ensure that the charges to Media User are net of all agency commissions and discounts.

B. Charges for production materials and services shall be billed by Agency upon completion of the production job or, if cash discounts are available, upon receipt of the supplier's invoice.

C. On all outside purchases other than for media, Agency shall attach to the invoice evidence of the supplier's charges.

D. All cash discounts on Agency's purchases including, but not limited to, media, art, printing and mechanical work, shall be available to Media User, provided that Media User meets Agency's requisite billing terms and there is no outstanding undisputed indebtedness of Media User to Agency at the time of the payment to the supplier.

E. Rate or billing adjustments shall be credited or charged to Media User on the next regular invoice date or as soon thereafter as otherwise practical.

F. Invoices shall be submitted in an itemized format and shall be paid by Media User within sixty (60) days of the invoice date.

6. Competitors.

During the term of this Agreement, Agency shall not accept employment from, render services to, represent or otherwise be affiliated with any person, firm, corporation or entity in connection with any product or service directly or indirectly competitive with or similar to any product or service of Media User with respect to which the Agency is providing any service pursuant to this Agreement, without the advance approval of the Media User. Media User shall not unreasonably withhold this approval.

7. Cost Estimates.

Agency shall not initiate billable work on any project pursuant to this Agreement without first estimating costs for preparation, including copy, service, layout, art, engraving, typography, processing, paste up and production. After determining the estimated cost, completion of the work shall be subject to Media User's prior approval.

8. Audit Rights.

Agency agrees that following reasonable prior notice any and all contracts, agreements, correspondence, books, accounts and other information relating to Media User's business or this Agreement shall be available for inspection by Media User and Media User's outside accountants, at Media User's expense and during the normal business hours of the Agency.

9. Ownership and Use.

A. Agency shall insure, to the fullest extent possible under law, that Media User shall own all right, title and interest in and to, including copyrights, trade secret, patent and other intellectual property rights, with respect to any copy, photograph, advertisement, music, lyrics, video, or other work or thing created by Agency or at Agency's direction for Media User pursuant to this Agreement and utilized by Media User.

B. Upon termination, Media User agrees that any advertising, merchandising, package, plan or idea prepared by Agency and submitted to Media User (whether submitted separately or in conjunction with or as a part of other material) which Media User has elected not to utilize, shall remain the property of Agency, unless Media User has paid Agency for its services in preparing such item. Media User agrees to return to Agency any copy, artwork, plates or other physical embodiment of such creative work relating to any such idea or plan which may be in Media User's possession at termination or expiration of this Agreement. Notwithstanding this, Media User has the unconditional right to pay for any of these materials or activities at the rate agreed upon in this Agreement and thereby these materials and activities would fall under the Section 9.A ownership and use rights accruing to Media User.

C. Materials and advertisements created by Agency pursuant to this Agreement may be used by Media User outside the United States without additional compensation, provided that Media User shall

be responsible for any additional expense associated with such use, such as charges for translation and amounts due talent.

10. Indemnification and Insurance.

A. Agency shall indemnify and hold Media User harmless with respect to any claims, loss, suit, liability or judgment suffered by Media User, including reasonable attorney's fees and costs, based upon or related to any item prepared by Agency or at Agency's direction, including, but not limited to, any claim of libel, slander, piracy, plagiarism, invasion of privacy, or infringement of copyright or other intellectual property interest, except where any such claim arises out of material supplied by Media User and incorporated into any materials or advertisement prepared by Agency. Agency agrees to procure and maintain in force during the term of this Agreement, at Agency's expense, an Agency liability policy or policies having a minimum limit of at least _____, naming Media User as an additional insured and loss payee under such policy or policies.

B. Media User agrees to indemnify and hold Agency harmless with respect to any claims, loss, liability, damage or judgment suffered by Agency, including reasonable attorney's fees and court costs, which results from the use by Agency of any material furnished by Media User or where material created by Agency or at the direction of Agency subject to the indemnification in subsection A. above is materially changed by Media User. Information or data obtained by Agency from Media User to substantiate claims made in advertising shall be deemed to be "material furnished by Media User to Agency."

C. In the event of any proceeding, litigation or suit against Media User by any regulatory agency or in the event of any court action or other proceeding challenging any advertising prepared by Agency, Agency shall assist in the preparation of the defense of such action or proceeding and cooperate with Media User and Media User's attorneys.

11. Term.

The term of this Agreement shall commence on _____ and shall continue in full force and effect until terminated by either party upon at least sixty (60) days prior written notice, provided that in no event (except breach) may this Agreement be terminated prior to _____. The rights, duties and obligations of the parties shall continue in full force during or following the period of the termination notice until termination, including the ordering and billing of advertising in media whose closing dates follow then such period.

12. Rights Upon Termination.

A. Upon termination of the Agreement, Agency shall transfer, assign and make available to Media User all property and materials in Agency's possession or subject to Agency's control that are the property of Media User, subject to payment in full of amounts due pursuant to this Agreement.

B. Upon termination, Agency agrees to provide reasonable cooperation in arranging for the transfer or approval of third party's interest in all contracts, agreements and other arrangements with advertising media, suppliers, talent and others not then utilized, and all rights and claims thereto and therein, following appropriate release from the obligations therein.

13. Default.

In the event of any default of any material obligation by or owed by a party pursuant to this Agreement, then the other party may provide written notice of such default and if such default is not cured within ten (10) days of the written notice, then the nondefaulting party may terminate this Agreement. In addition, the only damages collectible by Agency shall be the exact amounts due; no other damages,

for any reason whatsoever, may be assessed against Media User including, but limited to, punitive damages and unreasonable termination charges, and any other such claim. This provision shall be broadly interpreted in the favor of the Media User by any Court of competent jurisdiction.

14. <u>Notices</u>.

Any notice required by this Agreement or given in connection with it, shall be in writing and shall be given to the appropriate party by personal delivery or by postage prepaid, or recognized overnight delivery services such as Federal Express.

If to Media User: _____

_____

If to Agency: _____

_____

15. <u>Headings in this Agreement</u>.

The headings in this Agreement are for convenience only, confirm no rights or obligations in either party, and do not alter any terms of this Agreement.

16. <u>Entirety of Agreement</u>.

The terms and conditions set forth herein constitute the entire agreement between the parties and supersede any communications or previous agreements with respect to the subject matter of this Agreement. There are no written or oral understandings directly or indirectly related to this Agreement that are not set forth herein. No change can be made to this Agreement other than in writing and signed by both parties.

17. <u>Governing Law</u>.

This Agreement shall be construed and enforced according to the laws of the State of _____ and any dispute under this Agreement must be brought in this venue and in no other.

In Witness whereof, the parties have executed this Agreement as of the date first written above.

_____ _____
Agency   Media User

Ad or other Media Agency Agreement

This Agency Agreement ("Agreement") is made and effective this _____ (Date), by and between ("Agency") and _____ (Your Firm) ("Media User").

Agency is in the business of providing media agency services for a fee.

Media User desires to engage Agency to render, and Agency desires to render to Media User, certain Agency services, all as set forth.

NOW, THEREFORE, in consideration of the mutual agreements and covenants herein contained, the parties hereto agree as follows:

1. <u>Engagement</u>.

Media User engages Agency to render, and Agency agrees to render to Media User, services in connection with Media User's planning, preparing and placing of advertising and other media services for certain of Media User's products as follows:

_____

A. Analyze Media User's current and proposed products and services and presentations and potential markets.

B. Create, prepare and submit to Media User for its prior approval advertising ideas, media suggestions, and other such related programs.

C. Prepare and submit to Media User for its prior approval estimates of costs and expenses associated with proposed advertising ideas and programs prior to any such implementation or financial commitment.

D. Design and prepare, or arrange for the design and preparation of advertisements, public relations, and other such materials.

E. Perform such other services as Media User may request from time to time such as, but not limited to, direct mail ad preparations, speech writing, publicity and public relations work, market research and analysis, and other similar and related activities.

F. Order advertising space, time or other means to be used for publication of Media User's advertisements, at all times endeavoring to secure the most efficient and advantageous rates available. All such activities to be approved in advance by the Media User unless otherwise written and stipulated.

G. Proof for accuracy and completeness of insertions, displays, broadcasts, or other forms of advertisements.

H. Audit invoices for proper and agreed upon space, time, material preparation and charges.

2. <u>Products</u>.

Agency's engagement shall relate to the following products and services of Media User:

_____.

3. Exclusivity.

Agency shall be the Agency in the United States and worldwide for Media User with respect to the products described in Section 2 above, unless otherwise specified in this section:

_____.

4. Compensation.

A. Agency shall receive an amount equal to ___ percentage of the gross charges levied by media for advertising placed by Agency pursuant to this Agreement; and _____ after volume discount, of the charges of suppliers of services or properties, such as finished art, comprehensive layouts, type composition, photostats, engravings, printing, radio and television programs, talent, literary, dramatic and musical works, records and exhibits, purchased by Agency on Media User's authorization during the term of this Agreement; provided that: No percentage will be added to Agency charges for packing, shipping, express, postage, telephone, telex, fax, travel expenses and other out of pocket expenses of Agency personnel.

B. For those items where Agency is not compensated on a commission basis, Media User shall pay Agency on an hourly basis for services provided hereunder. The rate will be determined by the type of services provided and the person or persons providing such services, but in no event shall the rate exceed _____ per hour. Media User may elect in advance to be charged on this hourly rate basis. If Media User fails to notify Agency of its choice, it shall be presumed that Media User elected to be charged on a percentage basis.

C. In the event that Agency undertakes, at Media User's request subject to Media User's prior approval, special projects such as those described in Section I.F above, Agency shall prepare an estimate of total charges for any such special project in advance, including any charges for materials or services purchased from outside vendors. In the event that Media User elects to proceed with the special project based upon Agency's estimated cost, Agency shall perform the services with respect to such special project at its estimated cost, subject to modification as mutually agreed by the parties.

D. For any special project or other services provided by Agency pursuant to this Agreement upon which the parties have not agreed as to charges, Media User shall pay
Agency at its regular percentage rates, as stated in Section 4.A above.

E. Media User shall not be obligated to reimburse Agency for any travel or other out-of-pocket expenses incurred in the performance of services pursuant to this Agreement unless expressly agreed by Media User in advance.

5. Billing.

A. Agency shall invoice Media User for all media costs where possible in advance of Agency's payment date to allow for prepayment by the Media User so that Media User may receive the benefit of any available prepayment or similar discount. For any media purchase or service for which Agency is not entitled to a commission, Agency shall ensure that the charges to Media User are net of all agency commissions and discounts.

B. Charges for production materials and services shall be billed by Agency upon completion of the production job or, if cash discounts are available, upon receipt of the supplier's invoice.

C. On all outside purchases other than for media, Agency shall attach to the invoice evidence of the supplier's charges.

D.   All cash discounts on Agency's purchases including, but not limited to, media, art, printing and mechanical work, shall be available to Media User, provided that Media User meets Agency's requisite billing terms and there is no outstanding undisputed indebtedness of Media User to Agency at the time of the payment to the supplier.

E. Rate or billing adjustments shall be credited or charged to Media User on the next regular invoice date or as soon thereafter as otherwise practical.

F. Invoices shall be submitted in an itemized format and shall be paid by Media User within sixty (60) days of the invoice date.

6. Competitors.

During the term of this Agreement, Agency shall not accept employment from, render services to, represent or otherwise be affiliated with any person, firm, corporation or entity in connection with any product or service directly or indirectly competitive with or similar to any product or service of Media User with respect to which the Agency is providing any service pursuant to this Agreement, without the advance approval of the Media User. Media User shall not unreasonably withhold this approval.

7. Cost Estimates.

Agency shall not initiate billable work on any project pursuant to this Agreement without first estimating costs for preparation, including copy, service, layout, art, engraving, typography, processing, paste up and production. After determining the estimated cost, completion of the work shall be subject to Media User's prior approval.

8. Audit Rights.

Agency agrees that following reasonable prior notice any and all contracts, agreements, correspondence, books, accounts and other information relating to Media User's business or this Agreement shall be available for inspection by Media User and Media User's outside accountants, at Media User's expense and during the normal business hours of the Agency.

9. Ownership and Use.

A.   Agency shall insure, to the fullest extent possible under law, that Media User shall own all right, title and interest in and to, including copyrights, trade secret, patent and other intellectual property rights, with respect to any copy, photograph, advertisement, music, lyrics, video, or other work or thing created by Agency or at Agency's direction for Media User pursuant to this Agreement and utilized by Media User.

B.   Upon termination, Media User agrees that any advertising, merchandising, package, plan or idea prepared by Agency and submitted to Media User (whether submitted separately or in conjunction with or as a part of other material) which Media User has elected not to utilize, shall remain the property of Agency, unless Media User has paid Agency for its services in preparing such item. Media User agrees to return to Agency any copy, artwork, plates or other physical embodiment of such creative work relating to any such idea or plan which may be in Media User's possession at termination or expiration of this Agreement. Notwithstanding this, Media User has the unconditional right to pay for any of these materials or activities at the rate agreed upon in this Agreement and thereby these materials and activities would fall under the Section 9.A ownership and use rights accruing to Media User.

C.   Materials and advertisements created by Agency pursuant to this Agreement may be used by Media User outside the United States without additional compensation, provided that Media User shall

be responsible for any additional expense associated with such use, such as charges for translation and amounts due talent.

10. Indemnification and Insurance.

A. Agency shall indemnify and hold Media User harmless with respect to any claims, loss, suit, liability or judgment suffered by Media User, including reasonable attorney's fees and costs, based upon or related to any item prepared by Agency or at Agency's direction, including, but not limited to, any claim of libel, slander, piracy, plagiarism, invasion of privacy, or infringement of copyright or other intellectual property interest, except where any such claim arises out of material supplied by Media User and incorporated into any materials or advertisement prepared by Agency. Agency agrees to procure and maintain in force during the term of this Agreement, at Agency's expense, an Agency liability policy or policies having a minimum limit of at least _____, naming Media User as an additional insured and loss payee under such policy or policies.

B. Media User agrees to indemnify and hold Agency harmless with respect to any claims, loss, liability, damage or judgment suffered by Agency, including reasonable attorney's fees and court costs, which results from the use by Agency of any material furnished by Media User or where material created by Agency or at the direction of Agency subject to the indemnification in subsection A. above is materially changed by Media User. Information or data obtained by Agency from Media User to substantiate claims made in advertising shall be deemed to be "material furnished by Media User to Agency."

C. In the event of any proceeding, litigation or suit against Media User by any regulatory agency or in the event of any court action or other proceeding challenging any advertising prepared by Agency, Agency shall assist in the preparation of the defense of such action or proceeding and cooperate with Media User and Media User's attorneys.

11. Term.

The term of this Agreement shall commence on _____ and shall continue in full force and effect until terminated by either party upon at least sixty (60) days prior written notice, provided that in no event (except breach) may this Agreement be terminated prior to _____. The rights, duties and obligations of the parties shall continue in full force during or following the period of the termination notice until termination, including the ordering and billing of advertising in media whose closing dates follow then such period.

12. Rights Upon Termination.

A. Upon termination of the Agreement, Agency shall transfer, assign and make available to Media User all property and materials in Agency's possession or subject to Agency's control that are the property of Media User, subject to payment in full of amounts due pursuant to this Agreement.

B. Upon termination, Agency agrees to provide reasonable cooperation in arranging for the transfer or approval of third party's interest in all contracts, agreements and other arrangements with advertising media, suppliers, talent and others not then utilized, and all rights and claims thereto and therein, following appropriate release from the obligations therein.

13. Default.

In the event of any default of any material obligation by or owed by a party pursuant to this Agreement, then the other party may provide written notice of such default and if such default is not cured within ten (10) days of the written notice, then the nondefaulting party may terminate this Agreement. In addition, the only damages collectible by Agency shall be the exact amounts due; no other damages,

for any reason whatsoever, may be assessed against Media User including, but limited to, punitive damages and unreasonable termination charges, and any other such claim. This provision shall be broadly interpreted in the favor of the Media User by any Court of competent jurisdiction.

14. Notices.

Any notice required by this Agreement or given in connection with it, shall be in writing and shall be given to the appropriate party by personal delivery or by postage prepaid, or recognized overnight delivery services such as Federal Express.

If to Media User: _____

_____

If to Agency: _____

_____

15. Headings in this Agreement.

The headings in this Agreement are for convenience only, confirm no rights or obligations in either party, and do not alter any terms of this Agreement.

16. Entirety of Agreement.

The terms and conditions set forth herein constitute the entire agreement between the parties and supersede any communications or previous agreements with respect to the subject matter of this Agreement. There are no written or oral understandings directly or indirectly related to this Agreement that are not set forth herein. No change can be made to this Agreement other than in writing and signed by both parties.

17. Governing Law.

This Agreement shall be construed and enforced according to the laws of the State of _____ and any dispute under this Agreement must be brought in this venue and in no other.

In Witness whereof, the parties have executed this Agreement as of the date first written above.

_____ _____
Agency   Media User

Ad or other Media Agency Agreement

This Agency Agreement ("Agreement") is made and effective this _____ (Date), by and between ("Agency") and _____ (Your Firm) ("Media User").

Agency is in the business of providing media agency services for a fee.

Media User desires to engage Agency to render, and Agency desires to render to Media User, certain Agency services, all as set forth.

NOW, THEREFORE, in consideration of the mutual agreements and covenants herein contained, the parties hereto agree as follows:

1. <u>Engagement</u>.

Media User engages Agency to render, and Agency agrees to render to Media User, services in connection with Media User's planning, preparing and placing of advertising and other media services for certain of Media User's products as follows:

_____

A. Analyze Media User's current and proposed products and services and presentations and potential markets.

B. Create, prepare and submit to Media User for its prior approval advertising ideas, media suggestions, and other such related programs.

C. Prepare and submit to Media User for its prior approval estimates of costs and expenses associated with proposed advertising ideas and programs prior to any such implementation or financial commitment.

D. Design and prepare, or arrange for the design and preparation of advertisements, public relations, and other such materials.

E. Perform such other services as Media User may request from time to time such as, but not limited to, direct mail ad preparations, speech writing, publicity and public relations work, market research and analysis, and other similar and related activities.

F. Order advertising space, time or other means to be used for publication of Media User's advertisements, at all times endeavoring to secure the most efficient and advantageous rates available. All such activities to be approved in advance by the Media User unless otherwise written and stipulated.

G. Proof for accuracy and completeness of insertions, displays, broadcasts, or other forms of advertisements.

H. Audit invoices for proper and agreed upon space, time, material preparation and charges.

2. <u>Products</u>.

Agency's engagement shall relate to the following products and services of Media User:

_____.

3. <u>Exclusivity</u>.

Agency shall be the Agency in the United States and worldwide for Media User with respect to the products described in Section 2 above, unless otherwise specified in this section:

_____.

4.   <u>Compensation</u>.

A.   Agency shall receive an amount equal to ___ percentage of the gross charges levied by media for advertising placed by Agency pursuant to this Agreement; and   after volume discount, of the charges of suppliers of services or properties, such as finished art, comprehensive layouts, type composition, photostats, engravings, printing, radio and television programs, talent, literary, dramatic and musical works, records and exhibits, purchased by Agency on Media User's authorization during the term of this Agreement; provided that: No percentage will be added to Agency charges for packing, shipping, express, postage, telephone, telex, fax, travel expenses and other out of pocket expenses of Agency personnel.

B.   For those items where Agency is not compensated on a commission basis, Media User shall pay Agency on an hourly basis for services provided hereunder. The rate will be determined by the type of services provided and the person or persons providing such services, but in no event shall the rate exceed _____ per hour. Media User may elect in advance to be charged on this hourly rate basis. If Media User fails to notify Agency of its choice, it shall be presumed that Media User elected to be charged on a percentage basis.

C.   In the event that Agency undertakes, at Media User's request subject to Media User's prior approval, special projects such as those described in Section I.F above, Agency shall prepare an estimate of total charges for any such special project in advance, including any charges for materials or services purchased from outside vendors. In the event that Media User elects to proceed with the special project based upon Agency's estimated cost, Agency shall perform the services with respect to such special project at its estimated cost, subject to modification as mutually agreed by the parties.

D. For any special project or other services provided by Agency pursuant to this Agreement upon which the parties have not agreed as to charges, Media User shall pay
Agency at its regular percentage rates, as stated in Section 4.A above.

E.   Media User shall not be obligated to reimburse Agency for any travel or other out-of-pocket expenses incurred in the performance of services pursuant to this Agreement unless expressly agreed by Media User in advance.

5. <u>Billing</u>.

A.   Agency shall invoice Media User for all media costs where possible in advance of Agency's payment date to allow for prepayment by the Media User so that Media User may receive the benefit of any available prepayment or similar discount. For any media purchase or service for which Agency is not entitled to a commission, Agency shall ensure that the charges to Media User are net of all agency commissions and discounts.

B.   Charges for production materials and services shall be billed by Agency upon completion of the production job or, if cash discounts are available, upon receipt of the supplier's invoice.

C. On all outside purchases other than for media, Agency shall attach to the invoice evidence of the supplier's charges.

D.   All cash discounts on Agency's purchases including, but not limited to, media, art, printing and mechanical work, shall be available to Media User, provided that Media User meets Agency's requisite billing terms and there is no outstanding undisputed indebtedness of Media User to Agency at the time of the payment to the supplier.

E. Rate or billing adjustments shall be credited or charged to Media User on the next regular invoice date or as soon thereafter as otherwise practical.

F. Invoices shall be submitted in an itemized format and shall be paid by Media User within sixty (60) days of the invoice date.

6. Competitors.

During the term of this Agreement, Agency shall not accept employment from, render services to, represent or otherwise be affiliated with any person, firm, corporation or entity in connection with any product or service directly or indirectly competitive with or similar to any product or service of Media User with respect to which the Agency is providing any service pursuant to this Agreement, without the advance approval of the Media User. Media User shall not unreasonably withhold this approval.

7. Cost Estimates.

Agency shall not initiate billable work on any project pursuant to this Agreement without first estimating costs for preparation, including copy, service, layout, art, engraving, typography, processing, paste up and production. After determining the estimated cost, completion of the work shall be subject to Media User's prior approval.

8. Audit Rights.

Agency agrees that following reasonable prior notice any and all contracts, agreements, correspondence, books, accounts and other information relating to Media User's business or this Agreement shall be available for inspection by Media User and Media User's outside accountants, at Media User's expense and during the normal business hours of the Agency.

9. Ownership and Use.

A.   Agency shall insure, to the fullest extent possible under law, that Media User shall own all right, title and interest in and to, including copyrights, trade secret, patent and other intellectual property rights, with respect to any copy, photograph, advertisement, music, lyrics, video, or other work or thing created by Agency or at Agency's direction for Media User pursuant to this Agreement and utilized by Media User.

B.   Upon termination, Media User agrees that any advertising, merchandising, package, plan or idea prepared by Agency and submitted to Media User (whether submitted separately or in conjunction with or as a part of other material) which Media User has elected not to utilize, shall remain the property of Agency, unless Media User has paid Agency for its services in preparing such item. Media User agrees to return to Agency any copy, artwork, plates or other physical embodiment of such creative work relating to any such idea or plan which may be in Media User's possession at termination or expiration of this Agreement. Notwithstanding this, Media User has the unconditional right to pay for any of these materials or activities at the rate agreed upon in this Agreement and thereby these materials and activities would fall under the Section 9.A ownership and use rights accruing to Media User.

C.   Materials and advertisements created by Agency pursuant to this Agreement may be used by Media User outside the United States without additional compensation, provided that Media User shall

be responsible for any additional expense associated with such use, such as charges for translation and amounts due talent.

10. Indemnification and Insurance.

A. Agency shall indemnify and hold Media User harmless with respect to any claims, loss, suit, liability or judgment suffered by Media User, including reasonable attorney's fees and costs, based upon or related to any item prepared by Agency or at Agency's direction, including, but not limited to, any claim of libel, slander, piracy, plagiarism, invasion of privacy, or infringement of copyright or other intellectual property interest, except where any such claim arises out of material supplied by Media User and incorporated into any materials or advertisement prepared by Agency. Agency agrees to procure and maintain in force during the term of this Agreement, at Agency's expense, an Agency liability policy or policies having a minimum limit of at least _____, naming Media User as an additional insured and loss payee under such policy or policies.

B. Media User agrees to indemnify and hold Agency harmless with respect to any claims, loss, liability, damage or judgment suffered by Agency, including reasonable attorney's fees and court costs, which results from the use by Agency of any material furnished by Media User or where material created by Agency or at the direction of Agency subject to the indemnification in subsection A. above is materially changed by Media User. Information or data obtained by Agency from Media User to substantiate claims made in advertising shall be deemed to be "material furnished by Media User to Agency."

C. In the event of any proceeding, litigation or suit against Media User by any regulatory agency or in the event of any court action or other proceeding challenging any advertising prepared by Agency, Agency shall assist in the preparation of the defense of such action or proceeding and cooperate with Media User and Media User's attorneys.

11. Term.

The term of this Agreement shall commence on _____ and shall continue in full force and effect until terminated by either party upon at least sixty (60) days prior written notice, provided that in no event (except breach) may this Agreement be terminated prior to _____. The rights, duties and obligations of the parties shall continue in full force during or following the period of the termination notice until termination, including the ordering and billing of advertising in media whose closing dates follow then such period.

12. Rights Upon Termination.

A. Upon termination of the Agreement, Agency shall transfer, assign and make available to Media User all property and materials in Agency's possession or subject to Agency's control that are the property of Media User, subject to payment in full of amounts due pursuant to this Agreement.

B. Upon termination, Agency agrees to provide reasonable cooperation in arranging for the transfer or approval of third party's interest in all contracts, agreements and other arrangements with advertising media, suppliers, talent and others not then utilized, and all rights and claims thereto and therein, following appropriate release from the obligations therein.

13. Default.

In the event of any default of any material obligation by or owed by a party pursuant to this Agreement, then the other party may provide written notice of such default and if such default is not cured within ten (10) days of the written notice, then the nondefaulting party may terminate this Agreement. In addition, the only damages collectible by Agency shall be the exact amounts due; no other damages,

for any reason whatsoever, may be assessed against Media User including, but limited to, punitive damages and unreasonable termination charges, and any other such claim. This provision shall be broadly interpreted in the favor of the Media User by any Court of competent jurisdiction.

14. Notices.

Any notice required by this Agreement or given in connection with it, shall be in writing and shall be given to the appropriate party by personal delivery or by postage prepaid, or recognized overnight delivery services such as Federal Express.

If to Media User: _____

_____

If to Agency: _____

_____

15. Headings in this Agreement.

The headings in this Agreement are for convenience only, confirm no rights or obligations in either party, and do not alter any terms of this Agreement.

16. Entirety of Agreement.

The terms and conditions set forth herein constitute the entire agreement between the parties and supersede any communications or previous agreements with respect to the subject matter of this Agreement. There are no written or oral understandings directly or indirectly related to this Agreement that are not set forth herein. No change can be made to this Agreement other than in writing and signed by both parties.

17. Governing Law.

This Agreement shall be construed and enforced according to the laws of the State of _____ and any dispute under this Agreement must be brought in this venue and in no other.

In Witness whereof, the parties have executed this Agreement as of the date first written above.

_____   _____
Agency   Media User

Ad or other Media Agency Agreement

This Agency Agreement ("Agreement") is made and effective this _____ (Date), by and between ("Agency") and _____ (Your Firm) ("Media User").

Agency is in the business of providing media agency services for a fee.

Media User desires to engage Agency to render, and Agency desires to render to Media User, certain Agency services, all as set forth.

NOW, THEREFORE, in consideration of the mutual agreements and covenants herein contained, the parties hereto agree as follows:

1. <u>Engagement</u>.

Media User engages Agency to render, and Agency agrees to render to Media User, services in connection with Media User's planning, preparing and placing of advertising and other media services for certain of Media User's products as follows:

_____

A. Analyze Media User's current and proposed products and services and presentations and potential markets.

B. Create, prepare and submit to Media User for its prior approval advertising ideas, media suggestions, and other such related programs.

C. Prepare and submit to Media User for its prior approval estimates of costs and expenses associated with proposed advertising ideas and programs prior to any such implementation or financial commitment.

D. Design and prepare, or arrange for the design and preparation of advertisements, public relations, and other such materials.

E. Perform such other services as Media User may request from time to time such as, but not limited to, direct mail ad preparations, speech writing, publicity and public relations work, market research and analysis, and other similar and related activities.

F. Order advertising space, time or other means to be used for publication of Media User's advertisements, at all times endeavoring to secure the most efficient and advantageous rates available. All such activities to be approved in advance by the Media User unless otherwise written and stipulated.

G. Proof for accuracy and completeness of insertions, displays, broadcasts, or other forms of advertisements.

H. Audit invoices for proper and agreed upon space, time, material preparation and charges.

2. <u>Products</u>.

Agency's engagement shall relate to the following products and services of Media User:

_____.

3. Exclusivity.

Agency shall be the Agency in the United States and worldwide for Media User with respect to the products described in Section 2 above, unless otherwise specified in this section:

_____.

4.   Compensation.

A.   Agency shall receive an amount equal to ___ percentage of the gross charges levied by media for advertising placed by Agency pursuant to this Agreement; and   after volume discount, of the charges of suppliers of services or properties, such as finished art, comprehensive layouts, type composition, photostats, engravings, printing, radio and television programs, talent, literary, dramatic and musical works, records and exhibits, purchased by Agency on Media User's authorization during the term of this Agreement; provided that: No percentage will be added to Agency charges for packing, shipping, express, postage, telephone, telex, fax, travel expenses and other out of pocket expenses of Agency personnel.

B.   For those items where Agency is not compensated on a commission basis, Media User shall pay Agency on an hourly basis for services provided hereunder. The rate will be determined by the type of services provided and the person or persons providing such services, but in no event shall the rate exceed _____ per hour. Media User may elect in advance to be charged on this hourly rate basis. If Media User fails to notify Agency of its choice, it shall be presumed that Media User elected to be charged on a percentage basis.

C.   In the event that Agency undertakes, at Media User's request subject to Media User's prior approval, special projects such as those described in Section I.F above, Agency shall prepare an estimate of total charges for any such special project in advance, including any charges for materials or services purchased from outside vendors. In the event that Media User elects to proceed with the special project based upon Agency's estimated cost, Agency shall perform the services with respect to such special project at its estimated cost, subject to modification as mutually agreed by the parties.

D. For any special project or other services provided by Agency pursuant to this Agreement upon which the parties have not agreed as to charges, Media User shall pay
Agency at its regular percentage rates, as stated in Section 4.A above.

E.   Media User shall not be obligated to reimburse Agency for any travel or other out-of-pocket expenses incurred in the performance of services pursuant to this Agreement unless expressly agreed by Media User in advance.

5. Billing.

A.   Agency shall invoice Media User for all media costs where possible in advance of Agency's payment date to allow for prepayment by the Media User so that Media User may receive the benefit of any available prepayment or similar discount. For any media purchase or service for which Agency is not entitled to a commission, Agency shall ensure that the charges to Media User are net of all agency commissions and discounts.

B.   Charges for production materials and services shall be billed by Agency upon completion of the production job or, if cash discounts are available, upon receipt of the supplier's invoice.

C. On all outside purchases other than for media, Agency shall attach to the invoice evidence of the supplier's charges.

D. All cash discounts on Agency's purchases including, but not limited to, media, art, printing and mechanical work, shall be available to Media User, provided that Media User meets Agency's requisite billing terms and there is no outstanding undisputed indebtedness of Media User to Agency at the time of the payment to the supplier.

E. Rate or billing adjustments shall be credited or charged to Media User on the next regular invoice date or as soon thereafter as otherwise practical.

F. Invoices shall be submitted in an itemized format and shall be paid by Media User within sixty (60) days of the invoice date.

6. Competitors.

During the term of this Agreement, Agency shall not accept employment from, render services to, represent or otherwise be affiliated with any person, firm, corporation or entity in connection with any product or service directly or indirectly competitive with or similar to any product or service of Media User with respect to which the Agency is providing any service pursuant to this Agreement, without the advance approval of the Media User. Media User shall not unreasonably withhold this approval.

7. Cost Estimates.

Agency shall not initiate billable work on any project pursuant to this Agreement without first estimating costs for preparation, including copy, service, layout, art, engraving, typography, processing, paste up and production. After determining the estimated cost, completion of the work shall be subject to Media User's prior approval.

8. Audit Rights.

Agency agrees that following reasonable prior notice any and all contracts, agreements, correspondence, books, accounts and other information relating to Media User's business or this Agreement shall be available for inspection by Media User and Media User's outside accountants, at Media User's expense and during the normal business hours of the Agency.

9. Ownership and Use.

A. Agency shall insure, to the fullest extent possible under law, that Media User shall own all right, title and interest in and to, including copyrights, trade secret, patent and other intellectual property rights, with respect to any copy, photograph, advertisement, music, lyrics, video, or other work or thing created by Agency or at Agency's direction for Media User pursuant to this Agreement and utilized by Media User.

B. Upon termination, Media User agrees that any advertising, merchandising, package, plan or idea prepared by Agency and submitted to Media User (whether submitted separately or in conjunction with or as a part of other material) which Media User has elected not to utilize, shall remain the property of Agency, unless Media User has paid Agency for its services in preparing such item. Media User agrees to return to Agency any copy, artwork, plates or other physical embodiment of such creative work relating to any such idea or plan which may be in Media User's possession at termination or expiration of this Agreement. Notwithstanding this, Media User has the unconditional right to pay for any of these materials or activities at the rate agreed upon in this Agreement and thereby these materials and activities would fall under the Section 9.A ownership and use rights accruing to Media User.

C. Materials and advertisements created by Agency pursuant to this Agreement may be used by Media User outside the United States without additional compensation, provided that Media User shall

be responsible for any additional expense associated with such use, such as charges for translation and amounts due talent.

10. Indemnification and Insurance.

A. Agency shall indemnify and hold Media User harmless with respect to any claims, loss, suit, liability or judgment suffered by Media User, including reasonable attorney's fees and costs, based upon or related to any item prepared by Agency or at Agency's direction, including, but not limited to, any claim of libel, slander, piracy, plagiarism, invasion of privacy, or infringement of copyright or other intellectual property interest, except where any such claim arises out of material supplied by Media User and incorporated into any materials or advertisement prepared by Agency. Agency agrees to procure and maintain in force during the term of this Agreement, at Agency's expense, an Agency liability policy or policies having a minimum limit of at least _____, naming Media User as an additional insured and loss payee under such policy or policies.

B. Media User agrees to indemnify and hold Agency harmless with respect to any claims, loss, liability, damage or judgment suffered by Agency, including reasonable attorney's fees and court costs, which results from the use by Agency of any material furnished by Media User or where material created by Agency or at the direction of Agency subject to the indemnification in subsection A. above is materially changed by Media User. Information or data obtained by Agency from Media User to substantiate claims made in advertising shall be deemed to be "material furnished by Media User to Agency."

C. In the event of any proceeding, litigation or suit against Media User by any regulatory agency or in the event of any court action or other proceeding challenging any advertising prepared by Agency, Agency shall assist in the preparation of the defense of such action or proceeding and cooperate with Media User and Media User's attorneys.

11. Term.

The term of this Agreement shall commence on _____ and shall continue in full force and effect until terminated by either party upon at least sixty (60) days prior written notice, provided that in no event (except breach) may this Agreement be terminated prior to _____. The rights, duties and obligations of the parties shall continue in full force during or following the period of the termination notice until termination, including the ordering and billing of advertising in media whose closing dates follow then such period.

12. Rights Upon Termination.

A. Upon termination of the Agreement, Agency shall transfer, assign and make available to Media User all property and materials in Agency's possession or subject to Agency's control that are the property of Media User, subject to payment in full of amounts due pursuant to this Agreement.

B. Upon termination, Agency agrees to provide reasonable cooperation in arranging for the transfer or approval of third party's interest in all contracts, agreements and other arrangements with advertising media, suppliers, talent and others not then utilized, and all rights and claims thereto and therein, following appropriate release from the obligations therein.

13. Default.

In the event of any default of any material obligation by or owed by a party pursuant to this Agreement, then the other party may provide written notice of such default and if such default is not cured within ten (10) days of the written notice, then the nondefaulting party may terminate this Agreement. In addition, the only damages collectible by Agency shall be the exact amounts due; no other damages,

for any reason whatsoever, may be assessed against Media User including, but limited to, punitive damages and unreasonable termination charges, and any other such claim. This provision shall be broadly interpreted in the favor of the Media User by any Court of competent jurisdiction.

14. <u>Notices</u>.

Any notice required by this Agreement or given in connection with it, shall be in writing and shall be given to the appropriate party by personal delivery or by postage prepaid, or recognized overnight delivery services such as Federal Express.

If to Media User: _____

_____

If to Agency: _____

_____

15. <u>Headings in this Agreement</u>.

The headings in this Agreement are for convenience only, confirm no rights or obligations in either party, and do not alter any terms of this Agreement.

16. <u>Entirety of Agreement</u>.

The terms and conditions set forth herein constitute the entire agreement between the parties and supersede any communications or previous agreements with respect to the subject matter of this Agreement. There are no written or oral understandings directly or indirectly related to this Agreement that are not set forth herein. No change can be made to this Agreement other than in writing and signed by both parties.

17. <u>Governing Law</u>.

This Agreement shall be construed and enforced according to the laws of the State of _____ and any dispute under this Agreement must be brought in this venue and in no other.

In Witness whereof, the parties have executed this Agreement as of the date first written above.

_____   _____
Agency   Media User

Ad or other Media Agency Agreement

This Agency Agreement ("Agreement") is made and effective this _____ (Date), by and between ("Agency") and _____ (Your Firm) ("Media User").

Agency is in the business of providing media agency services for a fee.

Media User desires to engage Agency to render, and Agency desires to render to Media User, certain Agency services, all as set forth.

NOW, THEREFORE, in consideration of the mutual agreements and covenants herein contained, the parties hereto agree as follows:

1. Engagement.

Media User engages Agency to render, and Agency agrees to render to Media User, services in connection with Media User's planning, preparing and placing of advertising and other media services for certain of Media User's products as follows:

_____

A. Analyze Media User's current and proposed products and services and presentations and potential markets.

B. Create, prepare and submit to Media User for its prior approval advertising ideas, media suggestions, and other such related programs.

C. Prepare and submit to Media User for its prior approval estimates of costs and expenses associated with proposed advertising ideas and programs prior to any such implementation or financial commitment.

D. Design and prepare, or arrange for the design and preparation of advertisements, public relations, and other such materials.

E. Perform such other services as Media User may request from time to time such as, but not limited to, direct mail ad preparations, speech writing, publicity and public relations work, market research and analysis, and other similar and related activities.

F. Order advertising space, time or other means to be used for publication of Media User's advertisements, at all times endeavoring to secure the most efficient and advantageous rates available. All such activities to be approved in advance by the Media User unless otherwise written and stipulated.

G. Proof for accuracy and completeness of insertions, displays, broadcasts, or other forms of advertisements.

H. Audit invoices for proper and agreed upon space, time, material preparation and charges.

2. Products.

Agency's engagement shall relate to the following products and services of Media User:

_____.

3. Exclusivity.

Agency shall be the Agency in the United States and worldwide for Media User with respect to the products described in Section 2 above, unless otherwise specified in this section:

_____.

4.   Compensation.

A.   Agency shall receive an amount equal to ___ percentage of the gross charges levied by media for advertising placed by Agency pursuant to this Agreement; and   after volume discount, of the charges of suppliers of services or properties, such as finished art, comprehensive layouts, type composition, photostats, engravings, printing, radio and television programs, talent, literary, dramatic and musical works, records and exhibits, purchased by Agency on Media User's authorization during the term of this Agreement; provided that: No percentage will be added to Agency charges for packing, shipping, express, postage, telephone, telex, fax, travel expenses and other out of pocket expenses of Agency personnel.

B.   For those items where Agency is not compensated on a commission basis, Media User shall pay Agency on an hourly basis for services provided hereunder. The rate will be determined by the type of services provided and the person or persons providing such services, but in no event shall the rate exceed _____ per hour. Media User may elect in advance to be charged on this hourly rate basis. If Media User fails to notify Agency of its choice, it shall be presumed that Media User elected to be charged on a percentage basis.

C.   In the event that Agency undertakes, at Media User's request subject to Media User's prior approval, special projects such as those described in Section I.F above, Agency shall prepare an estimate of total charges for any such special project in advance, including any charges for materials or services purchased from outside vendors. In the event that Media User elects to proceed with the special project based upon Agency's estimated cost, Agency shall perform the services with respect to such special project at its estimated cost, subject to modification as mutually agreed by the parties.

D. For any special project or other services provided by Agency pursuant to this Agreement upon which the parties have not agreed as to charges, Media User shall pay
Agency at its regular percentage rates, as stated in Section 4.A above.

E.   Media User shall not be obligated to reimburse Agency for any travel or other out-of-pocket expenses incurred in the performance of services pursuant to this Agreement unless expressly agreed by Media User in advance.

5. Billing.

A.   Agency shall invoice Media User for all media costs where possible in advance of Agency's payment date to allow for prepayment by the Media User so that Media User may receive the benefit of any available prepayment or similar discount. For any media purchase or service for which Agency is not entitled to a commission, Agency shall ensure that the charges to Media User are net of all agency commissions and discounts.

B.   Charges for production materials and services shall be billed by Agency upon completion of the production job or, if cash discounts are available, upon receipt of the supplier's invoice.

C. On all outside purchases other than for media, Agency shall attach to the invoice evidence of the supplier's charges.

D. All cash discounts on Agency's purchases including, but not limited to, media, art, printing and mechanical work, shall be available to Media User, provided that Media User meets Agency's requisite billing terms and there is no outstanding undisputed indebtedness of Media User to Agency at the time of the payment to the supplier.

E. Rate or billing adjustments shall be credited or charged to Media User on the next regular invoice date or as soon thereafter as otherwise practical.

F. Invoices shall be submitted in an itemized format and shall be paid by Media User within sixty (60) days of the invoice date.

6. Competitors.

During the term of this Agreement, Agency shall not accept employment from, render services to, represent or otherwise be affiliated with any person, firm, corporation or entity in connection with any product or service directly or indirectly competitive with or similar to any product or service of Media User with respect to which the Agency is providing any service pursuant to this Agreement, without the advance approval of the Media User. Media User shall not unreasonably withhold this approval.

7. Cost Estimates.

Agency shall not initiate billable work on any project pursuant to this Agreement without first estimating costs for preparation, including copy, service, layout, art, engraving, typography, processing, paste up and production. After determining the estimated cost, completion of the work shall be subject to Media User's prior approval.

8. Audit Rights.

Agency agrees that following reasonable prior notice any and all contracts, agreements, correspondence, books, accounts and other information relating to Media User's business or this Agreement shall be available for inspection by Media User and Media User's outside accountants, at Media User's expense and during the normal business hours of the Agency.

9. Ownership and Use.

A. Agency shall insure, to the fullest extent possible under law, that Media User shall own all right, title and interest in and to, including copyrights, trade secret, patent and other intellectual property rights, with respect to any copy, photograph, advertisement, music, lyrics, video, or other work or thing created by Agency or at Agency's direction for Media User pursuant to this Agreement and utilized by Media User.

B. Upon termination, Media User agrees that any advertising, merchandising, package, plan or idea prepared by Agency and submitted to Media User (whether submitted separately or in conjunction with or as a part of other material) which Media User has elected not to utilize, shall remain the property of Agency, unless Media User has paid Agency for its services in preparing such item. Media User agrees to return to Agency any copy, artwork, plates or other physical embodiment of such creative work relating to any such idea or plan which may be in Media User's possession at termination or expiration of this Agreement. Notwithstanding this, Media User has the unconditional right to pay for any of these materials or activities at the rate agreed upon in this Agreement and thereby these materials and activities would fall under the Section 9.A ownership and use rights accruing to Media User.

C. Materials and advertisements created by Agency pursuant to this Agreement may be used by Media User outside the United States without additional compensation, provided that Media User shall

be responsible for any additional expense associated with such use, such as charges for translation and amounts due talent.

10. Indemnification and Insurance.

A. Agency shall indemnify and hold Media User harmless with respect to any claims, loss, suit, liability or judgment suffered by Media User, including reasonable attorney's fees and costs, based upon or related to any item prepared by Agency or at Agency's direction, including, but not limited to, any claim of libel, slander, piracy, plagiarism, invasion of privacy, or infringement of copyright or other intellectual property interest, except where any such claim arises out of material supplied by Media User and incorporated into any materials or advertisement prepared by Agency. Agency agrees to procure and maintain in force during the term of this Agreement, at Agency's expense, an Agency liability policy or policies having a minimum limit of at least _____, naming Media User as an additional insured and loss payee under such policy or policies.

B. Media User agrees to indemnify and hold Agency harmless with respect to any claims, loss, liability, damage or judgment suffered by Agency, including reasonable attorney's fees and court costs, which results from the use by Agency of any material furnished by Media User or where material created by Agency or at the direction of Agency subject to the indemnification in subsection A. above is materially changed by Media User. Information or data obtained by Agency from Media User to substantiate claims made in advertising shall be deemed to be "material furnished by Media User to Agency."

C. In the event of any proceeding, litigation or suit against Media User by any regulatory agency or in the event of any court action or other proceeding challenging any advertising prepared by Agency, Agency shall assist in the preparation of the defense of such action or proceeding and cooperate with Media User and Media User's attorneys.

11. Term.

The term of this Agreement shall commence on _____ and shall continue in full force and effect until terminated by either party upon at least sixty (60) days prior written notice, provided that in no event (except breach) may this Agreement be terminated prior to _____. The rights, duties and obligations of the parties shall continue in full force during or following the period of the termination notice until termination, including the ordering and billing of advertising in media whose closing dates follow then such period.

12. Rights Upon Termination.

A. Upon termination of the Agreement, Agency shall transfer, assign and make available to Media User all property and materials in Agency's possession or subject to Agency's control that are the property of Media User, subject to payment in full of amounts due pursuant to this Agreement.

B. Upon termination, Agency agrees to provide reasonable cooperation in arranging for the transfer or approval of third party's interest in all contracts, agreements and other arrangements with advertising media, suppliers, talent and others not then utilized, and all rights and claims thereto and therein, following appropriate release from the obligations therein.

13. Default.

In the event of any default of any material obligation by or owed by a party pursuant to this Agreement, then the other party may provide written notice of such default and if such default is not cured within ten (10) days of the written notice, then the nondefaulting party may terminate this Agreement. In addition, the only damages collectible by Agency shall be the exact amounts due; no other damages,

for any reason whatsoever, may be assessed against Media User including, but limited to, punitive damages and unreasonable termination charges, and any other such claim. This provision shall be broadly interpreted in the favor of the Media User by any Court of competent jurisdiction.

14. Notices.

Any notice required by this Agreement or given in connection with it, shall be in writing and shall be given to the appropriate party by personal delivery or by postage prepaid, or recognized overnight delivery services such as Federal Express.

If to Media User: _____

_____

If to Agency: _____

_____

15. Headings in this Agreement.

The headings in this Agreement are for convenience only, confirm no rights or obligations in either party, and do not alter any terms of this Agreement.

16. Entirety of Agreement.

The terms and conditions set forth herein constitute the entire agreement between the parties and supersede any communications or previous agreements with respect to the subject matter of this Agreement. There are no written or oral understandings directly or indirectly related to this Agreement that are not set forth herein. No change can be made to this Agreement other than in writing and signed by both parties.

17. Governing Law.

This Agreement shall be construed and enforced according to the laws of the State of _____ and any dispute under this Agreement must be brought in this venue and in no other.

In Witness whereof, the parties have executed this Agreement as of the date first written above.

_____   _____
Agency   Media User

Ad or other Media Agency Agreement

This Agency Agreement ("Agreement") is made and effective this _____ (Date), by and between ("Agency") and _____ (Your Firm) ("Media User").

Agency is in the business of providing media agency services for a fee.

Media User desires to engage Agency to render, and Agency desires to render to Media User, certain Agency services, all as set forth.

NOW, THEREFORE, in consideration of the mutual agreements and covenants herein contained, the parties hereto agree as follows:

1. <u>Engagement</u>.

Media User engages Agency to render, and Agency agrees to render to Media User, services in connection with Media User's planning, preparing and placing of advertising and other media services for certain of Media User's products as follows:

_____

A. Analyze Media User's current and proposed products and services and presentations and potential markets.

B. Create, prepare and submit to Media User for its prior approval advertising ideas, media suggestions, and other such related programs.

C. Prepare and submit to Media User for its prior approval estimates of costs and expenses associated with proposed advertising ideas and programs prior to any such implementation or financial commitment.

D. Design and prepare, or arrange for the design and preparation of advertisements, public relations, and other such materials.

E. Perform such other services as Media User may request from time to time such as, but not limited to, direct mail ad preparations, speech writing, publicity and public relations work, market research and analysis, and other similar and related activities.

F. Order advertising space, time or other means to be used for publication of Media User's advertisements, at all times endeavoring to secure the most efficient and advantageous rates available. All such activities to be approved in advance by the Media User unless otherwise written and stipulated.

G. Proof for accuracy and completeness of insertions, displays, broadcasts, or other forms of advertisements.

H. Audit invoices for proper and agreed upon space, time, material preparation and charges.

2. <u>Products</u>.

Agency's engagement shall relate to the following products and services of Media User:

_____.

3. Exclusivity.

Agency shall be the Agency in the United States and worldwide for Media User with respect to the products described in Section 2 above, unless otherwise specified in this section:

_____.

4.   Compensation.

A.   Agency shall receive an amount equal to ___ percentage of the gross charges levied by media for advertising placed by Agency pursuant to this Agreement; and ___ after volume discount, of the charges of suppliers of services or properties, such as finished art, comprehensive layouts, type composition, photostats, engravings, printing, radio and television programs, talent, literary, dramatic and musical works, records and exhibits, purchased by Agency on Media User's authorization during the term of this Agreement; provided that: No percentage will be added to Agency charges for packing, shipping, express, postage, telephone, telex, fax, travel expenses and other out of pocket expenses of Agency personnel.

B.   For those items where Agency is not compensated on a commission basis, Media User shall pay Agency on an hourly basis for services provided hereunder. The rate will be determined by the type of services provided and the person or persons providing such services, but in no event shall the rate exceed _____ per hour. Media User may elect in advance to be charged on this hourly rate basis. If Media User fails to notify Agency of its choice, it shall be presumed that Media User elected to be charged on a percentage basis.

C.   In the event that Agency undertakes, at Media User's request subject to Media User's prior approval, special projects such as those described in Section I.F above, Agency shall prepare an estimate of total charges for any such special project in advance, including any charges for materials or services purchased from outside vendors. In the event that Media User elects to proceed with the special project based upon Agency's estimated cost, Agency shall perform the services with respect to such special project at its estimated cost, subject to modification as mutually agreed by the parties.

D. For any special project or other services provided by Agency pursuant to this Agreement upon which the parties have not agreed as to charges, Media User shall pay
Agency at its regular percentage rates, as stated in Section 4.A above.

E.   Media User shall not be obligated to reimburse Agency for any travel or other out-of-pocket expenses incurred in the performance of services pursuant to this Agreement unless expressly agreed by Media User in advance.

5. Billing.

A.   Agency shall invoice Media User for all media costs where possible in advance of Agency's payment date to allow for prepayment by the Media User so that Media User may receive the benefit of any available prepayment or similar discount. For any media purchase or service for which Agency is not entitled to a commission, Agency shall ensure that the charges to Media User are net of all agency commissions and discounts.

B.   Charges for production materials and services shall be billed by Agency upon completion of the production job or, if cash discounts are available, upon receipt of the supplier's invoice.

C. On all outside purchases other than for media, Agency shall attach to the invoice evidence of the supplier's charges.

D. All cash discounts on Agency's purchases including, but not limited to, media, art, printing and mechanical work, shall be available to Media User, provided that Media User meets Agency's requisite billing terms and there is no outstanding undisputed indebtedness of Media User to Agency at the time of the payment to the supplier.

E. Rate or billing adjustments shall be credited or charged to Media User on the next regular invoice date or as soon thereafter as otherwise practical.

F. Invoices shall be submitted in an itemized format and shall be paid by Media User within sixty (60) days of the invoice date.

6. <u>Competitors</u>.

During the term of this Agreement, Agency shall not accept employment from, render services to, represent or otherwise be affiliated with any person, firm, corporation or entity in connection with any product or service directly or indirectly competitive with or similar to any product or service of Media User with respect to which the Agency is providing any service pursuant to this Agreement, without the advance approval of the Media User. Media User shall not unreasonably withhold this approval.

7. <u>Cost Estimates</u>.

Agency shall not initiate billable work on any project pursuant to this Agreement without first estimating costs for preparation, including copy, service, layout, art, engraving, typography, processing, paste up and production. After determining the estimated cost, completion of the work shall be subject to Media User's prior approval.

8. <u>Audit Rights</u>.

Agency agrees that following reasonable prior notice any and all contracts, agreements, correspondence, books, accounts and other information relating to Media User's business or this Agreement shall be available for inspection by Media User and Media User's outside accountants, at Media User's expense and during the normal business hours of the Agency.

9.<u>Ownership and Use.</u>

A. Agency shall insure, to the fullest extent possible under law, that Media User shall own all right, title and interest in and to, including copyrights, trade secret, patent and other intellectual property rights, with respect to any copy, photograph, advertisement, music, lyrics, video, or other work or thing created by Agency or at Agency's direction for Media User pursuant to this Agreement and utilized by Media User.

B. Upon termination, Media User agrees that any advertising, merchandising, package, plan or idea prepared by Agency and submitted to Media User (whether submitted separately or in conjunction with or as a part of other material) which Media User has elected not to utilize, shall remain the property of Agency, unless Media User has paid Agency for its services in preparing such item. Media User agrees to return to Agency any copy, artwork, plates or other physical embodiment of such creative work relating to any such idea or plan which may be in Media User's possession at termination or expiration of this Agreement. Notwithstanding this, Media User has the unconditional right to pay for any of these materials or activities at the rate agreed upon in this Agreement and thereby these materials and activities would fall under the Section 9.A ownership and use rights accruing to Media User.

C. Materials and advertisements created by Agency pursuant to this Agreement may be used by Media User outside the United States without additional compensation, provided that Media User shall

be responsible for any additional expense associated with such use, such as charges for translation and amounts due talent.

10. Indemnification and Insurance.

A.   Agency shall indemnify and hold Media User harmless with respect to any claims, loss, suit, liability or judgment suffered by Media User, including reasonable attorney's fees and costs, based upon or related to any item prepared by Agency or at Agency's direction, including, but not limited to, any claim of libel, slander, piracy, plagiarism, invasion of privacy, or infringement of copyright or other intellectual property interest, except where any such claim arises out of material supplied by Media User and incorporated into any materials or advertisement prepared by Agency. Agency agrees to procure and maintain in force during the term of this Agreement, at Agency's expense, an Agency liability policy or policies having a minimum limit of at least _____, naming Media User as an additional insured and loss payee under such policy or policies.

B.   Media User agrees to indemnify and hold Agency harmless with respect to any claims, loss, liability, damage or judgment suffered by Agency, including reasonable attorney's fees and court costs, which results from the use by Agency of any material furnished by Media User or where material created by Agency or at the direction of Agency subject to the indemnification in subsection A. above is materially changed by Media User. Information or data obtained by Agency from Media User to substantiate claims made in advertising shall be deemed to be "material furnished by Media User to Agency."

C.   In the event of any proceeding, litigation or suit against Media User by any regulatory agency or in the event of any court action or other proceeding challenging any advertising prepared by Agency, Agency shall assist in the preparation of the defense of such action or proceeding and cooperate with Media User and Media User's attorneys.

11. Term.

The term of this Agreement shall commence on _____ and shall continue in full force and effect until terminated by either party upon at least sixty (60) days prior written notice, provided that in no event (except breach) may this Agreement be terminated prior to _____. The rights, duties and obligations of the parties shall continue in full force during or following the period of the termination notice until termination, including the ordering and billing of advertising in media whose closing dates follow then such period.

12. Rights Upon Termination.

A.   Upon termination of the Agreement, Agency shall transfer, assign and make available to Media User all property and materials in Agency's possession or subject to Agency's control that are the property of Media User, subject to payment in full of amounts due pursuant to this Agreement.

B.   Upon termination, Agency agrees to provide reasonable cooperation in arranging for the transfer or approval of third party's interest in all contracts, agreements and other arrangements with advertising media, suppliers, talent and others not then utilized, and all rights and claims thereto and therein, following appropriate release from the obligations therein.

13. Default.

In the event of any default of any material obligation by or owed by a party pursuant to this Agreement, then the other party may provide written notice of such default and if such default is not cured within ten (10) days of the written notice, then the nondefaulting party may terminate this Agreement. In addition, the only damages collectible by Agency shall be the exact amounts due; no other damages,

for any reason whatsoever, may be assessed against Media User including, but limited to, punitive damages and unreasonable termination charges, and any other such claim. This provision shall be broadly interpreted in the favor of the Media User by any Court of competent jurisdiction.

14. Notices.

Any notice required by this Agreement or given in connection with it, shall be in writing and shall be given to the appropriate party by personal delivery or by postage prepaid, or recognized overnight delivery services such as Federal Express.

If to Media User: _____

_____

If to Agency: _____

_____

15. Headings in this Agreement.

The headings in this Agreement are for convenience only, confirm no rights or obligations in either party, and do not alter any terms of this Agreement.

16. Entirety of Agreement.

The terms and conditions set forth herein constitute the entire agreement between the parties and supersede any communications or previous agreements with respect to the subject matter of this Agreement. There are no written or oral understandings directly or indirectly related to this Agreement that are not set forth herein. No change can be made to this Agreement other than in writing and signed by both parties.

17. Governing Law.

This Agreement shall be construed and enforced according to the laws of the State of _____ and any dispute under this Agreement must be brought in this venue and in no other.

In Witness whereof, the parties have executed this Agreement as of the date first written above.

_____   _____
Agency   Media User

Ad or other Media Agency Agreement

This Agency Agreement ("Agreement") is made and effective this _____ (Date), by and between ("Agency") and _____ (Your Firm) ("Media User").

Agency is in the business of providing media agency services for a fee.

Media User desires to engage Agency to render, and Agency desires to render to Media User, certain Agency services, all as set forth.

NOW, THEREFORE, in consideration of the mutual agreements and covenants herein contained, the parties hereto agree as follows:

1. Engagement.

Media User engages Agency to render, and Agency agrees to render to Media User, services in connection with Media User's planning, preparing and placing of advertising and other media services for certain of Media User's products as follows:

_____

A. Analyze Media User's current and proposed products and services and presentations and potential markets.

B. Create, prepare and submit to Media User for its prior approval advertising ideas, media suggestions, and other such related programs.

C. Prepare and submit to Media User for its prior approval estimates of costs and expenses associated with proposed advertising ideas and programs prior to any such implementation or financial commitment.

D. Design and prepare, or arrange for the design and preparation of advertisements, public relations, and other such materials.

E. Perform such other services as Media User may request from time to time such as, but not limited to, direct mail ad preparations, speech writing, publicity and public relations work, market research and analysis, and other similar and related activities.

F. Order advertising space, time or other means to be used for publication of Media User's advertisements, at all times endeavoring to secure the most efficient and advantageous rates available. All such activities to be approved in advance by the Media User unless otherwise written and stipulated.

G. Proof for accuracy and completeness of insertions, displays, broadcasts, or other forms of advertisements.

H. Audit invoices for proper and agreed upon space, time, material preparation and charges.

2. Products.

Agency's engagement shall relate to the following products and services of Media User:

_____.

3. <u>Exclusivity</u>.

Agency shall be the Agency in the United States and worldwide for Media User with respect to the products described in Section 2 above, unless otherwise specified in this section:

_____.

4.   <u>Compensation</u>.

A.   Agency shall receive an amount equal to ___ percentage of the gross charges levied by media for advertising placed by Agency pursuant to this Agreement; and   after volume discount, of the charges of suppliers of services or properties, such as finished art, comprehensive layouts, type composition, photostats, engravings, printing, radio and television programs, talent, literary, dramatic and musical works, records and exhibits, purchased by Agency on Media User's authorization during the term of this Agreement; provided that: No percentage will be added to Agency charges for packing, shipping, express, postage, telephone, telex, fax, travel expenses and other out of pocket expenses of Agency personnel.

B.   For those items where Agency is not compensated on a commission basis, Media User shall pay Agency on an hourly basis for services provided hereunder. The rate will be determined by the type of services provided and the person or persons providing such services, but in no event shall the rate exceed _____ per hour. Media User may elect in advance to be charged on this hourly rate basis. If Media User fails to notify Agency of its choice, it shall be presumed that Media User elected to be charged on a percentage basis.

C.   In the event that Agency undertakes, at Media User's request subject to Media User's prior approval, special projects such as those described in Section I.F above, Agency shall prepare an estimate of total charges for any such special project in advance, including any charges for materials or services purchased from outside vendors. In the event that Media User elects to proceed with the special project based upon Agency's estimated cost, Agency shall perform the services with respect to such special project at its estimated cost, subject to modification as mutually agreed by the parties.

D. For any special project or other services provided by Agency pursuant to this Agreement upon which the parties have not agreed as to charges, Media User shall pay
Agency at its regular percentage rates, as stated in Section 4.A above.

E.   Media User shall not be obligated to reimburse Agency for any travel or other out-of-pocket expenses incurred in the performance of services pursuant to this Agreement unless expressly agreed by Media User in advance.

5. <u>Billing</u>.

A.   Agency shall invoice Media User for all media costs where possible in advance of Agency's payment date to allow for prepayment by the Media User so that Media User may receive the benefit of any available prepayment or similar discount. For any media purchase or service for which Agency is not entitled to a commission, Agency shall ensure that the charges to Media User are net of all agency commissions and discounts.

B.   Charges for production materials and services shall be billed by Agency upon completion of the production job or, if cash discounts are available, upon receipt of the supplier's invoice.

C. On all outside purchases other than for media, Agency shall attach to the invoice evidence of the supplier's charges.

D. All cash discounts on Agency's purchases including, but not limited to, media, art, printing and mechanical work, shall be available to Media User, provided that Media User meets Agency's requisite billing terms and there is no outstanding undisputed indebtedness of Media User to Agency at the time of the payment to the supplier.

E. Rate or billing adjustments shall be credited or charged to Media User on the next regular invoice date or as soon thereafter as otherwise practical.

F. Invoices shall be submitted in an itemized format and shall be paid by Media User within sixty (60) days of the invoice date.

6. Competitors.

During the term of this Agreement, Agency shall not accept employment from, render services to, represent or otherwise be affiliated with any person, firm, corporation or entity in connection with any product or service directly or indirectly competitive with or similar to any product or service of Media User with respect to which the Agency is providing any service pursuant to this Agreement, without the advance approval of the Media User. Media User shall not unreasonably withhold this approval.

7. Cost Estimates.

Agency shall not initiate billable work on any project pursuant to this Agreement without first estimating costs for preparation, including copy, service, layout, art, engraving, typography, processing, paste up and production. After determining the estimated cost, completion of the work shall be subject to Media User's prior approval.

8. Audit Rights.

Agency agrees that following reasonable prior notice any and all contracts, agreements, correspondence, books, accounts and other information relating to Media User's business or this Agreement shall be available for inspection by Media User and Media User's outside accountants, at Media User's expense and during the normal business hours of the Agency.

9. Ownership and Use.

A. Agency shall insure, to the fullest extent possible under law, that Media User shall own all right, title and interest in and to, including copyrights, trade secret, patent and other intellectual property rights, with respect to any copy, photograph, advertisement, music, lyrics, video, or other work or thing created by Agency or at Agency's direction for Media User pursuant to this Agreement and utilized by Media User.

B. Upon termination, Media User agrees that any advertising, merchandising, package, plan or idea prepared by Agency and submitted to Media User (whether submitted separately or in conjunction with or as a part of other material) which Media User has elected not to utilize, shall remain the property of Agency, unless Media User has paid Agency for its services in preparing such item. Media User agrees to return to Agency any copy, artwork, plates or other physical embodiment of such creative work relating to any such idea or plan which may be in Media User's possession at termination or expiration of this Agreement. Notwithstanding this, Media User has the unconditional right to pay for any of these materials or activities at the rate agreed upon in this Agreement and thereby these materials and activities would fall under the Section 9.A ownership and use rights accruing to Media User.

C. Materials and advertisements created by Agency pursuant to this Agreement may be used by Media User outside the United States without additional compensation, provided that Media User shall

be responsible for any additional expense associated with such use, such as charges for translation and amounts due talent.

10. Indemnification and Insurance.

A. Agency shall indemnify and hold Media User harmless with respect to any claims, loss, suit, liability or judgment suffered by Media User, including reasonable attorney's fees and costs, based upon or related to any item prepared by Agency or at Agency's direction, including, but not limited to, any claim of libel, slander, piracy, plagiarism, invasion of privacy, or infringement of copyright or other intellectual property interest, except where any such claim arises out of material supplied by Media User and incorporated into any materials or advertisement prepared by Agency. Agency agrees to procure and maintain in force during the term of this Agreement, at Agency's expense, an Agency liability policy or policies having a minimum limit of at least _____, naming Media User as an additional insured and loss payee under such policy or policies.

B. Media User agrees to indemnify and hold Agency harmless with respect to any claims, loss, liability, damage or judgment suffered by Agency, including reasonable attorney's fees and court costs, which results from the use by Agency of any material furnished by Media User or where material created by Agency or at the direction of Agency subject to the indemnification in subsection A. above is materially changed by Media User. Information or data obtained by Agency from Media User to substantiate claims made in advertising shall be deemed to be "material furnished by Media User to Agency."

C. In the event of any proceeding, litigation or suit against Media User by any regulatory agency or in the event of any court action or other proceeding challenging any advertising prepared by Agency, Agency shall assist in the preparation of the defense of such action or proceeding and cooperate with Media User and Media User's attorneys.

11. Term.

The term of this Agreement shall commence on _____ and shall continue in full force and effect until terminated by either party upon at least sixty (60) days prior written notice, provided that in no event (except breach) may this Agreement be terminated prior to _____. The rights, duties and obligations of the parties shall continue in full force during or following the period of the termination notice until termination, including the ordering and billing of advertising in media whose closing dates follow then such period.

12. Rights Upon Termination.

A. Upon termination of the Agreement, Agency shall transfer, assign and make available to Media User all property and materials in Agency's possession or subject to Agency's control that are the property of Media User, subject to payment in full of amounts due pursuant to this Agreement.

B. Upon termination, Agency agrees to provide reasonable cooperation in arranging for the transfer or approval of third party's interest in all contracts, agreements and other arrangements with advertising media, suppliers, talent and others not then utilized, and all rights and claims thereto and therein, following appropriate release from the obligations therein.

13. Default.

In the event of any default of any material obligation by or owed by a party pursuant to this Agreement, then the other party may provide written notice of such default and if such default is not cured within ten (10) days of the written notice, then the nondefaulting party may terminate this Agreement. In addition, the only damages collectible by Agency shall be the exact amounts due; no other damages,

for any reason whatsoever, may be assessed against Media User including, but limited to, punitive damages and unreasonable termination charges, and any other such claim. This provision shall be broadly interpreted in the favor of the Media User by any Court of competent jurisdiction.

14. Notices.

Any notice required by this Agreement or given in connection with it, shall be in writing and shall be given to the appropriate party by personal delivery or by postage prepaid, or recognized overnight delivery services such as Federal Express.

If to Media User: _____

_____

If to Agency: _____

_____

15. Headings in this Agreement.

The headings in this Agreement are for convenience only, confirm no rights or obligations in either party, and do not alter any terms of this Agreement.

16. Entirety of Agreement.

The terms and conditions set forth herein constitute the entire agreement between the parties and supersede any communications or previous agreements with respect to the subject matter of this Agreement. There are no written or oral understandings directly or indirectly related to this Agreement that are not set forth herein. No change can be made to this Agreement other than in writing and signed by both parties.

17. Governing Law.

This Agreement shall be construed and enforced according to the laws of the State of _____ and any dispute under this Agreement must be brought in this venue and in no other.

In Witness whereof, the parties have executed this Agreement as of the date first written above.

_____   _____
Agency   Media User

Ad or other Media Agency Agreement

This Agency Agreement ("Agreement") is made and effective this _____ (Date), by and between ("Agency") and _____ (Your Firm) ("Media User").

Agency is in the business of providing media agency services for a fee.

Media User desires to engage Agency to render, and Agency desires to render to Media User, certain Agency services, all as set forth.

NOW, THEREFORE, in consideration of the mutual agreements and covenants herein contained, the parties hereto agree as follows:

1. <u>Engagement</u>.

Media User engages Agency to render, and Agency agrees to render to Media User, services in connection with Media User's planning, preparing and placing of advertising and other media services for certain of Media User's products as follows:

_____

A. Analyze Media User's current and proposed products and services and presentations and potential markets.

B. Create, prepare and submit to Media User for its prior approval advertising ideas, media suggestions, and other such related programs.

C. Prepare and submit to Media User for its prior approval estimates of costs and expenses associated with proposed advertising ideas and programs prior to any such implementation or financial commitment.

D. Design and prepare, or arrange for the design and preparation of advertisements, public relations, and other such materials.

E. Perform such other services as Media User may request from time to time such as, but not limited to, direct mail ad preparations, speech writing, publicity and public relations work, market research and analysis, and other similar and related activities.

F. Order advertising space, time or other means to be used for publication of Media User's advertisements, at all times endeavoring to secure the most efficient and advantageous rates available. All such activities to be approved in advance by the Media User unless otherwise written and stipulated.

G. Proof for accuracy and completeness of insertions, displays, broadcasts, or other forms of advertisements.

H. Audit invoices for proper and agreed upon space, time, material preparation and charges.

2. <u>Products</u>.

Agency's engagement shall relate to the following products and services of Media User:

_____.

3. Exclusivity.

Agency shall be the Agency in the United States and worldwide for Media User with respect to the products described in Section 2 above, unless otherwise specified in this section:

_____.

4. Compensation.

A. Agency shall receive an amount equal to ___ percentage of the gross charges levied by media for advertising placed by Agency pursuant to this Agreement; and _____ after volume discount, of the charges of suppliers of services or properties, such as finished art, comprehensive layouts, type composition, photostats, engravings, printing, radio and television programs, talent, literary, dramatic and musical works, records and exhibits, purchased by Agency on Media User's authorization during the term of this Agreement; provided that: No percentage will be added to Agency charges for packing, shipping, express, postage, telephone, telex, fax, travel expenses and other out of pocket expenses of Agency personnel.

B. For those items where Agency is not compensated on a commission basis, Media User shall pay Agency on an hourly basis for services provided hereunder. The rate will be determined by the type of services provided and the person or persons providing such services, but in no event shall the rate exceed _____ per hour. Media User may elect in advance to be charged on this hourly rate basis. If Media User fails to notify Agency of its choice, it shall be presumed that Media User elected to be charged on a percentage basis.

C. In the event that Agency undertakes, at Media User's request subject to Media User's prior approval, special projects such as those described in Section I.F above, Agency shall prepare an estimate of total charges for any such special project in advance, including any charges for materials or services purchased from outside vendors. In the event that Media User elects to proceed with the special project based upon Agency's estimated cost, Agency shall perform the services with respect to such special project at its estimated cost, subject to modification as mutually agreed by the parties.

D. For any special project or other services provided by Agency pursuant to this Agreement upon which the parties have not agreed as to charges, Media User shall pay
Agency at its regular percentage rates, as stated in Section 4.A above.

E. Media User shall not be obligated to reimburse Agency for any travel or other out-of-pocket expenses incurred in the performance of services pursuant to this Agreement unless expressly agreed by Media User in advance.

5. Billing.

A. Agency shall invoice Media User for all media costs where possible in advance of Agency's payment date to allow for prepayment by the Media User so that Media User may receive the benefit of any available prepayment or similar discount. For any media purchase or service for which Agency is not entitled to a commission, Agency shall ensure that the charges to Media User are net of all agency commissions and discounts.

B. Charges for production materials and services shall be billed by Agency upon completion of the production job or, if cash discounts are available, upon receipt of the supplier's invoice.

C. On all outside purchases other than for media, Agency shall attach to the invoice evidence of the supplier's charges.

D.   All cash discounts on Agency's purchases including, but not limited to, media, art, printing and mechanical work, shall be available to Media User, provided that Media User meets Agency's requisite billing terms and there is no outstanding undisputed indebtedness of Media User to Agency at the time of the payment to the supplier.

E. Rate or billing adjustments shall be credited or charged to Media User on the next regular invoice date or as soon thereafter as otherwise practical.

F. Invoices shall be submitted in an itemized format and shall be paid by Media User within sixty (60) days of the invoice date.

6. Competitors.

During the term of this Agreement, Agency shall not accept employment from, render services to, represent or otherwise be affiliated with any person, firm, corporation or entity in connection with any product or service directly or indirectly competitive with or similar to any product or service of Media User with respect to which the Agency is providing any service pursuant to this Agreement, without the advance approval of the Media User. Media User shall not unreasonably withhold this approval.

7. Cost Estimates.

Agency shall not initiate billable work on any project pursuant to this Agreement without first estimating costs for preparation, including copy, service, layout, art, engraving, typography, processing, paste up and production. After determining the estimated cost, completion of the work shall be subject to Media User's prior approval.

8. Audit Rights.

Agency agrees that following reasonable prior notice any and all contracts, agreements, correspondence, books, accounts and other information relating to Media User's business or this Agreement shall be available for inspection by Media User and Media User's outside accountants, at Media User's expense and during the normal business hours of the Agency.

9. Ownership and Use.

A.   Agency shall insure, to the fullest extent possible under law, that Media User shall own all right, title and interest in and to, including copyrights, trade secret, patent and other intellectual property rights, with respect to any copy, photograph, advertisement, music, lyrics, video, or other work or thing created by Agency or at Agency's direction for Media User pursuant to this Agreement and utilized by Media User.

B.   Upon termination, Media User agrees that any advertising, merchandising, package, plan or idea prepared by Agency and submitted to Media User (whether submitted separately or in conjunction with or as a part of other material) which Media User has elected not to utilize, shall remain the property of Agency, unless Media User has paid Agency for its services in preparing such item. Media User agrees to return to Agency any copy, artwork, plates or other physical embodiment of such creative work relating to any such idea or plan which may be in Media User's possession at termination or expiration of this Agreement. Notwithstanding this, Media User has the unconditional right to pay for any of these materials or activities at the rate agreed upon in this Agreement and thereby these materials and activities would fall under the Section 9.A ownership and use rights accruing to Media User.

C.   Materials and advertisements created by Agency pursuant to this Agreement may be used by Media User outside the United States without additional compensation, provided that Media User shall

be responsible for any additional expense associated with such use, such as charges for translation and amounts due talent.

10. Indemnification and Insurance.

A.   Agency shall indemnify and hold Media User harmless with respect to any claims, loss, suit, liability or judgment suffered by Media User, including reasonable attorney's fees and costs, based upon or related to any item prepared by Agency or at Agency's direction, including, but not limited to, any claim of libel, slander, piracy, plagiarism, invasion of privacy, or infringement of copyright or other intellectual property interest, except where any such claim arises out of material supplied by Media User and incorporated into any materials or advertisement prepared by Agency. Agency agrees to procure and maintain in force during the term of this Agreement, at Agency's expense, an Agency liability policy or policies having a minimum limit of at least _____, naming Media User as an additional insured and loss payee under such policy or policies.

B.   Media User agrees to indemnify and hold Agency harmless with respect to any claims, loss, liability, damage or judgment suffered by Agency, including reasonable attorney's fees and court costs, which results from the use by Agency of any material furnished by Media User or where material created by Agency or at the direction of Agency subject to the indemnification in subsection A. above is materially changed by Media User. Information or data obtained by Agency from Media User to substantiate claims made in advertising shall be deemed to be "material furnished by Media User to Agency."

C.   In the event of any proceeding, litigation or suit against Media User by any regulatory agency or in the event of any court action or other proceeding challenging any advertising prepared by Agency, Agency shall assist in the preparation of the defense of such action or proceeding and cooperate with Media User and Media User's attorneys.

11. Term.

The term of this Agreement shall commence on _____ and shall continue in full force and effect until terminated by either party upon at least sixty (60) days prior written notice, provided that in no event (except breach) may this Agreement be terminated prior to _____. The rights, duties and obligations of the parties shall continue in full force during or following the period of the termination notice until termination, including the ordering and billing of advertising in media whose closing dates follow then such period.

12. Rights Upon Termination.

A.   Upon termination of the Agreement, Agency shall transfer, assign and make available to Media User all property and materials in Agency's possession or subject to Agency's control that are the property of Media User, subject to payment in full of amounts due pursuant to this Agreement.

B.   Upon termination, Agency agrees to provide reasonable cooperation in arranging for the transfer or approval of third party's interest in all contracts, agreements and other arrangements with advertising media, suppliers, talent and others not then utilized, and all rights and claims thereto and therein, following appropriate release from the obligations therein.

13. Default.

In the event of any default of any material obligation by or owed by a party pursuant to this Agreement, then the other party may provide written notice of such default and if such default is not cured within ten (10) days of the written notice, then the nondefaulting party may terminate this Agreement. In addition, the only damages collectible by Agency shall be the exact amounts due; no other damages,

for any reason whatsoever, may be assessed against Media User including, but limited to, punitive damages and unreasonable termination charges, and any other such claim. This provision shall be broadly interpreted in the favor of the Media User by any Court of competent jurisdiction.

14. <u>Notices</u>.

Any notice required by this Agreement or given in connection with it, shall be in writing and shall be given to the appropriate party by personal delivery or by postage prepaid, or recognized overnight delivery services such as Federal Express.

If to Media User: _____

_____

If to Agency: _____

_____

15. <u>Headings in this Agreement</u>.

The headings in this Agreement are for convenience only, confirm no rights or obligations in either party, and do not alter any terms of this Agreement.

16. <u>Entirety of Agreement</u>.

The terms and conditions set forth herein constitute the entire agreement between the parties and supersede any communications or previous agreements with respect to the subject matter of this Agreement. There are no written or oral understandings directly or indirectly related to this Agreement that are not set forth herein. No change can be made to this Agreement other than in writing and signed by both parties.

17. <u>Governing Law</u>.

This Agreement shall be construed and enforced according to the laws of the State of _____ and any dispute under this Agreement must be brought in this venue and in no other.

In Witness whereof, the parties have executed this Agreement as of the date first written above.

_____ _____
Agency   Media User

Ad or other Media Agency Agreement

This Agency Agreement ("Agreement") is made and effective this _____ (Date), by and between ("Agency") and _____ (Your Firm) ("Media User").

Agency is in the business of providing media agency services for a fee.

Media User desires to engage Agency to render, and Agency desires to render to Media User, certain Agency services, all as set forth.

NOW, THEREFORE, in consideration of the mutual agreements and covenants herein contained, the parties hereto agree as follows:

1. Engagement.

Media User engages Agency to render, and Agency agrees to render to Media User, services in connection with Media User's planning, preparing and placing of advertising and other media services for certain of Media User's products as follows:

_____

A. Analyze Media User's current and proposed products and services and presentations and potential markets.

B. Create, prepare and submit to Media User for its prior approval advertising ideas, media suggestions, and other such related programs.

C. Prepare and submit to Media User for its prior approval estimates of costs and expenses associated with proposed advertising ideas and programs prior to any such implementation or financial commitment.

D. Design and prepare, or arrange for the design and preparation of advertisements, public relations, and other such materials.

E. Perform such other services as Media User may request from time to time such as, but not limited to, direct mail ad preparations, speech writing, publicity and public relations work, market research and analysis, and other similar and related activities.

F. Order advertising space, time or other means to be used for publication of Media User's advertisements, at all times endeavoring to secure the most efficient and advantageous rates available. All such activities to be approved in advance by the Media User unless otherwise written and stipulated.

G. Proof for accuracy and completeness of insertions, displays, broadcasts, or other forms of advertisements.

H. Audit invoices for proper and agreed upon space, time, material preparation and charges.

2. Products.

Agency's engagement shall relate to the following products and services of Media User:

_____.

3. Exclusivity.

Agency shall be the Agency in the United States and worldwide for Media User with respect to the products described in Section 2 above, unless otherwise specified in this section:

_____.

4.   Compensation.

A.   Agency shall receive an amount equal to ___ percentage of the gross charges levied by media for advertising placed by Agency pursuant to this Agreement; and   after volume discount, of the charges of suppliers of services or properties, such as finished art, comprehensive layouts, type composition, photostats, engravings, printing, radio and television programs, talent, literary, dramatic and musical works, records and exhibits, purchased by Agency on Media User's authorization during the term of this Agreement; provided that: No percentage will be added to Agency charges for packing, shipping, express, postage, telephone, telex, fax, travel expenses and other out of pocket expenses of Agency personnel.

B.   For those items where Agency is not compensated on a commission basis, Media User shall pay Agency on an hourly basis for services provided hereunder. The rate will be determined by the type of services provided and the person or persons providing such services, but in no event shall the rate exceed _____ per hour. Media User may elect in advance to be charged on this hourly rate basis. If Media User fails to notify Agency of its choice, it shall be presumed that Media User elected to be charged on a percentage basis.

C.   In the event that Agency undertakes, at Media User's request subject to Media User's prior approval, special projects such as those described in Section I.F above, Agency shall prepare an estimate of total charges for any such special project in advance, including any charges for materials or services purchased from outside vendors. In the event that Media User elects to proceed with the special project based upon Agency's estimated cost, Agency shall perform the services with respect to such special project at its estimated cost, subject to modification as mutually agreed by the parties.

D. For any special project or other services provided by Agency pursuant to this Agreement upon which the parties have not agreed as to charges, Media User shall pay
Agency at its regular percentage rates, as stated in Section 4.A above.

E.   Media User shall not be obligated to reimburse Agency for any travel or other out-of-pocket expenses incurred in the performance of services pursuant to this Agreement unless expressly agreed by Media User in advance.

5. Billing.

A.   Agency shall invoice Media User for all media costs where possible in advance of Agency's payment date to allow for prepayment by the Media User so that Media User may receive the benefit of any available prepayment or similar discount. For any media purchase or service for which Agency is not entitled to a commission, Agency shall ensure that the charges to Media User are net of all agency commissions and discounts.

B.   Charges for production materials and services shall be billed by Agency upon completion of the production job or, if cash discounts are available, upon receipt of the supplier's invoice.

C. On all outside purchases other than for media, Agency shall attach to the invoice evidence of the supplier's charges.

D. All cash discounts on Agency's purchases including, but not limited to, media, art, printing and mechanical work, shall be available to Media User, provided that Media User meets Agency's requisite billing terms and there is no outstanding undisputed indebtedness of Media User to Agency at the time of the payment to the supplier.

E. Rate or billing adjustments shall be credited or charged to Media User on the next regular invoice date or as soon thereafter as otherwise practical.

F. Invoices shall be submitted in an itemized format and shall be paid by Media User within sixty (60) days of the invoice date.

6. Competitors.

During the term of this Agreement, Agency shall not accept employment from, render services to, represent or otherwise be affiliated with any person, firm, corporation or entity in connection with any product or service directly or indirectly competitive with or similar to any product or service of Media User with respect to which the Agency is providing any service pursuant to this Agreement, without the advance approval of the Media User. Media User shall not unreasonably withhold this approval.

7. Cost Estimates.

Agency shall not initiate billable work on any project pursuant to this Agreement without first estimating costs for preparation, including copy, service, layout, art, engraving, typography, processing, paste up and production. After determining the estimated cost, completion of the work shall be subject to Media User's prior approval.

8. Audit Rights.

Agency agrees that following reasonable prior notice any and all contracts, agreements, correspondence, books, accounts and other information relating to Media User's business or this Agreement shall be available for inspection by Media User and Media User's outside accountants, at Media User's expense and during the normal business hours of the Agency.

9. Ownership and Use.

A. Agency shall insure, to the fullest extent possible under law, that Media User shall own all right, title and interest in and to, including copyrights, trade secret, patent and other intellectual property rights, with respect to any copy, photograph, advertisement, music, lyrics, video, or other work or thing created by Agency or at Agency's direction for Media User pursuant to this Agreement and utilized by Media User.

B. Upon termination, Media User agrees that any advertising, merchandising, package, plan or idea prepared by Agency and submitted to Media User (whether submitted separately or in conjunction with or as a part of other material) which Media User has elected not to utilize, shall remain the property of Agency, unless Media User has paid Agency for its services in preparing such item. Media User agrees to return to Agency any copy, artwork, plates or other physical embodiment of such creative work relating to any such idea or plan which may be in Media User's possession at termination or expiration of this Agreement. Notwithstanding this, Media User has the unconditional right to pay for any of these materials or activities at the rate agreed upon in this Agreement and thereby these materials and activities would fall under the Section 9.A ownership and use rights accruing to Media User.

C. Materials and advertisements created by Agency pursuant to this Agreement may be used by Media User outside the United States without additional compensation, provided that Media User shall

be responsible for any additional expense associated with such use, such as charges for translation and amounts due talent.

10. Indemnification and Insurance.

A. Agency shall indemnify and hold Media User harmless with respect to any claims, loss, suit, liability or judgment suffered by Media User, including reasonable attorney's fees and costs, based upon or related to any item prepared by Agency or at Agency's direction, including, but not limited to, any claim of libel, slander, piracy, plagiarism, invasion of privacy, or infringement of copyright or other intellectual property interest, except where any such claim arises out of material supplied by Media User and incorporated into any materials or advertisement prepared by Agency. Agency agrees to procure and maintain in force during the term of this Agreement, at Agency's expense, an Agency liability policy or policies having a minimum limit of at least _____, naming Media User as an additional insured and loss payee under such policy or policies.

B. Media User agrees to indemnify and hold Agency harmless with respect to any claims, loss, liability, damage or judgment suffered by Agency, including reasonable attorney's fees and court costs, which results from the use by Agency of any material furnished by Media User or where material created by Agency or at the direction of Agency subject to the indemnification in subsection A. above is materially changed by Media User. Information or data obtained by Agency from Media User to substantiate claims made in advertising shall be deemed to be "material furnished by Media User to Agency."

C. In the event of any proceeding, litigation or suit against Media User by any regulatory agency or in the event of any court action or other proceeding challenging any advertising prepared by Agency, Agency shall assist in the preparation of the defense of such action or proceeding and cooperate with Media User and Media User's attorneys.

11. Term.

The term of this Agreement shall commence on _____ and shall continue in full force and effect until terminated by either party upon at least sixty (60) days prior written notice, provided that in no event (except breach) may this Agreement be terminated prior to _____. The rights, duties and obligations of the parties shall continue in full force during or following the period of the termination notice until termination, including the ordering and billing of advertising in media whose closing dates follow then such period.

12. Rights Upon Termination.

A. Upon termination of the Agreement, Agency shall transfer, assign and make available to Media User all property and materials in Agency's possession or subject to Agency's control that are the property of Media User, subject to payment in full of amounts due pursuant to this Agreement.

B. Upon termination, Agency agrees to provide reasonable cooperation in arranging for the transfer or approval of third party's interest in all contracts, agreements and other arrangements with advertising media, suppliers, talent and others not then utilized, and all rights and claims thereto and therein, following appropriate release from the obligations therein.

13. Default.

In the event of any default of any material obligation by or owed by a party pursuant to this Agreement, then the other party may provide written notice of such default and if such default is not cured within ten (10) days of the written notice, then the nondefaulting party may terminate this Agreement. In addition, the only damages collectible by Agency shall be the exact amounts due; no other damages,

for any reason whatsoever, may be assessed against Media User including, but limited to, punitive damages and unreasonable termination charges, and any other such claim. This provision shall be broadly interpreted in the favor of the Media User by any Court of competent jurisdiction.

14. Notices.

Any notice required by this Agreement or given in connection with it, shall be in writing and shall be given to the appropriate party by personal delivery or by postage prepaid, or recognized overnight delivery services such as Federal Express.

If to Media User: _____

_____

If to Agency: _____

_____

15. Headings in this Agreement.

The headings in this Agreement are for convenience only, confirm no rights or obligations in either party, and do not alter any terms of this Agreement.

16. Entirety of Agreement.

The terms and conditions set forth herein constitute the entire agreement between the parties and supersede any communications or previous agreements with respect to the subject matter of this Agreement. There are no written or oral understandings directly or indirectly related to this Agreement that are not set forth herein. No change can be made to this Agreement other than in writing and signed by both parties.

17. Governing Law.

This Agreement shall be construed and enforced according to the laws of the State of _____ and any dispute under this Agreement must be brought in this venue and in no other.

In Witness whereof, the parties have executed this Agreement as of the date first written above.

_____ _____
Agency   Media User

Ad or other Media Agency Agreement

This Agency Agreement ("Agreement") is made and effective this _____ (Date), by and between ("Agency") and _____ (Your Firm) ("Media User").

Agency is in the business of providing media agency services for a fee.

Media User desires to engage Agency to render, and Agency desires to render to Media User, certain Agency services, all as set forth.

NOW, THEREFORE, in consideration of the mutual agreements and covenants herein contained, the parties hereto agree as follows:

1. <u>Engagement</u>.

Media User engages Agency to render, and Agency agrees to render to Media User, services in connection with Media User's planning, preparing and placing of advertising and other media services for certain of Media User's products as follows:

_____

A. Analyze Media User's current and proposed products and services and presentations and potential markets.

B. Create, prepare and submit to Media User for its prior approval advertising ideas, media suggestions, and other such related programs.

C. Prepare and submit to Media User for its prior approval estimates of costs and expenses associated with proposed advertising ideas and programs prior to any such implementation or financial commitment.

D. Design and prepare, or arrange for the design and preparation of advertisements, public relations, and other such materials.

E. Perform such other services as Media User may request from time to time such as, but not limited to, direct mail ad preparations, speech writing, publicity and public relations work, market research and analysis, and other similar and related activities.

F. Order advertising space, time or other means to be used for publication of Media User's advertisements, at all times endeavoring to secure the most efficient and advantageous rates available. All such activities to be approved in advance by the Media User unless otherwise written and stipulated.

G. Proof for accuracy and completeness of insertions, displays, broadcasts, or other forms of advertisements.

H. Audit invoices for proper and agreed upon space, time, material preparation and charges.

2. <u>Products</u>.

Agency's engagement shall relate to the following products and services of Media User:

_____.

3. Exclusivity.

Agency shall be the Agency in the United States and worldwide for Media User with respect to the products described in Section 2 above, unless otherwise specified in this section:

_____.

4. Compensation.

A. Agency shall receive an amount equal to ___ percentage of the gross charges levied by media for advertising placed by Agency pursuant to this Agreement; and   after volume discount, of the charges of suppliers of services or properties, such as finished art, comprehensive layouts, type composition, photostats, engravings, printing, radio and television programs, talent, literary, dramatic and musical works, records and exhibits, purchased by Agency on Media User's authorization during the term of this Agreement; provided that: No percentage will be added to Agency charges for packing, shipping, express, postage, telephone, telex, fax, travel expenses and other out of pocket expenses of Agency personnel.

B. For those items where Agency is not compensated on a commission basis, Media User shall pay Agency on an hourly basis for services provided hereunder. The rate will be determined by the type of services provided and the person or persons providing such services, but in no event shall the rate exceed _____ per hour. Media User may elect in advance to be charged on this hourly rate basis. If Media User fails to notify Agency of its choice, it shall be presumed that Media User elected to be charged on a percentage basis.

C. In the event that Agency undertakes, at Media User's request subject to Media User's prior approval, special projects such as those described in Section I.F above, Agency shall prepare an estimate of total charges for any such special project in advance, including any charges for materials or services purchased from outside vendors. In the event that Media User elects to proceed with the special project based upon Agency's estimated cost, Agency shall perform the services with respect to such special project at its estimated cost, subject to modification as mutually agreed by the parties.

D. For any special project or other services provided by Agency pursuant to this Agreement upon which the parties have not agreed as to charges, Media User shall pay
Agency at its regular percentage rates, as stated in Section 4.A above.

E. Media User shall not be obligated to reimburse Agency for any travel or other out-of-pocket expenses incurred in the performance of services pursuant to this Agreement unless expressly agreed by Media User in advance.

5. Billing.

A. Agency shall invoice Media User for all media costs where possible in advance of Agency's payment date to allow for prepayment by the Media User so that Media User may receive the benefit of any available prepayment or similar discount. For any media purchase or service for which Agency is not entitled to a commission, Agency shall ensure that the charges to Media User are net of all agency commissions and discounts.

B. Charges for production materials and services shall be billed by Agency upon completion of the production job or, if cash discounts are available, upon receipt of the supplier's invoice.

C. On all outside purchases other than for media, Agency shall attach to the invoice evidence of the supplier's charges.

D.   All cash discounts on Agency's purchases including, but not limited to, media, art, printing and mechanical work, shall be available to Media User, provided that Media User meets Agency's requisite billing terms and there is no outstanding undisputed indebtedness of Media User to Agency at the time of the payment to the supplier.

E. Rate or billing adjustments shall be credited or charged to Media User on the next regular invoice date or as soon thereafter as otherwise practical.

F. Invoices shall be submitted in an itemized format and shall be paid by Media User within sixty (60) days of the invoice date.

6. Competitors.

During the term of this Agreement, Agency shall not accept employment from, render services to, represent or otherwise be affiliated with any person, firm, corporation or entity in connection with any product or service directly or indirectly competitive with or similar to any product or service of Media User with respect to which the Agency is providing any service pursuant to this Agreement, without the advance approval of the Media User. Media User shall not unreasonably withhold this approval.

7. Cost Estimates.

Agency shall not initiate billable work on any project pursuant to this Agreement without first estimating costs for preparation, including copy, service, layout, art, engraving, typography, processing, paste up and production. After determining the estimated cost, completion of the work shall be subject to Media User's prior approval.

8. Audit Rights.

Agency agrees that following reasonable prior notice any and all contracts, agreements, correspondence, books, accounts and other information relating to Media User's business or this Agreement shall be available for inspection by Media User and Media User's outside accountants, at Media User's expense and during the normal business hours of the Agency.

9. Ownership and Use.

A.   Agency shall insure, to the fullest extent possible under law, that Media User shall own all right, title and interest in and to, including copyrights, trade secret, patent and other intellectual property rights, with respect to any copy, photograph, advertisement, music, lyrics, video, or other work or thing created by Agency or at Agency's direction for Media User pursuant to this Agreement and utilized by Media User.

B.   Upon termination, Media User agrees that any advertising, merchandising, package, plan or idea prepared by Agency and submitted to Media User (whether submitted separately or in conjunction with or as a part of other material) which Media User has elected not to utilize, shall remain the property of Agency, unless Media User has paid Agency for its services in preparing such item. Media User agrees to return to Agency any copy, artwork, plates or other physical embodiment of such creative work relating to any such idea or plan which may be in Media User's possession at termination or expiration of this Agreement. Notwithstanding this, Media User has the unconditional right to pay for any of these materials or activities at the rate agreed upon in this Agreement and thereby these materials and activities would fall under the Section 9.A ownership and use rights accruing to Media User.

C.   Materials and advertisements created by Agency pursuant to this Agreement may be used by Media User outside the United States without additional compensation, provided that Media User shall

be responsible for any additional expense associated with such use, such as charges for translation and amounts due talent.

10. Indemnification and Insurance.

A. Agency shall indemnify and hold Media User harmless with respect to any claims, loss, suit, liability or judgment suffered by Media User, including reasonable attorney's fees and costs, based upon or related to any item prepared by Agency or at Agency's direction, including, but not limited to, any claim of libel, slander, piracy, plagiarism, invasion of privacy, or infringement of copyright or other intellectual property interest, except where any such claim arises out of material supplied by Media User and incorporated into any materials or advertisement prepared by Agency. Agency agrees to procure and maintain in force during the term of this Agreement, at Agency's expense, an Agency liability policy or policies having a minimum limit of at least _____, naming Media User as an additional insured and loss payee under such policy or policies.

B. Media User agrees to indemnify and hold Agency harmless with respect to any claims, loss, liability, damage or judgment suffered by Agency, including reasonable attorney's fees and court costs, which results from the use by Agency of any material furnished by Media User or where material created by Agency or at the direction of Agency subject to the indemnification in subsection A. above is materially changed by Media User. Information or data obtained by Agency from Media User to substantiate claims made in advertising shall be deemed to be "material furnished by Media User to Agency."

C. In the event of any proceeding, litigation or suit against Media User by any regulatory agency or in the event of any court action or other proceeding challenging any advertising prepared by Agency, Agency shall assist in the preparation of the defense of such action or proceeding and cooperate with Media User and Media User's attorneys.

11. Term.

The term of this Agreement shall commence on _____ and shall continue in full force and effect until terminated by either party upon at least sixty (60) days prior written notice, provided that in no event (except breach) may this Agreement be terminated prior to _____. The rights, duties and obligations of the parties shall continue in full force during or following the period of the termination notice until termination, including the ordering and billing of advertising in media whose closing dates follow then such period.

12. Rights Upon Termination.

A. Upon termination of the Agreement, Agency shall transfer, assign and make available to Media User all property and materials in Agency's possession or subject to Agency's control that are the property of Media User, subject to payment in full of amounts due pursuant to this Agreement.

B. Upon termination, Agency agrees to provide reasonable cooperation in arranging for the transfer or approval of third party's interest in all contracts, agreements and other arrangements with advertising media, suppliers, talent and others not then utilized, and all rights and claims thereto and therein, following appropriate release from the obligations therein.

13. Default.

In the event of any default of any material obligation by or owed by a party pursuant to this Agreement, then the other party may provide written notice of such default and if such default is not cured within ten (10) days of the written notice, then the nondefaulting party may terminate this Agreement. In addition, the only damages collectible by Agency shall be the exact amounts due; no other damages,

for any reason whatsoever, may be assessed against Media User including, but limited to, punitive damages and unreasonable termination charges, and any other such claim. This provision shall be broadly interpreted in the favor of the Media User by any Court of competent jurisdiction.

14. Notices.

Any notice required by this Agreement or given in connection with it, shall be in writing and shall be given to the appropriate party by personal delivery or by postage prepaid, or recognized overnight delivery services such as Federal Express.

If to Media User: _____

_____

If to Agency: _____

_____

15. Headings in this Agreement.

The headings in this Agreement are for convenience only, confirm no rights or obligations in either party, and do not alter any terms of this Agreement.

16. Entirety of Agreement.

The terms and conditions set forth herein constitute the entire agreement between the parties and supersede any communications or previous agreements with respect to the subject matter of this Agreement. There are no written or oral understandings directly or indirectly related to this Agreement that are not set forth herein. No change can be made to this Agreement other than in writing and signed by both parties.

17. Governing Law.

This Agreement shall be construed and enforced according to the laws of the State of _____ and any dispute under this Agreement must be brought in this venue and in no other.

In Witness whereof, the parties have executed this Agreement as of the date first written above.

_____ _____
Agency   Media User

Ad or other Media Agency Agreement

This Agency Agreement ("Agreement") is made and effective this _____ (Date), by and between ("Agency") and _____ (Your Firm) ("Media User").

Agency is in the business of providing media agency services for a fee.

Media User desires to engage Agency to render, and Agency desires to render to Media User, certain Agency services, all as set forth.

NOW, THEREFORE, in consideration of the mutual agreements and covenants herein contained, the parties hereto agree as follows:

1. Engagement.

Media User engages Agency to render, and Agency agrees to render to Media User, services in connection with Media User's planning, preparing and placing of advertising and other media services for certain of Media User's products as follows:

_____

A. Analyze Media User's current and proposed products and services and presentations and potential markets.

B. Create, prepare and submit to Media User for its prior approval advertising ideas, media suggestions, and other such related programs.

C. Prepare and submit to Media User for its prior approval estimates of costs and expenses associated with proposed advertising ideas and programs prior to any such implementation or financial commitment.

D. Design and prepare, or arrange for the design and preparation of advertisements, public relations, and other such materials.

E. Perform such other services as Media User may request from time to time such as, but not limited to, direct mail ad preparations, speech writing, publicity and public relations work, market research and analysis, and other similar and related activities.

F. Order advertising space, time or other means to be used for publication of Media User's advertisements, at all times endeavoring to secure the most efficient and advantageous rates available. All such activities to be approved in advance by the Media User unless otherwise written and stipulated.

G. Proof for accuracy and completeness of insertions, displays, broadcasts, or other forms of advertisements.

H. Audit invoices for proper and agreed upon space, time, material preparation and charges.

2. Products.

Agency's engagement shall relate to the following products and services of Media User:

_____.

3. <u>Exclusivity</u>.

Agency shall be the Agency in the United States and worldwide for Media User with respect to the products described in Section 2 above, unless otherwise specified in this section:

_____.

4.   <u>Compensation</u>.

A.   Agency shall receive an amount equal to ___ percentage of the gross charges levied by media for advertising placed by Agency pursuant to this Agreement; and _____ after volume discount, of the charges of suppliers of services or properties, such as finished art, comprehensive layouts, type composition, photostats, engravings, printing, radio and television programs, talent, literary, dramatic and musical works, records and exhibits, purchased by Agency on Media User's authorization during the term of this Agreement; provided that: No percentage will be added to Agency charges for packing, shipping, express, postage, telephone, telex, fax, travel expenses and other out of pocket expenses of Agency personnel.

B.   For those items where Agency is not compensated on a commission basis, Media User shall pay Agency on an hourly basis for services provided hereunder. The rate will be determined by the type of services provided and the person or persons providing such services, but in no event shall the rate exceed _____ per hour. Media User may elect in advance to be charged on this hourly rate basis. If Media User fails to notify Agency of its choice, it shall be presumed that Media User elected to be charged on a percentage basis.

C.   In the event that Agency undertakes, at Media User's request subject to Media User's prior approval, special projects such as those described in Section I.F above, Agency shall prepare an estimate of total charges for any such special project in advance, including any charges for materials or services purchased from outside vendors. In the event that Media User elects to proceed with the special project based upon Agency's estimated cost, Agency shall perform the services with respect to such special project at its estimated cost, subject to modification as mutually agreed by the parties.

D. For any special project or other services provided by Agency pursuant to this Agreement upon which the parties have not agreed as to charges, Media User shall pay
Agency at its regular percentage rates, as stated in Section 4.A above.

E.   Media User shall not be obligated to reimburse Agency for any travel or other out-of-pocket expenses incurred in the performance of services pursuant to this Agreement unless expressly agreed by Media User in advance.

5. <u>Billing</u>.

A.   Agency shall invoice Media User for all media costs where possible in advance of Agency's payment date to allow for prepayment by the Media User so that Media User may receive the benefit of any available prepayment or similar discount. For any media purchase or service for which Agency is not entitled to a commission, Agency shall ensure that the charges to Media User are net of all agency commissions and discounts.

B.   Charges for production materials and services shall be billed by Agency upon completion of the production job or, if cash discounts are available, upon receipt of the supplier's invoice.

C. On all outside purchases other than for media, Agency shall attach to the invoice evidence of the supplier's charges.

D. All cash discounts on Agency's purchases including, but not limited to, media, art, printing and mechanical work, shall be available to Media User, provided that Media User meets Agency's requisite billing terms and there is no outstanding undisputed indebtedness of Media User to Agency at the time of the payment to the supplier.

E. Rate or billing adjustments shall be credited or charged to Media User on the next regular invoice date or as soon thereafter as otherwise practical.

F. Invoices shall be submitted in an itemized format and shall be paid by Media User within sixty (60) days of the invoice date.

6. Competitors.

During the term of this Agreement, Agency shall not accept employment from, render services to, represent or otherwise be affiliated with any person, firm, corporation or entity in connection with any product or service directly or indirectly competitive with or similar to any product or service of Media User with respect to which the Agency is providing any service pursuant to this Agreement, without the advance approval of the Media User. Media User shall not unreasonably withhold this approval.

7. Cost Estimates.

Agency shall not initiate billable work on any project pursuant to this Agreement without first estimating costs for preparation, including copy, service, layout, art, engraving, typography, processing, paste up and production. After determining the estimated cost, completion of the work shall be subject to Media User's prior approval.

8. Audit Rights.

Agency agrees that following reasonable prior notice any and all contracts, agreements, correspondence, books, accounts and other information relating to Media User's business or this Agreement shall be available for inspection by Media User and Media User's outside accountants, at Media User's expense and during the normal business hours of the Agency.

9. Ownership and Use.

A. Agency shall insure, to the fullest extent possible under law, that Media User shall own all right, title and interest in and to, including copyrights, trade secret, patent and other intellectual property rights, with respect to any copy, photograph, advertisement, music, lyrics, video, or other work or thing created by Agency or at Agency's direction for Media User pursuant to this Agreement and utilized by Media User.

B. Upon termination, Media User agrees that any advertising, merchandising, package, plan or idea prepared by Agency and submitted to Media User (whether submitted separately or in conjunction with or as a part of other material) which Media User has elected not to utilize, shall remain the property of Agency, unless Media User has paid Agency for its services in preparing such item. Media User agrees to return to Agency any copy, artwork, plates or other physical embodiment of such creative work relating to any such idea or plan which may be in Media User's possession at termination or expiration of this Agreement. Notwithstanding this, Media User has the unconditional right to pay for any of these materials or activities at the rate agreed upon in this Agreement and thereby these materials and activities would fall under the Section 9.A ownership and use rights accruing to Media User.

C. Materials and advertisements created by Agency pursuant to this Agreement may be used by Media User outside the United States without additional compensation, provided that Media User shall

be responsible for any additional expense associated with such use, such as charges for translation and amounts due talent.

10. Indemnification and Insurance.

A. Agency shall indemnify and hold Media User harmless with respect to any claims, loss, suit, liability or judgment suffered by Media User, including reasonable attorney's fees and costs, based upon or related to any item prepared by Agency or at Agency's direction, including, but not limited to, any claim of libel, slander, piracy, plagiarism, invasion of privacy, or infringement of copyright or other intellectual property interest, except where any such claim arises out of material supplied by Media User and incorporated into any materials or advertisement prepared by Agency. Agency agrees to procure and maintain in force during the term of this Agreement, at Agency's expense, an Agency liability policy or policies having a minimum limit of at least _____, naming Media User as an additional insured and loss payee under such policy or policies.

B. Media User agrees to indemnify and hold Agency harmless with respect to any claims, loss, liability, damage or judgment suffered by Agency, including reasonable attorney's fees and court costs, which results from the use by Agency of any material furnished by Media User or where material created by Agency or at the direction of Agency subject to the indemnification in subsection A. above is materially changed by Media User. Information or data obtained by Agency from Media User to substantiate claims made in advertising shall be deemed to be "material furnished by Media User to Agency."

C. In the event of any proceeding, litigation or suit against Media User by any regulatory agency or in the event of any court action or other proceeding challenging any advertising prepared by Agency, Agency shall assist in the preparation of the defense of such action or proceeding and cooperate with Media User and Media User's attorneys.

11. Term.

The term of this Agreement shall commence on _____ and shall continue in full force and effect until terminated by either party upon at least sixty (60) days prior written notice, provided that in no event (except breach) may this Agreement be terminated prior to _____. The rights, duties and obligations of the parties shall continue in full force during or following the period of the termination notice until termination, including the ordering and billing of advertising in media whose closing dates follow then such period.

12. Rights Upon Termination.

A. Upon termination of the Agreement, Agency shall transfer, assign and make available to Media User all property and materials in Agency's possession or subject to Agency's control that are the property of Media User, subject to payment in full of amounts due pursuant to this Agreement.

B. Upon termination, Agency agrees to provide reasonable cooperation in arranging for the transfer or approval of third party's interest in all contracts, agreements and other arrangements with advertising media, suppliers, talent and others not then utilized, and all rights and claims thereto and therein, following appropriate release from the obligations therein.

13. Default.

In the event of any default of any material obligation by or owed by a party pursuant to this Agreement, then the other party may provide written notice of such default and if such default is not cured within ten (10) days of the written notice, then the nondefaulting party may terminate this Agreement. In addition, the only damages collectible by Agency shall be the exact amounts due; no other damages,

for any reason whatsoever, may be assessed against Media User including, but limited to, punitive damages and unreasonable termination charges, and any other such claim. This provision shall be broadly interpreted in the favor of the Media User by any Court of competent jurisdiction.

14. Notices.

Any notice required by this Agreement or given in connection with it, shall be in writing and shall be given to the appropriate party by personal delivery or by postage prepaid, or recognized overnight delivery services such as Federal Express.

If to Media User: _____

_____

If to Agency: _____

_____

15. Headings in this Agreement.

The headings in this Agreement are for convenience only, confirm no rights or obligations in either party, and do not alter any terms of this Agreement.

16. Entirety of Agreement.

The terms and conditions set forth herein constitute the entire agreement between the parties and supersede any communications or previous agreements with respect to the subject matter of this Agreement. There are no written or oral understandings directly or indirectly related to this Agreement that are not set forth herein. No change can be made to this Agreement other than in writing and signed by both parties.

17. Governing Law.

This Agreement shall be construed and enforced according to the laws of the State of _____ and any dispute under this Agreement must be brought in this venue and in no other.

In Witness whereof, the parties have executed this Agreement as of the date first written above.

_____   _____
Agency   Media User

Ad or other Media Agreement

This Agency Agreement ("Agreement") is made and effective this _____ (Date), by and between ("Agency") and _____ (Your Firm) ("Media User").

Agency is in the business of providing media agency services for a fee.

Media User desires to engage Agency to render, and Agency desires to render to Media User, certain Agency services, all as set forth.

NOW, THEREFORE, in consideration of the mutual agreements and covenants herein contained, the parties hereto agree as follows:

1. <u>Engagement</u>.

Media User engages Agency to render, and Agency agrees to render to Media User, services in connection with Media User's planning, preparing and placing of advertising and other media services for certain of Media User's products as follows:

_____

A. Analyze Media User's current and proposed products and services and presentations and potential markets.

B. Create, prepare and submit to Media User for its prior approval advertising ideas, media suggestions, and other such related programs.

C. Prepare and submit to Media User for its prior approval estimates of costs and expenses associated with proposed advertising ideas and programs prior to any such implementation or financial commitment.

D. Design and prepare, or arrange for the design and preparation of advertisements, public relations, and other such materials.

E. Perform such other services as Media User may request from time to time such as, but not limited to, direct mail ad preparations, speech writing, publicity and public relations work, market research and analysis, and other similar and related activities.

F. Order advertising space, time or other means to be used for publication of Media User's advertisements, at all times endeavoring to secure the most efficient and advantageous rates available. All such activities to be approved in advance by the Media User unless otherwise written and stipulated.

G. Proof for accuracy and completeness of insertions, displays, broadcasts, or other forms of advertisements.

H. Audit invoices for proper and agreed upon space, time, material preparation and charges.

2. <u>Products</u>.

Agency's engagement shall relate to the following products and services of Media User:

_____.

3. Exclusivity.

Agency shall be the Agency in the United States and worldwide for Media User with respect to the products described in Section 2 above, unless otherwise specified in this section:

_____.

4. Compensation.

A. Agency shall receive an amount equal to ___ percentage of the gross charges levied by media for advertising placed by Agency pursuant to this Agreement; and   after volume discount, of the charges of suppliers of services or properties, such as finished art, comprehensive layouts, type composition, photostats, engravings, printing, radio and television programs, talent, literary, dramatic and musical works, records and exhibits, purchased by Agency on Media User's authorization during the term of this Agreement; provided that: No percentage will be added to Agency charges for packing, shipping, express, postage, telephone, telex, fax, travel expenses and other out of pocket expenses of Agency personnel.

B. For those items where Agency is not compensated on a commission basis, Media User shall pay Agency on an hourly basis for services provided hereunder. The rate will be determined by the type of services provided and the person or persons providing such services, but in no event shall the rate exceed _____ per hour. Media User may elect in advance to be charged on this hourly rate basis. If Media User fails to notify Agency of its choice, it shall be presumed that Media User elected to be charged on a percentage basis.

C. In the event that Agency undertakes, at Media User's request subject to Media User's prior approval, special projects such as those described in Section I.F above, Agency shall prepare an estimate of total charges for any such special project in advance, including any charges for materials or services purchased from outside vendors. In the event that Media User elects to proceed with the special project based upon Agency's estimated cost, Agency shall perform the services with respect to such special project at its estimated cost, subject to modification as mutually agreed by the parties.

D. For any special project or other services provided by Agency pursuant to this Agreement upon which the parties have not agreed as to charges, Media User shall pay
Agency at its regular percentage rates, as stated in Section 4.A above.

E. Media User shall not be obligated to reimburse Agency for any travel or other out-of-pocket expenses incurred in the performance of services pursuant to this Agreement unless expressly agreed by Media User in advance.

5. Billing.

A. Agency shall invoice Media User for all media costs where possible in advance of Agency's payment date to allow for prepayment by the Media User so that Media User may receive the benefit of any available prepayment or similar discount. For any media purchase or service for which Agency is not entitled to a commission, Agency shall ensure that the charges to Media User are net of all agency commissions and discounts.

B. Charges for production materials and services shall be billed by Agency upon completion of the production job or, if cash discounts are available, upon receipt of the supplier's invoice.

C. On all outside purchases other than for media, Agency shall attach to the invoice evidence of the supplier's charges.

D. All cash discounts on Agency's purchases including, but not limited to, media, art, printing and mechanical work, shall be available to Media User, provided that Media User meets Agency's requisite billing terms and there is no outstanding undisputed indebtedness of Media User to Agency at the time of the payment to the supplier.

E. Rate or billing adjustments shall be credited or charged to Media User on the next regular invoice date or as soon thereafter as otherwise practical.

F. Invoices shall be submitted in an itemized format and shall be paid by Media User within sixty (60) days of the invoice date.

6. Competitors.

During the term of this Agreement, Agency shall not accept employment from, render services to, represent or otherwise be affiliated with any person, firm, corporation or entity in connection with any product or service directly or indirectly competitive with or similar to any product or service of Media User with respect to which the Agency is providing any service pursuant to this Agreement, without the advance approval of the Media User. Media User shall not unreasonably withhold this approval.

7. Cost Estimates.

Agency shall not initiate billable work on any project pursuant to this Agreement without first estimating costs for preparation, including copy, service, layout, art, engraving, typography, processing, paste up and production. After determining the estimated cost, completion of the work shall be subject to Media User's prior approval.

8. Audit Rights.

Agency agrees that following reasonable prior notice any and all contracts, agreements, correspondence, books, accounts and other information relating to Media User's business or this Agreement shall be available for inspection by Media User and Media User's outside accountants, at Media User's expense and during the normal business hours of the Agency.

9. Ownership and Use.

A. Agency shall insure, to the fullest extent possible under law, that Media User shall own all right, title and interest in and to, including copyrights, trade secret, patent and other intellectual property rights, with respect to any copy, photograph, advertisement, music, lyrics, video, or other work or thing created by Agency or at Agency's direction for Media User pursuant to this Agreement and utilized by Media User.

B. Upon termination, Media User agrees that any advertising, merchandising, package, plan or idea prepared by Agency and submitted to Media User (whether submitted separately or in conjunction with or as a part of other material) which Media User has elected not to utilize, shall remain the property of Agency, unless Media User has paid Agency for its services in preparing such item. Media User agrees to return to Agency any copy, artwork, plates or other physical embodiment of such creative work relating to any such idea or plan which may be in Media User's possession at termination or expiration of this Agreement. Notwithstanding this, Media User has the unconditional right to pay for any of these materials or activities at the rate agreed upon in this Agreement and thereby these materials and activities would fall under the Section 9.A ownership and use rights accruing to Media User.

C. Materials and advertisements created by Agency pursuant to this Agreement may be used by Media User outside the United States without additional compensation, provided that Media User shall

be responsible for any additional expense associated with such use, such as charges for translation and amounts due talent.

10. <u>Indemnification and Insurance</u>.

A. Agency shall indemnify and hold Media User harmless with respect to any claims, loss, suit, liability or judgment suffered by Media User, including reasonable attorney's fees and costs, based upon or related to any item prepared by Agency or at Agency's direction, including, but not limited to, any claim of libel, slander, piracy, plagiarism, invasion of privacy, or infringement of copyright or other intellectual property interest, except where any such claim arises out of material supplied by Media User and incorporated into any materials or advertisement prepared by Agency. Agency agrees to procure and maintain in force during the term of this Agreement, at Agency's expense, an Agency liability policy or policies having a minimum limit of at least _____, naming Media User as an additional insured and loss payee under such policy or policies.

B. Media User agrees to indemnify and hold Agency harmless with respect to any claims, loss, liability, damage or judgment suffered by Agency, including reasonable attorney's fees and court costs, which results from the use by Agency of any material furnished by Media User or where material created by Agency or at the direction of Agency subject to the indemnification in subsection A. above is materially changed by Media User. Information or data obtained by Agency from Media User to substantiate claims made in advertising shall be deemed to be "material furnished by Media User to Agency."

C. In the event of any proceeding, litigation or suit against Media User by any regulatory agency or in the event of any court action or other proceeding challenging any advertising prepared by Agency, Agency shall assist in the preparation of the defense of such action or proceeding and cooperate with Media User and Media User's attorneys.

11. <u>Term</u>.

The term of this Agreement shall commence on _____ and shall continue in full force and effect until terminated by either party upon at least sixty (60) days prior written notice, provided that in no event (except breach) may this Agreement be terminated prior to _____. The rights, duties and obligations of the parties shall continue in full force during or following the period of the termination notice until termination, including the ordering and billing of advertising in media whose closing dates follow then such period.

12. <u>Rights Upon Termination</u>.

A. Upon termination of the Agreement, Agency shall transfer, assign and make available to Media User all property and materials in Agency's possession or subject to Agency's control that are the property of Media User, subject to payment in full of amounts due pursuant to this Agreement.

B. Upon termination, Agency agrees to provide reasonable cooperation in arranging for the transfer or approval of third party's interest in all contracts, agreements and other arrangements with advertising media, suppliers, talent and others not then utilized, and all rights and claims thereto and therein, following appropriate release from the obligations therein.

13. <u>Default</u>.

In the event of any default of any material obligation by or owed by a party pursuant to this Agreement, then the other party may provide written notice of such default and if such default is not cured within ten (10) days of the written notice, then the nondefaulting party may terminate this Agreement. In addition, the only damages collectible by Agency shall be the exact amounts due; no other damages,

for any reason whatsoever, may be assessed against Media User including, but limited to, punitive damages and unreasonable termination charges, and any other such claim. This provision shall be broadly interpreted in the favor of the Media User by any Court of competent jurisdiction.

14. Notices.

Any notice required by this Agreement or given in connection with it, shall be in writing and shall be given to the appropriate party by personal delivery or by postage prepaid, or recognized overnight delivery services such as Federal Express.

If to Media User:　　　　_____

　　　　　　　　　　　　_____

If to Agency:　　　　　　 _____

　　　　　　　　　　　　_____

15. Headings in this Agreement.

The headings in this Agreement are for convenience only, confirm no rights or obligations in either party, and do not alter any terms of this Agreement.

16. Entirety of Agreement.

The terms and conditions set forth herein constitute the entire agreement between the parties and supersede any communications or previous agreements with respect to the subject matter of this Agreement. There are no written or oral understandings directly or indirectly related to this Agreement that are not set forth herein. No change can be made to this Agreement other than in writing and signed by both parties.

17. Governing Law.

This Agreement shall be construed and enforced according to the laws of the State of _____ and any dispute under this Agreement must be brought in this venue and in no other.

In Witness whereof, the parties have executed this Agreement as of the date first written above.

_____   _____
Agency   Media User

Ad or other Media Agency Agreement

This Agency Agreement ("Agreement") is made and effective this _____ (Date), by and between ("Agency") and _____ (Your Firm) ("Media User").

Agency is in the business of providing media agency services for a fee.

Media User desires to engage Agency to render, and Agency desires to render to Media User, certain Agency services, all as set forth.

NOW, THEREFORE, in consideration of the mutual agreements and covenants herein contained, the parties hereto agree as follows:

1. Engagement.

Media User engages Agency to render, and Agency agrees to render to Media User, services in connection with Media User's planning, preparing and placing of advertising and other media services for certain of Media User's products as follows:

_____

A. Analyze Media User's current and proposed products and services and presentations and potential markets.

B. Create, prepare and submit to Media User for its prior approval advertising ideas, media suggestions, and other such related programs.

C. Prepare and submit to Media User for its prior approval estimates of costs and expenses associated with proposed advertising ideas and programs prior to any such implementation or financial commitment.

D. Design and prepare, or arrange for the design and preparation of advertisements, public relations, and other such materials.

E. Perform such other services as Media User may request from time to time such as, but not limited to, direct mail ad preparations, speech writing, publicity and public relations work, market research and analysis, and other similar and related activities.

F. Order advertising space, time or other means to be used for publication of Media User's advertisements, at all times endeavoring to secure the most efficient and advantageous rates available. All such activities to be approved in advance by the Media User unless otherwise written and stipulated.

G. Proof for accuracy and completeness of insertions, displays, broadcasts, or other forms of advertisements.

H. Audit invoices for proper and agreed upon space, time, material preparation and charges.

2. Products.

Agency's engagement shall relate to the following products and services of Media User:

_____.

3. Exclusivity.

Agency shall be the Agency in the United States and worldwide for Media User with respect to the products described in Section 2 above, unless otherwise specified in this section:

_____.

4.   Compensation.

A.   Agency shall receive an amount equal to ___ percentage of the gross charges levied by media for advertising placed by Agency pursuant to this Agreement; and   after volume discount, of the charges of suppliers of services or properties, such as finished art, comprehensive layouts, type composition, photostats, engravings, printing, radio and television programs, talent, literary, dramatic and musical works, records and exhibits, purchased by Agency on Media User's authorization during the term of this Agreement; provided that: No percentage will be added to Agency charges for packing, shipping, express, postage, telephone, telex, fax, travel expenses and other out of pocket expenses of Agency personnel.

B.   For those items where Agency is not compensated on a commission basis, Media User shall pay Agency on an hourly basis for services provided hereunder. The rate will be determined by the type of services provided and the person or persons providing such services, but in no event shall the rate exceed _____ per hour. Media User may elect in advance to be charged on this hourly rate basis. If Media User fails to notify Agency of its choice, it shall be presumed that Media User elected to be charged on a percentage basis.

C.   In the event that Agency undertakes, at Media User's request subject to Media User's prior approval, special projects such as those described in Section I.F above, Agency shall prepare an estimate of total charges for any such special project in advance, including any charges for materials or services purchased from outside vendors. In the event that Media User elects to proceed with the special project based upon Agency's estimated cost, Agency shall perform the services with respect to such special project at its estimated cost, subject to modification as mutually agreed by the parties.

D. For any special project or other services provided by Agency pursuant to this Agreement upon which the parties have not agreed as to charges, Media User shall pay
Agency at its regular percentage rates, as stated in Section 4.A above.

E.   Media User shall not be obligated to reimburse Agency for any travel or other out-of-pocket expenses incurred in the performance of services pursuant to this Agreement unless expressly agreed by Media User in advance.

5. Billing.

A.   Agency shall invoice Media User for all media costs where possible in advance of Agency's payment date to allow for prepayment by the Media User so that Media User may receive the benefit of any available prepayment or similar discount. For any media purchase or service for which Agency is not entitled to a commission, Agency shall ensure that the charges to Media User are net of all agency commissions and discounts.

B.   Charges for production materials and services shall be billed by Agency upon completion of the production job or, if cash discounts are available, upon receipt of the supplier's invoice.

C. On all outside purchases other than for media, Agency shall attach to the invoice evidence of the supplier's charges.

D. All cash discounts on Agency's purchases including, but not limited to, media, art, printing and mechanical work, shall be available to Media User, provided that Media User meets Agency's requisite billing terms and there is no outstanding undisputed indebtedness of Media User to Agency at the time of the payment to the supplier.

E. Rate or billing adjustments shall be credited or charged to Media User on the next regular invoice date or as soon thereafter as otherwise practical.

F. Invoices shall be submitted in an itemized format and shall be paid by Media User within sixty (60) days of the invoice date.

6. Competitors.

During the term of this Agreement, Agency shall not accept employment from, render services to, represent or otherwise be affiliated with any person, firm, corporation or entity in connection with any product or service directly or indirectly competitive with or similar to any product or service of Media User with respect to which the Agency is providing any service pursuant to this Agreement, without the advance approval of the Media User. Media User shall not unreasonably withhold this approval.

7. Cost Estimates.

Agency shall not initiate billable work on any project pursuant to this Agreement without first estimating costs for preparation, including copy, service, layout, art, engraving, typography, processing, paste up and production. After determining the estimated cost, completion of the work shall be subject to Media User's prior approval.

8. Audit Rights.

Agency agrees that following reasonable prior notice any and all contracts, agreements, correspondence, books, accounts and other information relating to Media User's business or this Agreement shall be available for inspection by Media User and Media User's outside accountants, at Media User's expense and during the normal business hours of the Agency.

9. Ownership and Use.

A. Agency shall insure, to the fullest extent possible under law, that Media User shall own all right, title and interest in and to, including copyrights, trade secret, patent and other intellectual property rights, with respect to any copy, photograph, advertisement, music, lyrics, video, or other work or thing created by Agency or at Agency's direction for Media User pursuant to this Agreement and utilized by Media User.

B. Upon termination, Media User agrees that any advertising, merchandising, package, plan or idea prepared by Agency and submitted to Media User (whether submitted separately or in conjunction with or as a part of other material) which Media User has elected not to utilize, shall remain the property of Agency, unless Media User has paid Agency for its services in preparing such item. Media User agrees to return to Agency any copy, artwork, plates or other physical embodiment of such creative work relating to any such idea or plan which may be in Media User's possession at termination or expiration of this Agreement. Notwithstanding this, Media User has the unconditional right to pay for any of these materials or activities at the rate agreed upon in this Agreement and thereby these materials and activities would fall under the Section 9.A ownership and use rights accruing to Media User.

C. Materials and advertisements created by Agency pursuant to this Agreement may be used by Media User outside the United States without additional compensation, provided that Media User shall

be responsible for any additional expense associated with such use, such as charges for translation and amounts due talent.

10. Indemnification and Insurance.

A.   Agency shall indemnify and hold Media User harmless with respect to any claims, loss, suit, liability or judgment suffered by Media User, including reasonable attorney's fees and costs, based upon or related to any item prepared by Agency or at Agency's direction, including, but not limited to, any claim of libel, slander, piracy, plagiarism, invasion of privacy, or infringement of copyright or other intellectual property interest, except where any such claim arises out of material supplied by Media User and incorporated into any materials or advertisement prepared by Agency. Agency agrees to procure and maintain in force during the term of this Agreement, at Agency's expense, an Agency liability policy or policies having a minimum limit of at least _____, naming Media User as an additional insured and loss payee under such policy or policies.

B.   Media User agrees to indemnify and hold Agency harmless with respect to any claims, loss, liability, damage or judgment suffered by Agency, including reasonable attorney's fees and court costs, which results from the use by Agency of any material furnished by Media User or where material created by Agency or at the direction of Agency subject to the indemnification in subsection A. above is materially changed by Media User. Information or data obtained by Agency from Media User to substantiate claims made in advertising shall be deemed to be "material furnished by Media User to Agency."

C.   In the event of any proceeding, litigation or suit against Media User by any regulatory agency or in the event of any court action or other proceeding challenging any advertising prepared by Agency, Agency shall assist in the preparation of the defense of such action or proceeding and cooperate with Media User and Media User's attorneys.

11. Term.

The term of this Agreement shall commence on _____ and shall continue in full force and effect until terminated by either party upon at least sixty (60) days prior written notice, provided that in no event (except breach) may this Agreement be terminated prior to _____. The rights, duties and obligations of the parties shall continue in full force during or following the period of the termination notice until termination, including the ordering and billing of advertising in media whose closing dates follow then such period.

12. Rights Upon Termination.

A.   Upon termination of the Agreement, Agency shall transfer, assign and make available to Media User all property and materials in Agency's possession or subject to Agency's control that are the property of Media User, subject to payment in full of amounts due pursuant to this Agreement.

B.   Upon termination, Agency agrees to provide reasonable cooperation in arranging for the transfer or approval of third party's interest in all contracts, agreements and other arrangements with advertising media, suppliers, talent and others not then utilized, and all rights and claims thereto and therein, following appropriate release from the obligations therein.

13. Default.

In the event of any default of any material obligation by or owed by a party pursuant to this Agreement, then the other party may provide written notice of such default and if such default is not cured within ten (10) days of the written notice, then the nondefaulting party may terminate this Agreement. In addition, the only damages collectible by Agency shall be the exact amounts due; no other damages,

for any reason whatsoever, may be assessed against Media User including, but limited to, punitive damages and unreasonable termination charges, and any other such claim. This provision shall be broadly interpreted in the favor of the Media User by any Court of competent jurisdiction.

14. <u>Notices</u>.

Any notice required by this Agreement or given in connection with it, shall be in writing and shall be given to the appropriate party by personal delivery or by postage prepaid, or recognized overnight delivery services such as Federal Express.

If to Media User: _____

_____

If to Agency: _____

_____

15. <u>Headings in this Agreement</u>.

The headings in this Agreement are for convenience only, confirm no rights or obligations in either party, and do not alter any terms of this Agreement.

16. <u>Entirety of Agreement</u>.

The terms and conditions set forth herein constitute the entire agreement between the parties and supersede any communications or previous agreements with respect to the subject matter of this Agreement. There are no written or oral understandings directly or indirectly related to this Agreement that are not set forth herein. No change can be made to this Agreement other than in writing and signed by both parties.

17. <u>Governing Law</u>.

This Agreement shall be construed and enforced according to the laws of the State of _____ and any dispute under this Agreement must be brought in this venue and in no other.

In Witness whereof, the parties have executed this Agreement as of the date first written above.

_____ _____
Agency   Media User

Ad or other Media Agency Agreement

This Agency Agreement ("Agreement") is made and effective this _____ (Date), by and between ("Agency") and _____ (Your Firm) ("Media User").

Agency is in the business of providing media agency services for a fee.

Media User desires to engage Agency to render, and Agency desires to render to Media User, certain Agency services, all as set forth.

NOW, THEREFORE, in consideration of the mutual agreements and covenants herein contained, the parties hereto agree as follows:

1. <u>Engagement</u>.

Media User engages Agency to render, and Agency agrees to render to Media User, services in connection with Media User's planning, preparing and placing of advertising and other media services for certain of Media User's products as follows:

_____

A. Analyze Media User's current and proposed products and services and presentations and potential markets.

B. Create, prepare and submit to Media User for its prior approval advertising ideas, media suggestions, and other such related programs.

C. Prepare and submit to Media User for its prior approval estimates of costs and expenses associated with proposed advertising ideas and programs prior to any such implementation or financial commitment.

D. Design and prepare, or arrange for the design and preparation of advertisements, public relations, and other such materials.

E. Perform such other services as Media User may request from time to time such as, but not limited to, direct mail ad preparations, speech writing, publicity and public relations work, market research and analysis, and other similar and related activities.

F. Order advertising space, time or other means to be used for publication of Media User's advertisements, at all times endeavoring to secure the most efficient and advantageous rates available. All such activities to be approved in advance by the Media User unless otherwise written and stipulated.

G. Proof for accuracy and completeness of insertions, displays, broadcasts, or other forms of advertisements.

H. Audit invoices for proper and agreed upon space, time, material preparation and charges.

2. <u>Products</u>.

Agency's engagement shall relate to the following products and services of Media User:

_____.

3. Exclusivity.

Agency shall be the Agency in the United States and worldwide for Media User with respect to the products described in Section 2 above, unless otherwise specified in this section:

_____.

4.   Compensation.

A.   Agency shall receive an amount equal to ___ percentage of the gross charges levied by media for advertising placed by Agency pursuant to this Agreement; and after volume discount, of the charges of suppliers of services or properties, such as finished art, comprehensive layouts, type composition, photostats, engravings, printing, radio and television programs, talent, literary, dramatic and musical works, records and exhibits, purchased by Agency on Media User's authorization during the term of this Agreement; provided that: No percentage will be added to Agency charges for packing, shipping, express, postage, telephone, telex, fax, travel expenses and other out of pocket expenses of Agency personnel.

B.   For those items where Agency is not compensated on a commission basis, Media User shall pay Agency on an hourly basis for services provided hereunder. The rate will be determined by the type of services provided and the person or persons providing such services, but in no event shall the rate exceed _____ per hour. Media User may elect in advance to be charged on this hourly rate basis. If Media User fails to notify Agency of its choice, it shall be presumed that Media User elected to be charged on a percentage basis.

C.   In the event that Agency undertakes, at Media User's request subject to Media User's prior approval, special projects such as those described in Section I.F above, Agency shall prepare an estimate of total charges for any such special project in advance, including any charges for materials or services purchased from outside vendors. In the event that Media User elects to proceed with the special project based upon Agency's estimated cost, Agency shall perform the services with respect to such special project at its estimated cost, subject to modification as mutually agreed by the parties.

D. For any special project or other services provided by Agency pursuant to this Agreement upon which the parties have not agreed as to charges, Media User shall pay
Agency at its regular percentage rates, as stated in Section 4.A above.

E.   Media User shall not be obligated to reimburse Agency for any travel or other out-of-pocket expenses incurred in the performance of services pursuant to this Agreement unless expressly agreed by Media User in advance.

5. Billing.

A.   Agency shall invoice Media User for all media costs where possible in advance of Agency's payment date to allow for prepayment by the Media User so that Media User may receive the benefit of any available prepayment or similar discount. For any media purchase or service for which Agency is not entitled to a commission, Agency shall ensure that the charges to Media User are net of all agency commissions and discounts.

B.   Charges for production materials and services shall be billed by Agency upon completion of the production job or, if cash discounts are available, upon receipt of the supplier's invoice.

C. On all outside purchases other than for media, Agency shall attach to the invoice evidence of the supplier's charges.

D. All cash discounts on Agency's purchases including, but not limited to, media, art, printing and mechanical work, shall be available to Media User, provided that Media User meets Agency's requisite billing terms and there is no outstanding undisputed indebtedness of Media User to Agency at the time of the payment to the supplier.

E. Rate or billing adjustments shall be credited or charged to Media User on the next regular invoice date or as soon thereafter as otherwise practical.

F. Invoices shall be submitted in an itemized format and shall be paid by Media User within sixty (60) days of the invoice date.

6. Competitors.

During the term of this Agreement, Agency shall not accept employment from, render services to, represent or otherwise be affiliated with any person, firm, corporation or entity in connection with any product or service directly or indirectly competitive with or similar to any product or service of Media User with respect to which the Agency is providing any service pursuant to this Agreement, without the advance approval of the Media User. Media User shall not unreasonably withhold this approval.

7. Cost Estimates.

Agency shall not initiate billable work on any project pursuant to this Agreement without first estimating costs for preparation, including copy, service, layout, art, engraving, typography, processing, paste up and production. After determining the estimated cost, completion of the work shall be subject to Media User's prior approval.

8. Audit Rights.

Agency agrees that following reasonable prior notice any and all contracts, agreements, correspondence, books, accounts and other information relating to Media User's business or this Agreement shall be available for inspection by Media User and Media User's outside accountants, at Media User's expense and during the normal business hours of the Agency.

9. Ownership and Use.

A. Agency shall insure, to the fullest extent possible under law, that Media User shall own all right, title and interest in and to, including copyrights, trade secret, patent and other intellectual property rights, with respect to any copy, photograph, advertisement, music, lyrics, video, or other work or thing created by Agency or at Agency's direction for Media User pursuant to this Agreement and utilized by Media User.

B. Upon termination, Media User agrees that any advertising, merchandising, package, plan or idea prepared by Agency and submitted to Media User (whether submitted separately or in conjunction with or as a part of other material) which Media User has elected not to utilize, shall remain the property of Agency, unless Media User has paid Agency for its services in preparing such item. Media User agrees to return to Agency any copy, artwork, plates or other physical embodiment of such creative work relating to any such idea or plan which may be in Media User's possession at termination or expiration of this Agreement. Notwithstanding this, Media User has the unconditional right to pay for any of these materials or activities at the rate agreed upon in this Agreement and thereby these materials and activities would fall under the Section 9.A ownership and use rights accruing to Media User.

C. Materials and advertisements created by Agency pursuant to this Agreement may be used by Media User outside the United States without additional compensation, provided that Media User shall

be responsible for any additional expense associated with such use, such as charges for translation and amounts due talent.

10. Indemnification and Insurance.

A.   Agency shall indemnify and hold Media User harmless with respect to any claims, loss, suit, liability or judgment suffered by Media User, including reasonable attorney's fees and costs, based upon or related to any item prepared by Agency or at Agency's direction, including, but not limited to, any claim of libel, slander, piracy, plagiarism, invasion of privacy, or infringement of copyright or other intellectual property interest, except where any such claim arises out of material supplied by Media User and incorporated into any materials or advertisement prepared by Agency. Agency agrees to procure and maintain in force during the term of this Agreement, at Agency's expense, an Agency liability policy or policies having a minimum limit of at least _____, naming Media User as an additional insured and loss payee under such policy or policies.

B.   Media User agrees to indemnify and hold Agency harmless with respect to any claims, loss, liability, damage or judgment suffered by Agency, including reasonable attorney's fees and court costs, which results from the use by Agency of any material furnished by Media User or where material created by Agency or at the direction of Agency subject to the indemnification in subsection A. above is materially changed by Media User. Information or data obtained by Agency from Media User to substantiate claims made in advertising shall be deemed to be "material furnished by Media User to Agency."

C.   In the event of any proceeding, litigation or suit against Media User by any regulatory agency or in the event of any court action or other proceeding challenging any advertising prepared by Agency, Agency shall assist in the preparation of the defense of such action or proceeding and cooperate with Media User and Media User's attorneys.

11. Term.

The term of this Agreement shall commence on _____ and shall continue in full force and effect until terminated by either party upon at least sixty (60) days prior written notice, provided that in no event (except breach) may this Agreement be terminated prior to _____. The rights, duties and obligations of the parties shall continue in full force during or following the period of the termination notice until termination, including the ordering and billing of advertising in media whose closing dates follow then such period.

12. Rights Upon Termination.

A.   Upon termination of the Agreement, Agency shall transfer, assign and make available to Media User all property and materials in Agency's possession or subject to Agency's control that are the property of Media User, subject to payment in full of amounts due pursuant to this Agreement.

B.   Upon termination, Agency agrees to provide reasonable cooperation in arranging for the transfer or approval of third party's interest in all contracts, agreements and other arrangements with advertising media, suppliers, talent and others not then utilized, and all rights and claims thereto and therein, following appropriate release from the obligations therein.

13. Default.

In the event of any default of any material obligation by or owed by a party pursuant to this Agreement, then the other party may provide written notice of such default and if such default is not cured within ten (10) days of the written notice, then the nondefaulting party may terminate this Agreement. In addition, the only damages collectible by Agency shall be the exact amounts due; no other damages,

for any reason whatsoever, may be assessed against Media User including, but limited to, punitive damages and unreasonable termination charges, and any other such claim. This provision shall be broadly interpreted in the favor of the Media User by any Court of competent jurisdiction.

14. Notices.

Any notice required by this Agreement or given in connection with it, shall be in writing and shall be given to the appropriate party by personal delivery or by postage prepaid, or recognized overnight delivery services such as Federal Express.

If to Media User: _____

_____

If to Agency: _____

_____

15. Headings in this Agreement.

The headings in this Agreement are for convenience only, confirm no rights or obligations in either party, and do not alter any terms of this Agreement.

16. Entirety of Agreement.

The terms and conditions set forth herein constitute the entire agreement between the parties and supersede any communications or previous agreements with respect to the subject matter of this Agreement. There are no written or oral understandings directly or indirectly related to this Agreement that are not set forth herein. No change can be made to this Agreement other than in writing and signed by both parties.

17. Governing Law.

This Agreement shall be construed and enforced according to the laws of the State of _____ and any dispute under this Agreement must be brought in this venue and in no other.

In Witness whereof, the parties have executed this Agreement as of the date first written above.

_____ _____
Agency   Media User

Ad or other Media Agency Agreement

This Agency Agreement ("Agreement") is made and effective this _____ (Date), by and between ("Agency") and _____ (Your Firm) ("Media User").

Agency is in the business of providing media agency services for a fee.

Media User desires to engage Agency to render, and Agency desires to render to Media User, certain Agency services, all as set forth.

NOW, THEREFORE, in consideration of the mutual agreements and covenants herein contained, the parties hereto agree as follows:

1. <u>Engagement</u>.

Media User engages Agency to render, and Agency agrees to render to Media User, services in connection with Media User's planning, preparing and placing of advertising and other media services for certain of Media User's products as follows:

_____

A. Analyze Media User's current and proposed products and services and presentations and potential markets.

B. Create, prepare and submit to Media User for its prior approval advertising ideas, media suggestions, and other such related programs.

C. Prepare and submit to Media User for its prior approval estimates of costs and expenses associated with proposed advertising ideas and programs prior to any such implementation or financial commitment.

D. Design and prepare, or arrange for the design and preparation of advertisements, public relations, and other such materials.

E. Perform such other services as Media User may request from time to time such as, but not limited to, direct mail ad preparations, speech writing, publicity and public relations work, market research and analysis, and other similar and related activities.

F. Order advertising space, time or other means to be used for publication of Media User's advertisements, at all times endeavoring to secure the most efficient and advantageous rates available. All such activities to be approved in advance by the Media User unless otherwise written and stipulated.

G. Proof for accuracy and completeness of insertions, displays, broadcasts, or other forms of advertisements.

H. Audit invoices for proper and agreed upon space, time, material preparation and charges.

2. <u>Products</u>.

Agency's engagement shall relate to the following products and services of Media User:

_____.

3. Exclusivity.

Agency shall be the Agency in the United States and worldwide for Media User with respect to the products described in Section 2 above, unless otherwise specified in this section:

_____.

4.   Compensation.

A.   Agency shall receive an amount equal to ___ percentage of the gross charges levied by media for advertising placed by Agency pursuant to this Agreement; and   after volume discount, of the charges of suppliers of services or properties, such as finished art, comprehensive layouts, type composition, photostats, engravings, printing, radio and television programs, talent, literary, dramatic and musical works, records and exhibits, purchased by Agency on Media User's authorization during the term of this Agreement; provided that: No percentage will be added to Agency charges for packing, shipping, express, postage, telephone, telex, fax, travel expenses and other out of pocket expenses of Agency personnel.

B.   For those items where Agency is not compensated on a commission basis, Media User shall pay Agency on an hourly basis for services provided hereunder. The rate will be determined by the type of services provided and the person or persons providing such services, but in no event shall the rate exceed _____ per hour. Media User may elect in advance to be charged on this hourly rate basis. If Media User fails to notify Agency of its choice, it shall be presumed that Media User elected to be charged on a percentage basis.

C.   In the event that Agency undertakes, at Media User's request subject to Media User's prior approval, special projects such as those described in Section I.F above, Agency shall prepare an estimate of total charges for any such special project in advance, including any charges for materials or services purchased from outside vendors. In the event that Media User elects to proceed with the special project based upon Agency's estimated cost, Agency shall perform the services with respect to such special project at its estimated cost, subject to modification as mutually agreed by the parties.

D. For any special project or other services provided by Agency pursuant to this Agreement upon which the parties have not agreed as to charges, Media User shall pay
Agency at its regular percentage rates, as stated in Section 4.A above.

E.   Media User shall not be obligated to reimburse Agency for any travel or other out-of-pocket expenses incurred in the performance of services pursuant to this Agreement unless expressly agreed by Media User in advance.

5. Billing.

A.   Agency shall invoice Media User for all media costs where possible in advance of Agency's payment date to allow for prepayment by the Media User so that Media User may receive the benefit of any available prepayment or similar discount. For any media purchase or service for which Agency is not entitled to a commission, Agency shall ensure that the charges to Media User are net of all agency commissions and discounts.

B.   Charges for production materials and services shall be billed by Agency upon completion of the production job or, if cash discounts are available, upon receipt of the supplier's invoice.

C. On all outside purchases other than for media, Agency shall attach to the invoice evidence of the supplier's charges.

D.   All cash discounts on Agency's purchases including, but not limited to, media, art, printing and mechanical work, shall be available to Media User, provided that Media User meets Agency's requisite billing terms and there is no outstanding undisputed indebtedness of Media User to Agency at the time of the payment to the supplier.

E. Rate or billing adjustments shall be credited or charged to Media User on the next regular invoice date or as soon thereafter as otherwise practical.

F. Invoices shall be submitted in an itemized format and shall be paid by Media User within sixty (60) days of the invoice date.

6. Competitors.

During the term of this Agreement, Agency shall not accept employment from, render services to, represent or otherwise be affiliated with any person, firm, corporation or entity in connection with any product or service directly or indirectly competitive with or similar to any product or service of Media User with respect to which the Agency is providing any service pursuant to this Agreement, without the advance approval of the Media User. Media User shall not unreasonably withhold this approval.

7. Cost Estimates.

Agency shall not initiate billable work on any project pursuant to this Agreement without first estimating costs for preparation, including copy, service, layout, art, engraving, typography, processing, paste up and production. After determining the estimated cost, completion of the work shall be subject to Media User's prior approval.

8. Audit Rights.

Agency agrees that following reasonable prior notice any and all contracts, agreements, correspondence, books, accounts and other information relating to Media User's business or this Agreement shall be available for inspection by Media User and Media User's outside accountants, at Media User's expense and during the normal business hours of the Agency.

9. Ownership and Use.

A.   Agency shall insure, to the fullest extent possible under law, that Media User shall own all right, title and interest in and to, including copyrights, trade secret, patent and other intellectual property rights, with respect to any copy, photograph, advertisement, music, lyrics, video, or other work or thing created by Agency or at Agency's direction for Media User pursuant to this Agreement and utilized by Media User.

B.   Upon termination, Media User agrees that any advertising, merchandising, package, plan or idea prepared by Agency and submitted to Media User (whether submitted separately or in conjunction with or as a part of other material) which Media User has elected not to utilize, shall remain the property of Agency, unless Media User has paid Agency for its services in preparing such item. Media User agrees to return to Agency any copy, artwork, plates or other physical embodiment of such creative work relating to any such idea or plan which may be in Media User's possession at termination or expiration of this Agreement. Notwithstanding this, Media User has the unconditional right to pay for any of these materials or activities at the rate agreed upon in this Agreement and thereby these materials and activities would fall under the Section 9.A ownership and use rights accruing to Media User.

C.   Materials and advertisements created by Agency pursuant to this Agreement may be used by Media User outside the United States without additional compensation, provided that Media User shall

be responsible for any additional expense associated with such use, such as charges for translation and amounts due talent.

10. Indemnification and Insurance.

A. Agency shall indemnify and hold Media User harmless with respect to any claims, loss, suit, liability or judgment suffered by Media User, including reasonable attorney's fees and costs, based upon or related to any item prepared by Agency or at Agency's direction, including, but not limited to, any claim of libel, slander, piracy, plagiarism, invasion of privacy, or infringement of copyright or other intellectual property interest, except where any such claim arises out of material supplied by Media User and incorporated into any materials or advertisement prepared by Agency. Agency agrees to procure and maintain in force during the term of this Agreement, at Agency's expense, an Agency liability policy or policies having a minimum limit of at least _____, naming Media User as an additional insured and loss payee under such policy or policies.

B. Media User agrees to indemnify and hold Agency harmless with respect to any claims, loss, liability, damage or judgment suffered by Agency, including reasonable attorney's fees and court costs, which results from the use by Agency of any material furnished by Media User or where material created by Agency or at the direction of Agency subject to the indemnification in subsection A. above is materially changed by Media User. Information or data obtained by Agency from Media User to substantiate claims made in advertising shall be deemed to be "material furnished by Media User to Agency."

C. In the event of any proceeding, litigation or suit against Media User by any regulatory agency or in the event of any court action or other proceeding challenging any advertising prepared by Agency, Agency shall assist in the preparation of the defense of such action or proceeding and cooperate with Media User and Media User's attorneys.

11. Term.

The term of this Agreement shall commence on _____ and shall continue in full force and effect until terminated by either party upon at least sixty (60) days prior written notice, provided that in no event (except breach) may this Agreement be terminated prior to _____. The rights, duties and obligations of the parties shall continue in full force during or following the period of the termination notice until termination, including the ordering and billing of advertising in media whose closing dates follow then such period.

12. Rights Upon Termination.

A. Upon termination of the Agreement, Agency shall transfer, assign and make available to Media User all property and materials in Agency's possession or subject to Agency's control that are the property of Media User, subject to payment in full of amounts due pursuant to this Agreement.

B. Upon termination, Agency agrees to provide reasonable cooperation in arranging for the transfer or approval of third party's interest in all contracts, agreements and other arrangements with advertising media, suppliers, talent and others not then utilized, and all rights and claims thereto and therein, following appropriate release from the obligations therein.

13. Default.

In the event of any default of any material obligation by or owed by a party pursuant to this Agreement, then the other party may provide written notice of such default and if such default is not cured within ten (10) days of the written notice, then the nondefaulting party may terminate this Agreement. In addition, the only damages collectible by Agency shall be the exact amounts due; no other damages,

for any reason whatsoever, may be assessed against Media User including, but limited to, punitive damages and unreasonable termination charges, and any other such claim. This provision shall be broadly interpreted in the favor of the Media User by any Court of competent jurisdiction.

14. Notices.

Any notice required by this Agreement or given in connection with it, shall be in writing and shall be given to the appropriate party by personal delivery or by postage prepaid, or recognized overnight delivery services such as Federal Express.

If to Media User: _____

_____

If to Agency: _____

_____

15. Headings in this Agreement.

The headings in this Agreement are for convenience only, confirm no rights or obligations in either party, and do not alter any terms of this Agreement.

16. Entirety of Agreement.

The terms and conditions set forth herein constitute the entire agreement between the parties and supersede any communications or previous agreements with respect to the subject matter of this Agreement. There are no written or oral understandings directly or indirectly related to this Agreement that are not set forth herein. No change can be made to this Agreement other than in writing and signed by both parties.

17. Governing Law.

This Agreement shall be construed and enforced according to the laws of the State of _____ and any dispute under this Agreement must be brought in this venue and in no other.

In Witness whereof, the parties have executed this Agreement as of the date first written above.

_____   _____
Agency   Media User

Ad or other Media Agency Agreement

This Agency Agreement ("Agreement") is made and effective this _____ (Date), by and between ("Agency") and _____ (Your Firm) ("Media User").

Agency is in the business of providing media agency services for a fee.

Media User desires to engage Agency to render, and Agency desires to render to Media User, certain Agency services, all as set forth.

NOW, THEREFORE, in consideration of the mutual agreements and covenants herein contained, the parties hereto agree as follows:

1. <u>Engagement</u>.

Media User engages Agency to render, and Agency agrees to render to Media User, services in connection with Media User's planning, preparing and placing of advertising and other media services for certain of Media User's products as follows:

_____

A. Analyze Media User's current and proposed products and services and presentations and potential markets.

B. Create, prepare and submit to Media User for its prior approval advertising ideas, media suggestions, and other such related programs.

C. Prepare and submit to Media User for its prior approval estimates of costs and expenses associated with proposed advertising ideas and programs prior to any such implementation or financial commitment.

D. Design and prepare, or arrange for the design and preparation of advertisements, public relations, and other such materials.

E. Perform such other services as Media User may request from time to time such as, but not limited to, direct mail ad preparations, speech writing, publicity and public relations work, market research and analysis, and other similar and related activities.

F. Order advertising space, time or other means to be used for publication of Media User's advertisements, at all times endeavoring to secure the most efficient and advantageous rates available. All such activities to be approved in advance by the Media User unless otherwise written and stipulated.

G. Proof for accuracy and completeness of insertions, displays, broadcasts, or other forms of advertisements.

H. Audit invoices for proper and agreed upon space, time, material preparation and charges.

2. <u>Products</u>.

Agency's engagement shall relate to the following products and services of Media User:

_____.

3. Exclusivity.

Agency shall be the Agency in the United States and worldwide for Media User with respect to the products described in Section 2 above, unless otherwise specified in this section:

_____.

4. Compensation.

A. Agency shall receive an amount equal to ___ percentage of the gross charges levied by media for advertising placed by Agency pursuant to this Agreement; and ___ after volume discount, of the charges of suppliers of services or properties, such as finished art, comprehensive layouts, type composition, photostats, engravings, printing, radio and television programs, talent, literary, dramatic and musical works, records and exhibits, purchased by Agency on Media User's authorization during the term of this Agreement; provided that: No percentage will be added to Agency charges for packing, shipping, express, postage, telephone, telex, fax, travel expenses and other out of pocket expenses of Agency personnel.

B. For those items where Agency is not compensated on a commission basis, Media User shall pay Agency on an hourly basis for services provided hereunder. The rate will be determined by the type of services provided and the person or persons providing such services, but in no event shall the rate exceed _____ per hour. Media User may elect in advance to be charged on this hourly rate basis. If Media User fails to notify Agency of its choice, it shall be presumed that Media User elected to be charged on a percentage basis.

C. In the event that Agency undertakes, at Media User's request subject to Media User's prior approval, special projects such as those described in Section I.F above, Agency shall prepare an estimate of total charges for any such special project in advance, including any charges for materials or services purchased from outside vendors. In the event that Media User elects to proceed with the special project based upon Agency's estimated cost, Agency shall perform the services with respect to such special project at its estimated cost, subject to modification as mutually agreed by the parties.

D. For any special project or other services provided by Agency pursuant to this Agreement upon which the parties have not agreed as to charges, Media User shall pay Agency at its regular percentage rates, as stated in Section 4.A above.

E. Media User shall not be obligated to reimburse Agency for any travel or other out-of-pocket expenses incurred in the performance of services pursuant to this Agreement unless expressly agreed by Media User in advance.

5. Billing.

A. Agency shall invoice Media User for all media costs where possible in advance of Agency's payment date to allow for prepayment by the Media User so that Media User may receive the benefit of any available prepayment or similar discount. For any media purchase or service for which Agency is not entitled to a commission, Agency shall ensure that the charges to Media User are net of all agency commissions and discounts.

B. Charges for production materials and services shall be billed by Agency upon completion of the production job or, if cash discounts are available, upon receipt of the supplier's invoice.

C. On all outside purchases other than for media, Agency shall attach to the invoice evidence of the supplier's charges.

D.   All cash discounts on Agency's purchases including, but not limited to, media, art, printing and mechanical work, shall be available to Media User, provided that Media User meets Agency's requisite billing terms and there is no outstanding undisputed indebtedness of Media User to Agency at the time of the payment to the supplier.

E. Rate or billing adjustments shall be credited or charged to Media User on the next regular invoice date or as soon thereafter as otherwise practical.

F. Invoices shall be submitted in an itemized format and shall be paid by Media User within sixty (60) days of the invoice date.

6. <u>Competitors</u>.

During the term of this Agreement, Agency shall not accept employment from, render services to, represent or otherwise be affiliated with any person, firm, corporation or entity in connection with any product or service directly or indirectly competitive with or similar to any product or service of Media User with respect to which the Agency is providing any service pursuant to this Agreement, without the advance approval of the Media User. Media User shall not unreasonably withhold this approval.

7. <u>Cost Estimates</u>.

Agency shall not initiate billable work on any project pursuant to this Agreement without first estimating costs for preparation, including copy, service, layout, art, engraving, typography, processing, paste up and production. After determining the estimated cost, completion of the work shall be subject to Media User's prior approval.

8. <u>Audit Rights</u>.

Agency agrees that following reasonable prior notice any and all contracts, agreements, correspondence, books, accounts and other information relating to Media User's business or this Agreement shall be available for inspection by Media User and Media User's outside accountants, at Media User's expense and during the normal business hours of the Agency.

9.<u>Ownership and Use.</u>

A.   Agency shall insure, to the fullest extent possible under law, that Media User shall own all right, title and interest in and to, including copyrights, trade secret, patent and other intellectual property rights, with respect to any copy, photograph, advertisement, music, lyrics, video, or other work or thing created by Agency or at Agency's direction for Media User pursuant to this Agreement and utilized by Media User.

B.   Upon termination, Media User agrees that any advertising, merchandising, package, plan or idea prepared by Agency and submitted to Media User (whether submitted separately or in conjunction with or as a part of other material) which Media User has elected not to utilize, shall remain the property of Agency, unless Media User has paid Agency for its services in preparing such item. Media User agrees to return to Agency any copy, artwork, plates or other physical embodiment of such creative work relating to any such idea or plan which may be in Media User's possession at termination or expiration of this Agreement. Notwithstanding this, Media User has the unconditional right to pay for any of these materials or activities at the rate agreed upon in this Agreement and thereby these materials and activities would fall under the Section 9.A ownership and use rights accruing to Media User.

C.   Materials and advertisements created by Agency pursuant to this Agreement may be used by Media User outside the United States without additional compensation, provided that Media User shall

be responsible for any additional expense associated with such use, such as charges for translation and amounts due talent.

10. Indemnification and Insurance.

A. Agency shall indemnify and hold Media User harmless with respect to any claims, loss, suit, liability or judgment suffered by Media User, including reasonable attorney's fees and costs, based upon or related to any item prepared by Agency or at Agency's direction, including, but not limited to, any claim of libel, slander, piracy, plagiarism, invasion of privacy, or infringement of copyright or other intellectual property interest, except where any such claim arises out of material supplied by Media User and incorporated into any materials or advertisement prepared by Agency. Agency agrees to procure and maintain in force during the term of this Agreement, at Agency's expense, an Agency liability policy or policies having a minimum limit of at least _____, naming Media User as an additional insured and loss payee under such policy or policies.

B. Media User agrees to indemnify and hold Agency harmless with respect to any claims, loss, liability, damage or judgment suffered by Agency, including reasonable attorney's fees and court costs, which results from the use by Agency of any material furnished by Media User or where material created by Agency or at the direction of Agency subject to the indemnification in subsection A. above is materially changed by Media User. Information or data obtained by Agency from Media User to substantiate claims made in advertising shall be deemed to be "material furnished by Media User to Agency."

C. In the event of any proceeding, litigation or suit against Media User by any regulatory agency or in the event of any court action or other proceeding challenging any advertising prepared by Agency, Agency shall assist in the preparation of the defense of such action or proceeding and cooperate with Media User and Media User's attorneys.

11. Term.

The term of this Agreement shall commence on _____ and shall continue in full force and effect until terminated by either party upon at least sixty (60) days prior written notice, provided that in no event (except breach) may this Agreement be terminated prior to _____. The rights, duties and obligations of the parties shall continue in full force during or following the period of the termination notice until termination, including the ordering and billing of advertising in media whose closing dates follow then such period.

12. Rights Upon Termination.

A. Upon termination of the Agreement, Agency shall transfer, assign and make available to Media User all property and materials in Agency's possession or subject to Agency's control that are the property of Media User, subject to payment in full of amounts due pursuant to this Agreement.

B. Upon termination, Agency agrees to provide reasonable cooperation in arranging for the transfer or approval of third party's interest in all contracts, agreements and other arrangements with advertising media, suppliers, talent and others not then utilized, and all rights and claims thereto and therein, following appropriate release from the obligations therein.

13. Default.

In the event of any default of any material obligation by or owed by a party pursuant to this Agreement, then the other party may provide written notice of such default and if such default is not cured within ten (10) days of the written notice, then the nondefaulting party may terminate this Agreement. In addition, the only damages collectible by Agency shall be the exact amounts due; no other damages,

for any reason whatsoever, may be assessed against Media User including, but limited to, punitive damages and unreasonable termination charges, and any other such claim. This provision shall be broadly interpreted in the favor of the Media User by any Court of competent jurisdiction.

14. Notices.

Any notice required by this Agreement or given in connection with it, shall be in writing and shall be given to the appropriate party by personal delivery or by postage prepaid, or recognized overnight delivery services such as Federal Express.

If to Media User: _____

_____

If to Agency: _____

_____

15. Headings in this Agreement.

The headings in this Agreement are for convenience only, confirm no rights or obligations in either party, and do not alter any terms of this Agreement.

16. Entirety of Agreement.

The terms and conditions set forth herein constitute the entire agreement between the parties and supersede any communications or previous agreements with respect to the subject matter of this Agreement. There are no written or oral understandings directly or indirectly related to this Agreement that are not set forth herein. No change can be made to this Agreement other than in writing and signed by both parties.

17. Governing Law.

This Agreement shall be construed and enforced according to the laws of the State of _____ and any dispute under this Agreement must be brought in this venue and in no other.

In Witness whereof, the parties have executed this Agreement as of the date first written above.

_____ _____
Agency   Media User

Ad or other Media Agency Agreement

This Agency Agreement ("Agreement") is made and effective this _____ (Date), by and between ("Agency") and _____ (Your Firm) ("Media User").

Agency is in the business of providing media agency services for a fee.

Media User desires to engage Agency to render, and Agency desires to render to Media User, certain Agency services, all as set forth.

NOW, THEREFORE, in consideration of the mutual agreements and covenants herein contained, the parties hereto agree as follows:

1. Engagement.

Media User engages Agency to render, and Agency agrees to render to Media User, services in connection with Media User's planning, preparing and placing of advertising and other media services for certain of Media User's products as follows:

_____

A. Analyze Media User's current and proposed products and services and presentations and potential markets.

B. Create, prepare and submit to Media User for its prior approval advertising ideas, media suggestions, and other such related programs.

C. Prepare and submit to Media User for its prior approval estimates of costs and expenses associated with proposed advertising ideas and programs prior to any such implementation or financial commitment.

D. Design and prepare, or arrange for the design and preparation of advertisements, public relations, and other such materials.

E. Perform such other services as Media User may request from time to time such as, but not limited to, direct mail ad preparations, speech writing, publicity and public relations work, market research and analysis, and other similar and related activities.

F. Order advertising space, time or other means to be used for publication of Media User's advertisements, at all times endeavoring to secure the most efficient and advantageous rates available. All such activities to be approved in advance by the Media User unless otherwise written and stipulated.

G. Proof for accuracy and completeness of insertions, displays, broadcasts, or other forms of advertisements.

H. Audit invoices for proper and agreed upon space, time, material preparation and charges.

2. Products.

Agency's engagement shall relate to the following products and services of Media User:

_____.

3. Exclusivity.

Agency shall be the Agency in the United States and worldwide for Media User with respect to the products described in Section 2 above, unless otherwise specified in this section:

_____.

4.　Compensation.

A.　Agency shall receive an amount equal to ___ percentage of the gross charges levied by media for advertising placed by Agency pursuant to this Agreement; and　　　　　　　　　　　　after volume discount, of the charges of suppliers of services or properties, such as finished art, comprehensive layouts, type composition, photostats, engravings, printing, radio and television programs, talent, literary, dramatic and musical works, records and exhibits, purchased by Agency on Media User's authorization during the term of this Agreement; provided that: No percentage will be added to Agency charges for packing, shipping, express, postage, telephone, telex, fax, travel expenses and other out of pocket expenses of Agency personnel.

B.　For those items where Agency is not compensated on a commission basis, Media User shall pay Agency on an hourly basis for services provided hereunder. The rate will be determined by the type of services provided and the person or persons providing such services, but in no event shall the rate exceed _____ per hour. Media User may elect in advance to be charged on this hourly rate basis. If Media User fails to notify Agency of its choice, it shall be presumed that Media User elected to be charged on a percentage basis.

C.　In the event that Agency undertakes, at Media User's request subject to Media User's prior approval, special projects such as those described in Section I.F above, Agency shall prepare an estimate of total charges for any such special project in advance, including any charges for materials or services purchased from outside vendors. In the event that Media User elects to proceed with the special project based upon Agency's estimated cost, Agency shall perform the services with respect to such special project at its estimated cost, subject to modification as mutually agreed by the parties.

D. For any special project or other services provided by Agency pursuant to this Agreement upon which the parties have not agreed as to charges, Media User shall pay
Agency at its regular percentage rates, as stated in Section 4.A above.

E.　Media User shall not be obligated to reimburse Agency for any travel or other out-of-pocket expenses incurred in the performance of services pursuant to this Agreement unless expressly agreed by Media User in advance.

5. Billing.

A.　Agency shall invoice Media User for all media costs where possible in advance of Agency's payment date to allow for prepayment by the Media User so that Media User may receive the benefit of any available prepayment or similar discount. For any media purchase or service for which Agency is not entitled to a commission, Agency shall ensure that the charges to Media User are net of all agency commissions and discounts.

B.　Charges for production materials and services shall be billed by Agency upon completion of the production job or, if cash discounts are available, upon receipt of the supplier's invoice.

C. On all outside purchases other than for media, Agency shall attach to the invoice evidence of the supplier's charges.

D.   All cash discounts on Agency's purchases including, but not limited to, media, art, printing and mechanical work, shall be available to Media User, provided that Media User meets Agency's requisite billing terms and there is no outstanding undisputed indebtedness of Media User to Agency at the time of the payment to the supplier.

E. Rate or billing adjustments shall be credited or charged to Media User on the next regular invoice date or as soon thereafter as otherwise practical.

F. Invoices shall be submitted in an itemized format and shall be paid by Media User within sixty (60) days of the invoice date.

6. Competitors.

During the term of this Agreement, Agency shall not accept employment from, render services to, represent or otherwise be affiliated with any person, firm, corporation or entity in connection with any product or service directly or indirectly competitive with or similar to any product or service of Media User with respect to which the Agency is providing any service pursuant to this Agreement, without the advance approval of the Media User. Media User shall not unreasonably withhold this approval.

7. Cost Estimates.

Agency shall not initiate billable work on any project pursuant to this Agreement without first estimating costs for preparation, including copy, service, layout, art, engraving, typography, processing, paste up and production. After determining the estimated cost, completion of the work shall be subject to Media User's prior approval.

8. Audit Rights.

Agency agrees that following reasonable prior notice any and all contracts, agreements, correspondence, books, accounts and other information relating to Media User's business or this Agreement shall be available for inspection by Media User and Media User's outside accountants, at Media User's expense and during the normal business hours of the Agency.

9. Ownership and Use.

A.   Agency shall insure, to the fullest extent possible under law, that Media User shall own all right, title and interest in and to, including copyrights, trade secret, patent and other intellectual property rights, with respect to any copy, photograph, advertisement, music, lyrics, video, or other work or thing created by Agency or at Agency's direction for Media User pursuant to this Agreement and utilized by Media User.

B.   Upon termination, Media User agrees that any advertising, merchandising, package, plan or idea prepared by Agency and submitted to Media User (whether submitted separately or in conjunction with or as a part of other material) which Media User has elected not to utilize, shall remain the property of Agency, unless Media User has paid Agency for its services in preparing such item. Media User agrees to return to Agency any copy, artwork, plates or other physical embodiment of such creative work relating to any such idea or plan which may be in Media User's possession at termination or expiration of this Agreement. Notwithstanding this, Media User has the unconditional right to pay for any of these materials or activities at the rate agreed upon in this Agreement and thereby these materials and activities would fall under the Section 9.A ownership and use rights accruing to Media User.

C.   Materials and advertisements created by Agency pursuant to this Agreement may be used by Media User outside the United States without additional compensation, provided that Media User shall

be responsible for any additional expense associated with such use, such as charges for translation and amounts due talent.

10. Indemnification and Insurance.

A. Agency shall indemnify and hold Media User harmless with respect to any claims, loss, suit, liability or judgment suffered by Media User, including reasonable attorney's fees and costs, based upon or related to any item prepared by Agency or at Agency's direction, including, but not limited to, any claim of libel, slander, piracy, plagiarism, invasion of privacy, or infringement of copyright or other intellectual property interest, except where any such claim arises out of material supplied by Media User and incorporated into any materials or advertisement prepared by Agency. Agency agrees to procure and maintain in force during the term of this Agreement, at Agency's expense, an Agency liability policy or policies having a minimum limit of at least _____, naming Media User as an additional insured and loss payee under such policy or policies.

B. Media User agrees to indemnify and hold Agency harmless with respect to any claims, loss, liability, damage or judgment suffered by Agency, including reasonable attorney's fees and court costs, which results from the use by Agency of any material furnished by Media User or where material created by Agency or at the direction of Agency subject to the indemnification in subsection A. above is materially changed by Media User. Information or data obtained by Agency from Media User to substantiate claims made in advertising shall be deemed to be "material furnished by Media User to Agency."

C. In the event of any proceeding, litigation or suit against Media User by any regulatory agency or in the event of any court action or other proceeding challenging any advertising prepared by Agency, Agency shall assist in the preparation of the defense of such action or proceeding and cooperate with Media User and Media User's attorneys.

11. Term.

The term of this Agreement shall commence on _____ and shall continue in full force and effect until terminated by either party upon at least sixty (60) days prior written notice, provided that in no event (except breach) may this Agreement be terminated prior to _____. The rights, duties and obligations of the parties shall continue in full force during or following the period of the termination notice until termination, including the ordering and billing of advertising in media whose closing dates follow then such period.

12. Rights Upon Termination.

A. Upon termination of the Agreement, Agency shall transfer, assign and make available to Media User all property and materials in Agency's possession or subject to Agency's control that are the property of Media User, subject to payment in full of amounts due pursuant to this Agreement.

B. Upon termination, Agency agrees to provide reasonable cooperation in arranging for the transfer or approval of third party's interest in all contracts, agreements and other arrangements with advertising media, suppliers, talent and others not then utilized, and all rights and claims thereto and therein, following appropriate release from the obligations therein.

13. Default.

In the event of any default of any material obligation by or owed by a party pursuant to this Agreement, then the other party may provide written notice of such default and if such default is not cured within ten (10) days of the written notice, then the nondefaulting party may terminate this Agreement. In addition, the only damages collectible by Agency shall be the exact amounts due; no other damages,

for any reason whatsoever, may be assessed against Media User including, but limited to, punitive damages and unreasonable termination charges, and any other such claim. This provision shall be broadly interpreted in the favor of the Media User by any Court of competent jurisdiction.

14. Notices.

Any notice required by this Agreement or given in connection with it, shall be in writing and shall be given to the appropriate party by personal delivery or by postage prepaid, or recognized overnight delivery services such as Federal Express.

If to Media User: _____

_____

If to Agency: _____

_____

15. Headings in this Agreement.

The headings in this Agreement are for convenience only, confirm no rights or obligations in either party, and do not alter any terms of this Agreement.

16. Entirety of Agreement.

The terms and conditions set forth herein constitute the entire agreement between the parties and supersede any communications or previous agreements with respect to the subject matter of this Agreement. There are no written or oral understandings directly or indirectly related to this Agreement that are not set forth herein. No change can be made to this Agreement other than in writing and signed by both parties.

17. Governing Law.

This Agreement shall be construed and enforced according to the laws of the State of _____ and any dispute under this Agreement must be brought in this venue and in no other.

In Witness whereof, the parties have executed this Agreement as of the date first written above.

_____ _____
Agency   Media User

Ad or other Media Agency Agreement

This Agency Agreement ("Agreement") is made and effective this _____ (Date), by and between ("Agency") and _____ (Your Firm) ("Media User").

Agency is in the business of providing media agency services for a fee.

Media User desires to engage Agency to render, and Agency desires to render to Media User, certain Agency services, all as set forth.

NOW, THEREFORE, in consideration of the mutual agreements and covenants herein contained, the parties hereto agree as follows:

1. <u>Engagement</u>.

Media User engages Agency to render, and Agency agrees to render to Media User, services in connection with Media User's planning, preparing and placing of advertising and other media services for certain of Media User's products as follows:

_____

A. Analyze Media User's current and proposed products and services and presentations and potential markets.

B. Create, prepare and submit to Media User for its prior approval advertising ideas, media suggestions, and other such related programs.

C. Prepare and submit to Media User for its prior approval estimates of costs and expenses associated with proposed advertising ideas and programs prior to any such implementation or financial commitment.

D. Design and prepare, or arrange for the design and preparation of advertisements, public relations, and other such materials.

E. Perform such other services as Media User may request from time to time such as, but not limited to, direct mail ad preparations, speech writing, publicity and public relations work, market research and analysis, and other similar and related activities.

F. Order advertising space, time or other means to be used for publication of Media User's advertisements, at all times endeavoring to secure the most efficient and advantageous rates available. All such activities to be approved in advance by the Media User unless otherwise written and stipulated.

G. Proof for accuracy and completeness of insertions, displays, broadcasts, or other forms of advertisements.

H. Audit invoices for proper and agreed upon space, time, material preparation and charges.

2. <u>Products</u>.

Agency's engagement shall relate to the following products and services of Media User:

_____.

3. Exclusivity.

Agency shall be the Agency in the United States and worldwide for Media User with respect to the products described in Section 2 above, unless otherwise specified in this section:

_____.

4.   Compensation.

A.   Agency shall receive an amount equal to ___ percentage of the gross charges levied by media for advertising placed by Agency pursuant to this Agreement; and   after volume discount, of the charges of suppliers of services or properties, such as finished art, comprehensive layouts, type composition, photostats, engravings, printing, radio and television programs, talent, literary, dramatic and musical works, records and exhibits, purchased by Agency on Media User's authorization during the term of this Agreement; provided that: No percentage will be added to Agency charges for packing, shipping, express, postage, telephone, telex, fax, travel expenses and other out of pocket expenses of Agency personnel.

B.   For those items where Agency is not compensated on a commission basis, Media User shall pay Agency on an hourly basis for services provided hereunder. The rate will be determined by the type of services provided and the person or persons providing such services, but in no event shall the rate exceed _____ per hour. Media User may elect in advance to be charged on this hourly rate basis. If Media User fails to notify Agency of its choice, it shall be presumed that Media User elected to be charged on a percentage basis.

C.   In the event that Agency undertakes, at Media User's request subject to Media User's prior approval, special projects such as those described in Section I.F above, Agency shall prepare an estimate of total charges for any such special project in advance, including any charges for materials or services purchased from outside vendors. In the event that Media User elects to proceed with the special project based upon Agency's estimated cost, Agency shall perform the services with respect to such special project at its estimated cost, subject to modification as mutually agreed by the parties.

D. For any special project or other services provided by Agency pursuant to this Agreement upon which the parties have not agreed as to charges, Media User shall pay
Agency at its regular percentage rates, as stated in Section 4.A above.

E.   Media User shall not be obligated to reimburse Agency for any travel or other out-of-pocket expenses incurred in the performance of services pursuant to this Agreement unless expressly agreed by Media User in advance.

5. Billing.

A.   Agency shall invoice Media User for all media costs where possible in advance of Agency's payment date to allow for prepayment by the Media User so that Media User may receive the benefit of any available prepayment or similar discount. For any media purchase or service for which Agency is not entitled to a commission, Agency shall ensure that the charges to Media User are net of all agency commissions and discounts.

B.   Charges for production materials and services shall be billed by Agency upon completion of the production job or, if cash discounts are available, upon receipt of the supplier's invoice.

C. On all outside purchases other than for media, Agency shall attach to the invoice evidence of the supplier's charges.

D.   All cash discounts on Agency's purchases including, but not limited to, media, art, printing and mechanical work, shall be available to Media User, provided that Media User meets Agency's requisite billing terms and there is no outstanding undisputed indebtedness of Media User to Agency at the time of the payment to the supplier.

E. Rate or billing adjustments shall be credited or charged to Media User on the next regular invoice date or as soon thereafter as otherwise practical.

F. Invoices shall be submitted in an itemized format and shall be paid by Media User within sixty (60) days of the invoice date.

6. Competitors.

During the term of this Agreement, Agency shall not accept employment from, render services to, represent or otherwise be affiliated with any person, firm, corporation or entity in connection with any product or service directly or indirectly competitive with or similar to any product or service of Media User with respect to which the Agency is providing any service pursuant to this Agreement, without the advance approval of the Media User. Media User shall not unreasonably withhold this approval.

7. Cost Estimates.

Agency shall not initiate billable work on any project pursuant to this Agreement without first estimating costs for preparation, including copy, service, layout, art, engraving, typography, processing, paste up and production. After determining the estimated cost, completion of the work shall be subject to Media User's prior approval.

8. Audit Rights.

Agency agrees that following reasonable prior notice any and all contracts, agreements, correspondence, books, accounts and other information relating to Media User's business or this Agreement shall be available for inspection by Media User and Media User's outside accountants, at Media User's expense and during the normal business hours of the Agency.

9. Ownership and Use.

A.   Agency shall insure, to the fullest extent possible under law, that Media User shall own all right, title and interest in and to, including copyrights, trade secret, patent and other intellectual property rights, with respect to any copy, photograph, advertisement, music, lyrics, video, or other work or thing created by Agency or at Agency's direction for Media User pursuant to this Agreement and utilized by Media User.

B.   Upon termination, Media User agrees that any advertising, merchandising, package, plan or idea prepared by Agency and submitted to Media User (whether submitted separately or in conjunction with or as a part of other material) which Media User has elected not to utilize, shall remain the property of Agency, unless Media User has paid Agency for its services in preparing such item. Media User agrees to return to Agency any copy, artwork, plates or other physical embodiment of such creative work relating to any such idea or plan which may be in Media User's possession at termination or expiration of this Agreement. Notwithstanding this, Media User has the unconditional right to pay for any of these materials or activities at the rate agreed upon in this Agreement and thereby these materials and activities would fall under the Section 9.A ownership and use rights accruing to Media User.

C.   Materials and advertisements created by Agency pursuant to this Agreement may be used by Media User outside the United States without additional compensation, provided that Media User shall

be responsible for any additional expense associated with such use, such as charges for translation and amounts due talent.

10. Indemnification and Insurance.

A. Agency shall indemnify and hold Media User harmless with respect to any claims, loss, suit, liability or judgment suffered by Media User, including reasonable attorney's fees and costs, based upon or related to any item prepared by Agency or at Agency's direction, including, but not limited to, any claim of libel, slander, piracy, plagiarism, invasion of privacy, or infringement of copyright or other intellectual property interest, except where any such claim arises out of material supplied by Media User and incorporated into any materials or advertisement prepared by Agency. Agency agrees to procure and maintain in force during the term of this Agreement, at Agency's expense, an Agency liability policy or policies having a minimum limit of at least _____, naming Media User as an additional insured and loss payee under such policy or policies.

B. Media User agrees to indemnify and hold Agency harmless with respect to any claims, loss, liability, damage or judgment suffered by Agency, including reasonable attorney's fees and court costs, which results from the use by Agency of any material furnished by Media User or where material created by Agency or at the direction of Agency subject to the indemnification in subsection A. above is materially changed by Media User. Information or data obtained by Agency from Media User to substantiate claims made in advertising shall be deemed to be "material furnished by Media User to Agency."

C. In the event of any proceeding, litigation or suit against Media User by any regulatory agency or in the event of any court action or other proceeding challenging any advertising prepared by Agency, Agency shall assist in the preparation of the defense of such action or proceeding and cooperate with Media User and Media User's attorneys.

11. Term.

The term of this Agreement shall commence on _____ and shall continue in full force and effect until terminated by either party upon at least sixty (60) days prior written notice, provided that in no event (except breach) may this Agreement be terminated prior to _____. The rights, duties and obligations of the parties shall continue in full force during or following the period of the termination notice until termination, including the ordering and billing of advertising in media whose closing dates follow then such period.

12. Rights Upon Termination.

A. Upon termination of the Agreement, Agency shall transfer, assign and make available to Media User all property and materials in Agency's possession or subject to Agency's control that are the property of Media User, subject to payment in full of amounts due pursuant to this Agreement.

B. Upon termination, Agency agrees to provide reasonable cooperation in arranging for the transfer or approval of third party's interest in all contracts, agreements and other arrangements with advertising media, suppliers, talent and others not then utilized, and all rights and claims thereto and therein, following appropriate release from the obligations therein.

13. Default.

In the event of any default of any material obligation by or owed by a party pursuant to this Agreement, then the other party may provide written notice of such default and if such default is not cured within ten (10) days of the written notice, then the nondefaulting party may terminate this Agreement. In addition, the only damages collectible by Agency shall be the exact amounts due; no other damages,

for any reason whatsoever, may be assessed against Media User including, but limited to, punitive damages and unreasonable termination charges, and any other such claim. This provision shall be broadly interpreted in the favor of the Media User by any Court of competent jurisdiction.

14. <u>Notices</u>.

Any notice required by this Agreement or given in connection with it, shall be in writing and shall be given to the appropriate party by personal delivery or by postage prepaid, or recognized overnight delivery services such as Federal Express.

If to Media User: _____

_____

If to Agency: _____

_____

15. <u>Headings in this Agreement</u>.

The headings in this Agreement are for convenience only, confirm no rights or obligations in either party, and do not alter any terms of this Agreement.

16. <u>Entirety of Agreement</u>.

The terms and conditions set forth herein constitute the entire agreement between the parties and supersede any communications or previous agreements with respect to the subject matter of this Agreement. There are no written or oral understandings directly or indirectly related to this Agreement that are not set forth herein. No change can be made to this Agreement other than in writing and signed by both parties.

17. <u>Governing Law</u>.

This Agreement shall be construed and enforced according to the laws of the State of _____ and any dispute under this Agreement must be brought in this venue and in no other.

In Witness whereof, the parties have executed this Agreement as of the date first written above.

_____   _____
Agency   Media User

Ad or other Media Agency Agreement

This Agency Agreement ("Agreement") is made and effective this _____ (Date), by and between ("Agency") and _____ (Your Firm) ("Media User").

Agency is in the business of providing media agency services for a fee.

Media User desires to engage Agency to render, and Agency desires to render to Media User, certain Agency services, all as set forth.

NOW, THEREFORE, in consideration of the mutual agreements and covenants herein contained, the parties hereto agree as follows:

1. Engagement.

Media User engages Agency to render, and Agency agrees to render to Media User, services in connection with Media User's planning, preparing and placing of advertising and other media services for certain of Media User's products as follows:

_____

A. Analyze Media User's current and proposed products and services and presentations and potential markets.

B. Create, prepare and submit to Media User for its prior approval advertising ideas, media suggestions, and other such related programs.

C. Prepare and submit to Media User for its prior approval estimates of costs and expenses associated with proposed advertising ideas and programs prior to any such implementation or financial commitment.

D. Design and prepare, or arrange for the design and preparation of advertisements, public relations, and other such materials.

E. Perform such other services as Media User may request from time to time such as, but not limited to, direct mail ad preparations, speech writing, publicity and public relations work, market research and analysis, and other similar and related activities.

F. Order advertising space, time or other means to be used for publication of Media User's advertisements, at all times endeavoring to secure the most efficient and advantageous rates available. All such activities to be approved in advance by the Media User unless otherwise written and stipulated.

G. Proof for accuracy and completeness of insertions, displays, broadcasts, or other forms of advertisements.

H. Audit invoices for proper and agreed upon space, time, material preparation and charges.

2. Products.

Agency's engagement shall relate to the following products and services of Media User:

_____.

3. Exclusivity.

Agency shall be the Agency in the United States and worldwide for Media User with respect to the products described in Section 2 above, unless otherwise specified in this section:

_____.

4.   Compensation.

A.   Agency shall receive an amount equal to ___ percentage of the gross charges levied by media for advertising placed by Agency pursuant to this Agreement; and   after volume discount, of the charges of suppliers of services or properties, such as finished art, comprehensive layouts, type composition, photostats, engravings, printing, radio and television programs, talent, literary, dramatic and musical works, records and exhibits, purchased by Agency on Media User's authorization during the term of this Agreement; provided that: No percentage will be added to Agency charges for packing, shipping, express, postage, telephone, telex, fax, travel expenses and other out of pocket expenses of Agency personnel.

B.   For those items where Agency is not compensated on a commission basis, Media User shall pay Agency on an hourly basis for services provided hereunder. The rate will be determined by the type of services provided and the person or persons providing such services, but in no event shall the rate exceed _____ per hour. Media User may elect in advance to be charged on this hourly rate basis. If Media User fails to notify Agency of its choice, it shall be presumed that Media User elected to be charged on a percentage basis.

C.   In the event that Agency undertakes, at Media User's request subject to Media User's prior approval, special projects such as those described in Section I.F above, Agency shall prepare an estimate of total charges for any such special project in advance, including any charges for materials or services purchased from outside vendors. In the event that Media User elects to proceed with the special project based upon Agency's estimated cost, Agency shall perform the services with respect to such special project at its estimated cost, subject to modification as mutually agreed by the parties.

D. For any special project or other services provided by Agency pursuant to this Agreement upon which the parties have not agreed as to charges, Media User shall pay
Agency at its regular percentage rates, as stated in Section 4.A above.

E.   Media User shall not be obligated to reimburse Agency for any travel or other out-of-pocket expenses incurred in the performance of services pursuant to this Agreement unless expressly agreed by Media User in advance.

5. Billing.

A.   Agency shall invoice Media User for all media costs where possible in advance of Agency's payment date to allow for prepayment by the Media User so that Media User may receive the benefit of any available prepayment or similar discount. For any media purchase or service for which Agency is not entitled to a commission, Agency shall ensure that the charges to Media User are net of all agency commissions and discounts.

B.   Charges for production materials and services shall be billed by Agency upon completion of the production job or, if cash discounts are available, upon receipt of the supplier's invoice.

C. On all outside purchases other than for media, Agency shall attach to the invoice evidence of the supplier's charges.

D. All cash discounts on Agency's purchases including, but not limited to, media, art, printing and mechanical work, shall be available to Media User, provided that Media User meets Agency's requisite billing terms and there is no outstanding undisputed indebtedness of Media User to Agency at the time of the payment to the supplier.

E. Rate or billing adjustments shall be credited or charged to Media User on the next regular invoice date or as soon thereafter as otherwise practical.

F. Invoices shall be submitted in an itemized format and shall be paid by Media User within sixty (60) days of the invoice date.

6. Competitors.

During the term of this Agreement, Agency shall not accept employment from, render services to, represent or otherwise be affiliated with any person, firm, corporation or entity in connection with any product or service directly or indirectly competitive with or similar to any product or service of Media User with respect to which the Agency is providing any service pursuant to this Agreement, without the advance approval of the Media User. Media User shall not unreasonably withhold this approval.

7. Cost Estimates.

Agency shall not initiate billable work on any project pursuant to this Agreement without first estimating costs for preparation, including copy, service, layout, art, engraving, typography, processing, paste up and production. After determining the estimated cost, completion of the work shall be subject to Media User's prior approval.

8. Audit Rights.

Agency agrees that following reasonable prior notice any and all contracts, agreements, correspondence, books, accounts and other information relating to Media User's business or this Agreement shall be available for inspection by Media User and Media User's outside accountants, at Media User's expense and during the normal business hours of the Agency.

9. Ownership and Use.

A. Agency shall insure, to the fullest extent possible under law, that Media User shall own all right, title and interest in and to, including copyrights, trade secret, patent and other intellectual property rights, with respect to any copy, photograph, advertisement, music, lyrics, video, or other work or thing created by Agency or at Agency's direction for Media User pursuant to this Agreement and utilized by Media User.

B. Upon termination, Media User agrees that any advertising, merchandising, package, plan or idea prepared by Agency and submitted to Media User (whether submitted separately or in conjunction with or as a part of other material) which Media User has elected not to utilize, shall remain the property of Agency, unless Media User has paid Agency for its services in preparing such item. Media User agrees to return to Agency any copy, artwork, plates or other physical embodiment of such creative work relating to any such idea or plan which may be in Media User's possession at termination or expiration of this Agreement. Notwithstanding this, Media User has the unconditional right to pay for any of these materials or activities at the rate agreed upon in this Agreement and thereby these materials and activities would fall under the Section 9.A ownership and use rights accruing to Media User.

C. Materials and advertisements created by Agency pursuant to this Agreement may be used by Media User outside the United States without additional compensation, provided that Media User shall

be responsible for any additional expense associated with such use, such as charges for translation and amounts due talent.

10. <u>Indemnification and Insurance</u>.

A. Agency shall indemnify and hold Media User harmless with respect to any claims, loss, suit, liability or judgment suffered by Media User, including reasonable attorney's fees and costs, based upon or related to any item prepared by Agency or at Agency's direction, including, but not limited to, any claim of libel, slander, piracy, plagiarism, invasion of privacy, or infringement of copyright or other intellectual property interest, except where any such claim arises out of material supplied by Media User and incorporated into any materials or advertisement prepared by Agency. Agency agrees to procure and maintain in force during the term of this Agreement, at Agency's expense, an Agency liability policy or policies having a minimum limit of at least _____, naming Media User as an additional insured and loss payee under such policy or policies.

B. Media User agrees to indemnify and hold Agency harmless with respect to any claims, loss, liability, damage or judgment suffered by Agency, including reasonable attorney's fees and court costs, which results from the use by Agency of any material furnished by Media User or where material created by Agency or at the direction of Agency subject to the indemnification in subsection A. above is materially changed by Media User. Information or data obtained by Agency from Media User to substantiate claims made in advertising shall be deemed to be "material furnished by Media User to Agency."

C. In the event of any proceeding, litigation or suit against Media User by any regulatory agency or in the event of any court action or other proceeding challenging any advertising prepared by Agency, Agency shall assist in the preparation of the defense of such action or proceeding and cooperate with Media User and Media User's attorneys.

11. <u>Term</u>.

The term of this Agreement shall commence on _____ and shall continue in full force and effect until terminated by either party upon at least sixty (60) days prior written notice, provided that in no event (except breach) may this Agreement be terminated prior to _____. The rights, duties and obligations of the parties shall continue in full force during or following the period of the termination notice until termination, including the ordering and billing of advertising in media whose closing dates follow then such period.

12. <u>Rights Upon Termination</u>.

A. Upon termination of the Agreement, Agency shall transfer, assign and make available to Media User all property and materials in Agency's possession or subject to Agency's control that are the property of Media User, subject to payment in full of amounts due pursuant to this Agreement.

B. Upon termination, Agency agrees to provide reasonable cooperation in arranging for the transfer or approval of third party's interest in all contracts, agreements and other arrangements with advertising media, suppliers, talent and others not then utilized, and all rights and claims thereto and therein, following appropriate release from the obligations therein.

13. <u>Default</u>.

In the event of any default of any material obligation by or owed by a party pursuant to this Agreement, then the other party may provide written notice of such default and if such default is not cured within ten (10) days of the written notice, then the nondefaulting party may terminate this Agreement. In addition, the only damages collectible by Agency shall be the exact amounts due; no other damages,

for any reason whatsoever, may be assessed against Media User including, but limited to, punitive damages and unreasonable termination charges, and any other such claim. This provision shall be broadly interpreted in the favor of the Media User by any Court of competent jurisdiction.

14. Notices.

Any notice required by this Agreement or given in connection with it, shall be in writing and shall be given to the appropriate party by personal delivery or by postage prepaid, or recognized overnight delivery services such as Federal Express.

If to Media User: _____

_____

If to Agency: _____

_____

15. Headings in this Agreement.

The headings in this Agreement are for convenience only, confirm no rights or obligations in either party, and do not alter any terms of this Agreement.

16. Entirety of Agreement.

The terms and conditions set forth herein constitute the entire agreement between the parties and supersede any communications or previous agreements with respect to the subject matter of this Agreement. There are no written or oral understandings directly or indirectly related to this Agreement that are not set forth herein. No change can be made to this Agreement other than in writing and signed by both parties.

17. Governing Law.

This Agreement shall be construed and enforced according to the laws of the State of _____ and any dispute under this Agreement must be brought in this venue and in no other.

In Witness whereof, the parties have executed this Agreement as of the date first written above.

_____   _____
Agency   Media User

Ad or other Media Agency Agreement

This Agency Agreement ("Agreement") is made and effective this _____ (Date), by and between ("Agency") and _____ (Your Firm) ("Media User").

Agency is in the business of providing media agency services for a fee.

Media User desires to engage Agency to render, and Agency desires to render to Media User, certain Agency services, all as set forth.

NOW, THEREFORE, in consideration of the mutual agreements and covenants herein contained, the parties hereto agree as follows:

1. <u>Engagement</u>.

Media User engages Agency to render, and Agency agrees to render to Media User, services in connection with Media User's planning, preparing and placing of advertising and other media services for certain of Media User's products as follows:

_____

A. Analyze Media User's current and proposed products and services and presentations and potential markets.

B. Create, prepare and submit to Media User for its prior approval advertising ideas, media suggestions, and other such related programs.

C. Prepare and submit to Media User for its prior approval estimates of costs and expenses associated with proposed advertising ideas and programs prior to any such implementation or financial commitment.

D. Design and prepare, or arrange for the design and preparation of advertisements, public relations, and other such materials.

E. Perform such other services as Media User may request from time to time such as, but not limited to, direct mail ad preparations, speech writing, publicity and public relations work, market research and analysis, and other similar and related activities.

F. Order advertising space, time or other means to be used for publication of Media User's advertisements, at all times endeavoring to secure the most efficient and advantageous rates available. All such activities to be approved in advance by the Media User unless otherwise written and stipulated.

G. Proof for accuracy and completeness of insertions, displays, broadcasts, or other forms of advertisements.

H. Audit invoices for proper and agreed upon space, time, material preparation and charges.

2. <u>Products</u>.

Agency's engagement shall relate to the following products and services of Media User:

_____.

3. Exclusivity.

Agency shall be the Agency in the United States and worldwide for Media User with respect to the products described in Section 2 above, unless otherwise specified in this section:

_____.

4.   Compensation.

A.   Agency shall receive an amount equal to ___ percentage of the gross charges levied by media for advertising placed by Agency pursuant to this Agreement; and   after volume discount, of the charges of suppliers of services or properties, such as finished art, comprehensive layouts, type composition, photostats, engravings, printing, radio and television programs, talent, literary, dramatic and musical works, records and exhibits, purchased by Agency on Media User's authorization during the term of this Agreement; provided that: No percentage will be added to Agency charges for packing, shipping, express, postage, telephone, telex, fax, travel expenses and other out of pocket expenses of Agency personnel.

B.   For those items where Agency is not compensated on a commission basis, Media User shall pay Agency on an hourly basis for services provided hereunder. The rate will be determined by the type of services provided and the person or persons providing such services, but in no event shall the rate exceed _____ per hour. Media User may elect in advance to be charged on this hourly rate basis. If Media User fails to notify Agency of its choice, it shall be presumed that Media User elected to be charged on a percentage basis.

C.   In the event that Agency undertakes, at Media User's request subject to Media User's prior approval, special projects such as those described in Section I.F above, Agency shall prepare an estimate of total charges for any such special project in advance, including any charges for materials or services purchased from outside vendors. In the event that Media User elects to proceed with the special project based upon Agency's estimated cost, Agency shall perform the services with respect to such special project at its estimated cost, subject to modification as mutually agreed by the parties.

D. For any special project or other services provided by Agency pursuant to this Agreement upon which the parties have not agreed as to charges, Media User shall pay
Agency at its regular percentage rates, as stated in Section 4.A above.

E.   Media User shall not be obligated to reimburse Agency for any travel or other out-of-pocket expenses incurred in the performance of services pursuant to this Agreement unless expressly agreed by Media User in advance.

5. Billing.

A.   Agency shall invoice Media User for all media costs where possible in advance of Agency's payment date to allow for prepayment by the Media User so that Media User may receive the benefit of any available prepayment or similar discount. For any media purchase or service for which Agency is not entitled to a commission, Agency shall ensure that the charges to Media User are net of all agency commissions and discounts.

B.   Charges for production materials and services shall be billed by Agency upon completion of the production job or, if cash discounts are available, upon receipt of the supplier's invoice.

C. On all outside purchases other than for media, Agency shall attach to the invoice evidence of the supplier's charges.

D.   All cash discounts on Agency's purchases including, but not limited to, media, art, printing and mechanical work, shall be available to Media User, provided that Media User meets Agency's requisite billing terms and there is no outstanding undisputed indebtedness of Media User to Agency at the time of the payment to the supplier.

E. Rate or billing adjustments shall be credited or charged to Media User on the next regular invoice date or as soon thereafter as otherwise practical.

F. Invoices shall be submitted in an itemized format and shall be paid by Media User within sixty (60) days of the invoice date.

6. Competitors.

During the term of this Agreement, Agency shall not accept employment from, render services to, represent or otherwise be affiliated with any person, firm, corporation or entity in connection with any product or service directly or indirectly competitive with or similar to any product or service of Media User with respect to which the Agency is providing any service pursuant to this Agreement, without the advance approval of the Media User. Media User shall not unreasonably withhold this approval.

7. Cost Estimates.

Agency shall not initiate billable work on any project pursuant to this Agreement without first estimating costs for preparation, including copy, service, layout, art, engraving, typography, processing, paste up and production. After determining the estimated cost, completion of the work shall be subject to Media User's prior approval.

8. Audit Rights.

Agency agrees that following reasonable prior notice any and all contracts, agreements, correspondence, books, accounts and other information relating to Media User's business or this Agreement shall be available for inspection by Media User and Media User's outside accountants, at Media User's expense and during the normal business hours of the Agency.

9. Ownership and Use.

A.   Agency shall insure, to the fullest extent possible under law, that Media User shall own all right, title and interest in and to, including copyrights, trade secret, patent and other intellectual property rights, with respect to any copy, photograph, advertisement, music, lyrics, video, or other work or thing created by Agency or at Agency's direction for Media User pursuant to this Agreement and utilized by Media User.

B.   Upon termination, Media User agrees that any advertising, merchandising, package, plan or idea prepared by Agency and submitted to Media User (whether submitted separately or in conjunction with or as a part of other material) which Media User has elected not to utilize, shall remain the property of Agency, unless Media User has paid Agency for its services in preparing such item. Media User agrees to return to Agency any copy, artwork, plates or other physical embodiment of such creative work relating to any such idea or plan which may be in Media User's possession at termination or expiration of this Agreement. Notwithstanding this, Media User has the unconditional right to pay for any of these materials or activities at the rate agreed upon in this Agreement and thereby these materials and activities would fall under the Section 9.A ownership and use rights accruing to Media User.

C.   Materials and advertisements created by Agency pursuant to this Agreement may be used by Media User outside the United States without additional compensation, provided that Media User shall

be responsible for any additional expense associated with such use, such as charges for translation and amounts due talent.

10. Indemnification and Insurance.

A. Agency shall indemnify and hold Media User harmless with respect to any claims, loss, suit, liability or judgment suffered by Media User, including reasonable attorney's fees and costs, based upon or related to any item prepared by Agency or at Agency's direction, including, but not limited to, any claim of libel, slander, piracy, plagiarism, invasion of privacy, or infringement of copyright or other intellectual property interest, except where any such claim arises out of material supplied by Media User and incorporated into any materials or advertisement prepared by Agency. Agency agrees to procure and maintain in force during the term of this Agreement, at Agency's expense, an Agency liability policy or policies having a minimum limit of at least _____, naming Media User as an additional insured and loss payee under such policy or policies.

B. Media User agrees to indemnify and hold Agency harmless with respect to any claims, loss, liability, damage or judgment suffered by Agency, including reasonable attorney's fees and court costs, which results from the use by Agency of any material furnished by Media User or where material created by Agency or at the direction of Agency subject to the indemnification in subsection A. above is materially changed by Media User. Information or data obtained by Agency from Media User to substantiate claims made in advertising shall be deemed to be "material furnished by Media User to Agency."

C. In the event of any proceeding, litigation or suit against Media User by any regulatory agency or in the event of any court action or other proceeding challenging any advertising prepared by Agency, Agency shall assist in the preparation of the defense of such action or proceeding and cooperate with Media User and Media User's attorneys.

11. Term.

The term of this Agreement shall commence on _____ and shall continue in full force and effect until terminated by either party upon at least sixty (60) days prior written notice, provided that in no event (except breach) may this Agreement be terminated prior to _____. The rights, duties and obligations of the parties shall continue in full force during or following the period of the termination notice until termination, including the ordering and billing of advertising in media whose closing dates follow then such period.

12. Rights Upon Termination.

A. Upon termination of the Agreement, Agency shall transfer, assign and make available to Media User all property and materials in Agency's possession or subject to Agency's control that are the property of Media User, subject to payment in full of amounts due pursuant to this Agreement.

B. Upon termination, Agency agrees to provide reasonable cooperation in arranging for the transfer or approval of third party's interest in all contracts, agreements and other arrangements with advertising media, suppliers, talent and others not then utilized, and all rights and claims thereto and therein, following appropriate release from the obligations therein.

13. Default.

In the event of any default of any material obligation by or owed by a party pursuant to this Agreement, then the other party may provide written notice of such default and if such default is not cured within ten (10) days of the written notice, then the nondefaulting party may terminate this Agreement. In addition, the only damages collectible by Agency shall be the exact amounts due; no other damages,

for any reason whatsoever, may be assessed against Media User including, but limited to, punitive damages and unreasonable termination charges, and any other such claim. This provision shall be broadly interpreted in the favor of the Media User by any Court of competent jurisdiction.

14. <u>Notices</u>.

Any notice required by this Agreement or given in connection with it, shall be in writing and shall be given to the appropriate party by personal delivery or by postage prepaid, or recognized overnight delivery services such as Federal Express.

If to Media User: _____

_____

If to Agency: _____

_____

15. <u>Headings in this Agreement</u>.

The headings in this Agreement are for convenience only, confirm no rights or obligations in either party, and do not alter any terms of this Agreement.

16. <u>Entirety of Agreement</u>.

The terms and conditions set forth herein constitute the entire agreement between the parties and supersede any communications or previous agreements with respect to the subject matter of this Agreement. There are no written or oral understandings directly or indirectly related to this Agreement that are not set forth herein. No change can be made to this Agreement other than in writing and signed by both parties.

17. <u>Governing Law</u>.

This Agreement shall be construed and enforced according to the laws of the State of _____ and any dispute under this Agreement must be brought in this venue and in no other.

In Witness whereof, the parties have executed this Agreement as of the date first written above.

_____ _____
Agency   Media User

Ad or other Media Agency Agreement

This Agency Agreement ("Agreement") is made and effective this _____ (Date), by and between ("Agency") and _____ (Your Firm) ("Media User").

Agency is in the business of providing media agency services for a fee.

Media User desires to engage Agency to render, and Agency desires to render to Media User, certain Agency services, all as set forth.

NOW, THEREFORE, in consideration of the mutual agreements and covenants herein contained, the parties hereto agree as follows:

1. Engagement.

Media User engages Agency to render, and Agency agrees to render to Media User, services in connection with Media User's planning, preparing and placing of advertising and other media services for certain of Media User's products as follows:

_____

A. Analyze Media User's current and proposed products and services and presentations and potential markets.

B. Create, prepare and submit to Media User for its prior approval advertising ideas, media suggestions, and other such related programs.

C. Prepare and submit to Media User for its prior approval estimates of costs and expenses associated with proposed advertising ideas and programs prior to any such implementation or financial commitment.

D. Design and prepare, or arrange for the design and preparation of advertisements, public relations, and other such materials.

E. Perform such other services as Media User may request from time to time such as, but not limited to, direct mail ad preparations, speech writing, publicity and public relations work, market research and analysis, and other similar and related activities.

F. Order advertising space, time or other means to be used for publication of Media User's advertisements, at all times endeavoring to secure the most efficient and advantageous rates available. All such activities to be approved in advance by the Media User unless otherwise written and stipulated.

G. Proof for accuracy and completeness of insertions, displays, broadcasts, or other forms of advertisements.

H. Audit invoices for proper and agreed upon space, time, material preparation and charges.

2. Products.

Agency's engagement shall relate to the following products and services of Media User:

_____.

3. Exclusivity.

Agency shall be the Agency in the United States and worldwide for Media User with respect to the products described in Section 2 above, unless otherwise specified in this section:

_____.

4.   Compensation.

A.   Agency shall receive an amount equal to ___ percentage of the gross charges levied by media for advertising placed by Agency pursuant to this Agreement; and   after volume discount, of the charges of suppliers of services or properties, such as finished art, comprehensive layouts, type composition, photostats, engravings, printing, radio and television programs, talent, literary, dramatic and musical works, records and exhibits, purchased by Agency on Media User's authorization during the term of this Agreement; provided that: No percentage will be added to Agency charges for packing, shipping, express, postage, telephone, telex, fax, travel expenses and other out of pocket expenses of Agency personnel.

B.   For those items where Agency is not compensated on a commission basis, Media User shall pay Agency on an hourly basis for services provided hereunder. The rate will be determined by the type of services provided and the person or persons providing such services, but in no event shall the rate exceed _____ per hour. Media User may elect in advance to be charged on this hourly rate basis. If Media User fails to notify Agency of its choice, it shall be presumed that Media User elected to be charged on a percentage basis.

C.   In the event that Agency undertakes, at Media User's request subject to Media User's prior approval, special projects such as those described in Section I.F above, Agency shall prepare an estimate of total charges for any such special project in advance, including any charges for materials or services purchased from outside vendors. In the event that Media User elects to proceed with the special project based upon Agency's estimated cost, Agency shall perform the services with respect to such special project at its estimated cost, subject to modification as mutually agreed by the parties.

D. For any special project or other services provided by Agency pursuant to this Agreement upon which the parties have not agreed as to charges, Media User shall pay
Agency at its regular percentage rates, as stated in Section 4.A above.

E.   Media User shall not be obligated to reimburse Agency for any travel or other out-of-pocket expenses incurred in the performance of services pursuant to this Agreement unless expressly agreed by Media User in advance.

5. Billing.

A.   Agency shall invoice Media User for all media costs where possible in advance of Agency's payment date to allow for prepayment by the Media User so that Media User may receive the benefit of any available prepayment or similar discount. For any media purchase or service for which Agency is not entitled to a commission, Agency shall ensure that the charges to Media User are net of all agency commissions and discounts.

B.   Charges for production materials and services shall be billed by Agency upon completion of the production job or, if cash discounts are available, upon receipt of the supplier's invoice.

C. On all outside purchases other than for media, Agency shall attach to the invoice evidence of the supplier's charges.

D. All cash discounts on Agency's purchases including, but not limited to, media, art, printing and mechanical work, shall be available to Media User, provided that Media User meets Agency's requisite billing terms and there is no outstanding undisputed indebtedness of Media User to Agency at the time of the payment to the supplier.

E. Rate or billing adjustments shall be credited or charged to Media User on the next regular invoice date or as soon thereafter as otherwise practical.

F. Invoices shall be submitted in an itemized format and shall be paid by Media User within sixty (60) days of the invoice date.

6. <u>Competitors</u>.

During the term of this Agreement, Agency shall not accept employment from, render services to, represent or otherwise be affiliated with any person, firm, corporation or entity in connection with any product or service directly or indirectly competitive with or similar to any product or service of Media User with respect to which the Agency is providing any service pursuant to this Agreement, without the advance approval of the Media User. Media User shall not unreasonably withhold this approval.

7. <u>Cost Estimates</u>.

Agency shall not initiate billable work on any project pursuant to this Agreement without first estimating costs for preparation, including copy, service, layout, art, engraving, typography, processing, paste up and production. After determining the estimated cost, completion of the work shall be subject to Media User's prior approval.

8. <u>Audit Rights</u>.

Agency agrees that following reasonable prior notice any and all contracts, agreements, correspondence, books, accounts and other information relating to Media User's business or this Agreement shall be available for inspection by Media User and Media User's outside accountants, at Media User's expense and during the normal business hours of the Agency.

9. <u>Ownership and Use.</u>

A. Agency shall insure, to the fullest extent possible under law, that Media User shall own all right, title and interest in and to, including copyrights, trade secret, patent and other intellectual property rights, with respect to any copy, photograph, advertisement, music, lyrics, video, or other work or thing created by Agency or at Agency's direction for Media User pursuant to this Agreement and utilized by Media User.

B. Upon termination, Media User agrees that any advertising, merchandising, package, plan or idea prepared by Agency and submitted to Media User (whether submitted separately or in conjunction with or as a part of other material) which Media User has elected not to utilize, shall remain the property of Agency, unless Media User has paid Agency for its services in preparing such item. Media User agrees to return to Agency any copy, artwork, plates or other physical embodiment of such creative work relating to any such idea or plan which may be in Media User's possession at termination or expiration of this Agreement. Notwithstanding this, Media User has the unconditional right to pay for any of these materials or activities at the rate agreed upon in this Agreement and thereby these materials and activities would fall under the Section 9.A ownership and use rights accruing to Media User.

C. Materials and advertisements created by Agency pursuant to this Agreement may be used by Media User outside the United States without additional compensation, provided that Media User shall

be responsible for any additional expense associated with such use, such as charges for translation and amounts due talent.

10. <u>Indemnification and Insurance</u>.

A. Agency shall indemnify and hold Media User harmless with respect to any claims, loss, suit, liability or judgment suffered by Media User, including reasonable attorney's fees and costs, based upon or related to any item prepared by Agency or at Agency's direction, including, but not limited to, any claim of libel, slander, piracy, plagiarism, invasion of privacy, or infringement of copyright or other intellectual property interest, except where any such claim arises out of material supplied by Media User and incorporated into any materials or advertisement prepared by Agency. Agency agrees to procure and maintain in force during the term of this Agreement, at Agency's expense, an Agency liability policy or policies having a minimum limit of at least _____, naming Media User as an additional insured and loss payee under such policy or policies.

B. Media User agrees to indemnify and hold Agency harmless with respect to any claims, loss, liability, damage or judgment suffered by Agency, including reasonable attorney's fees and court costs, which results from the use by Agency of any material furnished by Media User or where material created by Agency or at the direction of Agency subject to the indemnification in subsection A. above is materially changed by Media User. Information or data obtained by Agency from Media User to substantiate claims made in advertising shall be deemed to be "material furnished by Media User to Agency."

C. In the event of any proceeding, litigation or suit against Media User by any regulatory agency or in the event of any court action or other proceeding challenging any advertising prepared by Agency, Agency shall assist in the preparation of the defense of such action or proceeding and cooperate with Media User and Media User's attorneys.

11. <u>Term</u>.

The term of this Agreement shall commence on _____ and shall continue in full force and effect until terminated by either party upon at least sixty (60) days prior written notice, provided that in no event (except breach) may this Agreement be terminated prior to _____. The rights, duties and obligations of the parties shall continue in full force during or following the period of the termination notice until termination, including the ordering and billing of advertising in media whose closing dates follow then such period.

12. <u>Rights Upon Termination</u>.

A. Upon termination of the Agreement, Agency shall transfer, assign and make available to Media User all property and materials in Agency's possession or subject to Agency's control that are the property of Media User, subject to payment in full of amounts due pursuant to this Agreement.

B. Upon termination, Agency agrees to provide reasonable cooperation in arranging for the transfer or approval of third party's interest in all contracts, agreements and other arrangements with advertising media, suppliers, talent and others not then utilized, and all rights and claims thereto and therein, following appropriate release from the obligations therein.

13. <u>Default</u>.

In the event of any default of any material obligation by or owed by a party pursuant to this Agreement, then the other party may provide written notice of such default and if such default is not cured within ten (10) days of the written notice, then the nondefaulting party may terminate this Agreement. In addition, the only damages collectible by Agency shall be the exact amounts due; no other damages,

for any reason whatsoever, may be assessed against Media User including, but limited to, punitive damages and unreasonable termination charges, and any other such claim. This provision shall be broadly interpreted in the favor of the Media User by any Court of competent jurisdiction.

14. Notices.

Any notice required by this Agreement or given in connection with it, shall be in writing and shall be given to the appropriate party by personal delivery or by postage prepaid, or recognized overnight delivery services such as Federal Express.

If to Media User: _____

_____

If to Agency: _____

_____

15. Headings in this Agreement.

The headings in this Agreement are for convenience only, confirm no rights or obligations in either party, and do not alter any terms of this Agreement.

16. Entirety of Agreement.

The terms and conditions set forth herein constitute the entire agreement between the parties and supersede any communications or previous agreements with respect to the subject matter of this Agreement. There are no written or oral understandings directly or indirectly related to this Agreement that are not set forth herein. No change can be made to this Agreement other than in writing and signed by both parties.

17. Governing Law.

This Agreement shall be construed and enforced according to the laws of the State of _____ and any dispute under this Agreement must be brought in this venue and in no other.

In Witness whereof, the parties have executed this Agreement as of the date first written above.

_____   _____
Agency   Media User

Ad or other Media Agency Agreement

This Agency Agreement ("Agreement") is made and effective this _____ (Date), by and between ("Agency") and _____ (Your Firm) ("Media User").

Agency is in the business of providing media agency services for a fee.

Media User desires to engage Agency to render, and Agency desires to render to Media User, certain Agency services, all as set forth.

NOW, THEREFORE, in consideration of the mutual agreements and covenants herein contained, the parties hereto agree as follows:

1. Engagement.

Media User engages Agency to render, and Agency agrees to render to Media User, services in connection with Media User's planning, preparing and placing of advertising and other media services for certain of Media User's products as follows:

_____

A. Analyze Media User's current and proposed products and services and presentations and potential markets.

B. Create, prepare and submit to Media User for its prior approval advertising ideas, media suggestions, and other such related programs.

C. Prepare and submit to Media User for its prior approval estimates of costs and expenses associated with proposed advertising ideas and programs prior to any such implementation or financial commitment.

D. Design and prepare, or arrange for the design and preparation of advertisements, public relations, and other such materials.

E. Perform such other services as Media User may request from time to time such as, but not limited to, direct mail ad preparations, speech writing, publicity and public relations work, market research and analysis, and other similar and related activities.

F. Order advertising space, time or other means to be used for publication of Media User's advertisements, at all times endeavoring to secure the most efficient and advantageous rates available. All such activities to be approved in advance by the Media User unless otherwise written and stipulated.

G. Proof for accuracy and completeness of insertions, displays, broadcasts, or other forms of advertisements.

H. Audit invoices for proper and agreed upon space, time, material preparation and charges.

2. Products.

Agency's engagement shall relate to the following products and services of Media User:

_____.

3. Exclusivity.

Agency shall be the Agency in the United States and worldwide for Media User with respect to the products described in Section 2 above, unless otherwise specified in this section:

_____.

4. Compensation.

A.   Agency shall receive an amount equal to ___ percentage of the gross charges levied by media for advertising placed by Agency pursuant to this Agreement; and   after volume discount, of the charges of suppliers of services or properties, such as finished art, comprehensive layouts, type composition, photostats, engravings, printing, radio and television programs, talent, literary, dramatic and musical works, records and exhibits, purchased by Agency on Media User's authorization during the term of this Agreement; provided that: No percentage will be added to Agency charges for packing, shipping, express, postage, telephone, telex, fax, travel expenses and other out of pocket expenses of Agency personnel.

B.   For those items where Agency is not compensated on a commission basis, Media User shall pay Agency on an hourly basis for services provided hereunder. The rate will be determined by the type of services provided and the person or persons providing such services, but in no event shall the rate exceed _____ per hour. Media User may elect in advance to be charged on this hourly rate basis. If Media User fails to notify Agency of its choice, it shall be presumed that Media User elected to be charged on a percentage basis.

C.   In the event that Agency undertakes, at Media User's request subject to Media User's prior approval, special projects such as those described in Section I.F above, Agency shall prepare an estimate of total charges for any such special project in advance, including any charges for materials or services purchased from outside vendors. In the event that Media User elects to proceed with the special project based upon Agency's estimated cost, Agency shall perform the services with respect to such special project at its estimated cost, subject to modification as mutually agreed by the parties.

D. For any special project or other services provided by Agency pursuant to this Agreement upon which the parties have not agreed as to charges, Media User shall pay
Agency at its regular percentage rates, as stated in Section 4.A above.

E.   Media User shall not be obligated to reimburse Agency for any travel or other out-of-pocket expenses incurred in the performance of services pursuant to this Agreement unless expressly agreed by Media User in advance.

5. Billing.

A.   Agency shall invoice Media User for all media costs where possible in advance of Agency's payment date to allow for prepayment by the Media User so that Media User may receive the benefit of any available prepayment or similar discount. For any media purchase or service for which Agency is not entitled to a commission, Agency shall ensure that the charges to Media User are net of all agency commissions and discounts.

B.   Charges for production materials and services shall be billed by Agency upon completion of the production job or, if cash discounts are available, upon receipt of the supplier's invoice.

C. On all outside purchases other than for media, Agency shall attach to the invoice evidence of the supplier's charges.

D. All cash discounts on Agency's purchases including, but not limited to, media, art, printing and mechanical work, shall be available to Media User, provided that Media User meets Agency's requisite billing terms and there is no outstanding undisputed indebtedness of Media User to Agency at the time of the payment to the supplier.

E. Rate or billing adjustments shall be credited or charged to Media User on the next regular invoice date or as soon thereafter as otherwise practical.

F. Invoices shall be submitted in an itemized format and shall be paid by Media User within sixty (60) days of the invoice date.

6. Competitors.

During the term of this Agreement, Agency shall not accept employment from, render services to, represent or otherwise be affiliated with any person, firm, corporation or entity in connection with any product or service directly or indirectly competitive with or similar to any product or service of Media User with respect to which the Agency is providing any service pursuant to this Agreement, without the advance approval of the Media User. Media User shall not unreasonably withhold this approval.

7. Cost Estimates.

Agency shall not initiate billable work on any project pursuant to this Agreement without first estimating costs for preparation, including copy, service, layout, art, engraving, typography, processing, paste up and production. After determining the estimated cost, completion of the work shall be subject to Media User's prior approval.

8. Audit Rights.

Agency agrees that following reasonable prior notice any and all contracts, agreements, correspondence, books, accounts and other information relating to Media User's business or this Agreement shall be available for inspection by Media User and Media User's outside accountants, at Media User's expense and during the normal business hours of the Agency.

9. Ownership and Use.

A. Agency shall insure, to the fullest extent possible under law, that Media User shall own all right, title and interest in and to, including copyrights, trade secret, patent and other intellectual property rights, with respect to any copy, photograph, advertisement, music, lyrics, video, or other work or thing created by Agency or at Agency's direction for Media User pursuant to this Agreement and utilized by Media User.

B. Upon termination, Media User agrees that any advertising, merchandising, package, plan or idea prepared by Agency and submitted to Media User (whether submitted separately or in conjunction with or as a part of other material) which Media User has elected not to utilize, shall remain the property of Agency, unless Media User has paid Agency for its services in preparing such item. Media User agrees to return to Agency any copy, artwork, plates or other physical embodiment of such creative work relating to any such idea or plan which may be in Media User's possession at termination or expiration of this Agreement. Notwithstanding this, Media User has the unconditional right to pay for any of these materials or activities at the rate agreed upon in this Agreement and thereby these materials and activities would fall under the Section 9.A ownership and use rights accruing to Media User.

C. Materials and advertisements created by Agency pursuant to this Agreement may be used by Media User outside the United States without additional compensation, provided that Media User shall

be responsible for any additional expense associated with such use, such as charges for translation and amounts due talent.

10. Indemnification and Insurance.

A. Agency shall indemnify and hold Media User harmless with respect to any claims, loss, suit, liability or judgment suffered by Media User, including reasonable attorney's fees and costs, based upon or related to any item prepared by Agency or at Agency's direction, including, but not limited to, any claim of libel, slander, piracy, plagiarism, invasion of privacy, or infringement of copyright or other intellectual property interest, except where any such claim arises out of material supplied by Media User and incorporated into any materials or advertisement prepared by Agency. Agency agrees to procure and maintain in force during the term of this Agreement, at Agency's expense, an Agency liability policy or policies having a minimum limit of at least _____, naming Media User as an additional insured and loss payee under such policy or policies.

B. Media User agrees to indemnify and hold Agency harmless with respect to any claims, loss, liability, damage or judgment suffered by Agency, including reasonable attorney's fees and court costs, which results from the use by Agency of any material furnished by Media User or where material created by Agency or at the direction of Agency subject to the indemnification in subsection A. above is materially changed by Media User. Information or data obtained by Agency from Media User to substantiate claims made in advertising shall be deemed to be "material furnished by Media User to Agency."

C. In the event of any proceeding, litigation or suit against Media User by any regulatory agency or in the event of any court action or other proceeding challenging any advertising prepared by Agency, Agency shall assist in the preparation of the defense of such action or proceeding and cooperate with Media User and Media User's attorneys.

11. Term.

The term of this Agreement shall commence on _____ and shall continue in full force and effect until terminated by either party upon at least sixty (60) days prior written notice, provided that in no event (except breach) may this Agreement be terminated prior to _____. The rights, duties and obligations of the parties shall continue in full force during or following the period of the termination notice until termination, including the ordering and billing of advertising in media whose closing dates follow then such period.

12. Rights Upon Termination.

A. Upon termination of the Agreement, Agency shall transfer, assign and make available to Media User all property and materials in Agency's possession or subject to Agency's control that are the property of Media User, subject to payment in full of amounts due pursuant to this Agreement.

B. Upon termination, Agency agrees to provide reasonable cooperation in arranging for the transfer or approval of third party's interest in all contracts, agreements and other arrangements with advertising media, suppliers, talent and others not then utilized, and all rights and claims thereto and therein, following appropriate release from the obligations therein.

13. Default.

In the event of any default of any material obligation by or owed by a party pursuant to this Agreement, then the other party may provide written notice of such default and if such default is not cured within ten (10) days of the written notice, then the nondefaulting party may terminate this Agreement. In addition, the only damages collectible by Agency shall be the exact amounts due; no other damages,

for any reason whatsoever, may be assessed against Media User including, but limited to, punitive damages and unreasonable termination charges, and any other such claim. This provision shall be broadly interpreted in the favor of the Media User by any Court of competent jurisdiction.

14. <u>Notices</u>.

Any notice required by this Agreement or given in connection with it, shall be in writing and shall be given to the appropriate party by personal delivery or by postage prepaid, or recognized overnight delivery services such as Federal Express.

If to Media User: _____

_____

If to Agency: _____

_____

15. <u>Headings in this Agreement</u>.

The headings in this Agreement are for convenience only, confirm no rights or obligations in either party, and do not alter any terms of this Agreement.

16. <u>Entirety of Agreement</u>.

The terms and conditions set forth herein constitute the entire agreement between the parties and supersede any communications or previous agreements with respect to the subject matter of this Agreement. There are no written or oral understandings directly or indirectly related to this Agreement that are not set forth herein. No change can be made to this Agreement other than in writing and signed by both parties.

17. <u>Governing Law</u>.

This Agreement shall be construed and enforced according to the laws of the State of _____ and any dispute under this Agreement must be brought in this venue and in no other.

In Witness whereof, the parties have executed this Agreement as of the date first written above.

_____   _____
Agency   Media User

Ad or other Media Agency Agreement

This Agency Agreement ("Agreement") is made and effective this _____ (Date), by and between ("Agency") and _____ (Your Firm) ("Media User").

Agency is in the business of providing media agency services for a fee.

Media User desires to engage Agency to render, and Agency desires to render to Media User, certain Agency services, all as set forth.

NOW, THEREFORE, in consideration of the mutual agreements and covenants herein contained, the parties hereto agree as follows:

1. Engagement.

Media User engages Agency to render, and Agency agrees to render to Media User, services in connection with Media User's planning, preparing and placing of advertising and other media services for certain of Media User's products as follows:

_____

A. Analyze Media User's current and proposed products and services and presentations and potential markets.

B. Create, prepare and submit to Media User for its prior approval advertising ideas, media suggestions, and other such related programs.

C. Prepare and submit to Media User for its prior approval estimates of costs and expenses associated with proposed advertising ideas and programs prior to any such implementation or financial commitment.

D. Design and prepare, or arrange for the design and preparation of advertisements, public relations, and other such materials.

E. Perform such other services as Media User may request from time to time such as, but not limited to, direct mail ad preparations, speech writing, publicity and public relations work, market research and analysis, and other similar and related activities.

F. Order advertising space, time or other means to be used for publication of Media User's advertisements, at all times endeavoring to secure the most efficient and advantageous rates available. All such activities to be approved in advance by the Media User unless otherwise written and stipulated.

G. Proof for accuracy and completeness of insertions, displays, broadcasts, or other forms of advertisements.

H. Audit invoices for proper and agreed upon space, time, material preparation and charges.

2. Products.

Agency's engagement shall relate to the following products and services of Media User:

_____.

3. <u>Exclusivity</u>.

Agency shall be the Agency in the United States and worldwide for Media User with respect to the products described in Section 2 above, unless otherwise specified in this section:

_____.

4.	Compensation.

A.	Agency shall receive an amount equal to ___ percentage of the gross charges levied by media for advertising placed by Agency pursuant to this Agreement; and _____ after volume discount, of the charges of suppliers of services or properties, such as finished art, comprehensive layouts, type composition, photostats, engravings, printing, radio and television programs, talent, literary, dramatic and musical works, records and exhibits, purchased by Agency on Media User's authorization during the term of this Agreement; provided that: No percentage will be added to Agency charges for packing, shipping, express, postage, telephone, telex, fax, travel expenses and other out of pocket expenses of Agency personnel.

B.	For those items where Agency is not compensated on a commission basis, Media User shall pay Agency on an hourly basis for services provided hereunder. The rate will be determined by the type of services provided and the person or persons providing such services, but in no event shall the rate exceed _____ per hour. Media User may elect in advance to be charged on this hourly rate basis. If Media User fails to notify Agency of its choice, it shall be presumed that Media User elected to be charged on a percentage basis.

C.	In the event that Agency undertakes, at Media User's request subject to Media User's prior approval, special projects such as those described in Section I.F above, Agency shall prepare an estimate of total charges for any such special project in advance, including any charges for materials or services purchased from outside vendors. In the event that Media User elects to proceed with the special project based upon Agency's estimated cost, Agency shall perform the services with respect to such special project at its estimated cost, subject to modification as mutually agreed by the parties.

D. For any special project or other services provided by Agency pursuant to this Agreement upon which the parties have not agreed as to charges, Media User shall pay
Agency at its regular percentage rates, as stated in Section 4.A above.

E.	Media User shall not be obligated to reimburse Agency for any travel or other out-of-pocket expenses incurred in the performance of services pursuant to this Agreement unless expressly agreed by Media User in advance.

5. <u>Billing</u>.

A.	Agency shall invoice Media User for all media costs where possible in advance of Agency's payment date to allow for prepayment by the Media User so that Media User may receive the benefit of any available prepayment or similar discount. For any media purchase or service for which Agency is not entitled to a commission, Agency shall ensure that the charges to Media User are net of all agency commissions and discounts.

B.	Charges for production materials and services shall be billed by Agency upon completion of the production job or, if cash discounts are available, upon receipt of the supplier's invoice.

C. On all outside purchases other than for media, Agency shall attach to the invoice evidence of the supplier's charges.

D. All cash discounts on Agency's purchases including, but not limited to, media, art, printing and mechanical work, shall be available to Media User, provided that Media User meets Agency's requisite billing terms and there is no outstanding undisputed indebtedness of Media User to Agency at the time of the payment to the supplier.

E. Rate or billing adjustments shall be credited or charged to Media User on the next regular invoice date or as soon thereafter as otherwise practical.

F. Invoices shall be submitted in an itemized format and shall be paid by Media User within sixty (60) days of the invoice date.

6. Competitors.

During the term of this Agreement, Agency shall not accept employment from, render services to, represent or otherwise be affiliated with any person, firm, corporation or entity in connection with any product or service directly or indirectly competitive with or similar to any product or service of Media User with respect to which the Agency is providing any service pursuant to this Agreement, without the advance approval of the Media User. Media User shall not unreasonably withhold this approval.

7. Cost Estimates.

Agency shall not initiate billable work on any project pursuant to this Agreement without first estimating costs for preparation, including copy, service, layout, art, engraving, typography, processing, paste up and production. After determining the estimated cost, completion of the work shall be subject to Media User's prior approval.

8. Audit Rights.

Agency agrees that following reasonable prior notice any and all contracts, agreements, correspondence, books, accounts and other information relating to Media User's business or this Agreement shall be available for inspection by Media User and Media User's outside accountants, at Media User's expense and during the normal business hours of the Agency.

9. Ownership and Use.

A. Agency shall insure, to the fullest extent possible under law, that Media User shall own all right, title and interest in and to, including copyrights, trade secret, patent and other intellectual property rights, with respect to any copy, photograph, advertisement, music, lyrics, video, or other work or thing created by Agency or at Agency's direction for Media User pursuant to this Agreement and utilized by Media User.

B. Upon termination, Media User agrees that any advertising, merchandising, package, plan or idea prepared by Agency and submitted to Media User (whether submitted separately or in conjunction with or as a part of other material) which Media User has elected not to utilize, shall remain the property of Agency, unless Media User has paid Agency for its services in preparing such item. Media User agrees to return to Agency any copy, artwork, plates or other physical embodiment of such creative work relating to any such idea or plan which may be in Media User's possession at termination or expiration of this Agreement. Notwithstanding this, Media User has the unconditional right to pay for any of these materials or activities at the rate agreed upon in this Agreement and thereby these materials and activities would fall under the Section 9.A ownership and use rights accruing to Media User.

C. Materials and advertisements created by Agency pursuant to this Agreement may be used by Media User outside the United States without additional compensation, provided that Media User shall

be responsible for any additional expense associated with such use, such as charges for translation and amounts due talent.

10. Indemnification and Insurance.

A. Agency shall indemnify and hold Media User harmless with respect to any claims, loss, suit, liability or judgment suffered by Media User, including reasonable attorney's fees and costs, based upon or related to any item prepared by Agency or at Agency's direction, including, but not limited to, any claim of libel, slander, piracy, plagiarism, invasion of privacy, or infringement of copyright or other intellectual property interest, except where any such claim arises out of material supplied by Media User and incorporated into any materials or advertisement prepared by Agency. Agency agrees to procure and maintain in force during the term of this Agreement, at Agency's expense, an Agency liability policy or policies having a minimum limit of at least _____, naming Media User as an additional insured and loss payee under such policy or policies.

B. Media User agrees to indemnify and hold Agency harmless with respect to any claims, loss, liability, damage or judgment suffered by Agency, including reasonable attorney's fees and court costs, which results from the use by Agency of any material furnished by Media User or where material created by Agency or at the direction of Agency subject to the indemnification in subsection A. above is materially changed by Media User. Information or data obtained by Agency from Media User to substantiate claims made in advertising shall be deemed to be "material furnished by Media User to Agency."

C. In the event of any proceeding, litigation or suit against Media User by any regulatory agency or in the event of any court action or other proceeding challenging any advertising prepared by Agency, Agency shall assist in the preparation of the defense of such action or proceeding and cooperate with Media User and Media User's attorneys.

11. Term.

The term of this Agreement shall commence on _____ and shall continue in full force and effect until terminated by either party upon at least sixty (60) days prior written notice, provided that in no event (except breach) may this Agreement be terminated prior to _____. The rights, duties and obligations of the parties shall continue in full force during or following the period of the termination notice until termination, including the ordering and billing of advertising in media whose closing dates follow then such period.

12. Rights Upon Termination.

A. Upon termination of the Agreement, Agency shall transfer, assign and make available to Media User all property and materials in Agency's possession or subject to Agency's control that are the property of Media User, subject to payment in full of amounts due pursuant to this Agreement.

B. Upon termination, Agency agrees to provide reasonable cooperation in arranging for the transfer or approval of third party's interest in all contracts, agreements and other arrangements with advertising media, suppliers, talent and others not then utilized, and all rights and claims thereto and therein, following appropriate release from the obligations therein.

13. Default.

In the event of any default of any material obligation by or owed by a party pursuant to this Agreement, then the other party may provide written notice of such default and if such default is not cured within ten (10) days of the written notice, then the nondefaulting party may terminate this Agreement. In addition, the only damages collectible by Agency shall be the exact amounts due; no other damages,

for any reason whatsoever, may be assessed against Media User including, but limited to, punitive damages and unreasonable termination charges, and any other such claim. This provision shall be broadly interpreted in the favor of the Media User by any Court of competent jurisdiction.

14. Notices.

Any notice required by this Agreement or given in connection with it, shall be in writing and shall be given to the appropriate party by personal delivery or by postage prepaid, or recognized overnight delivery services such as Federal Express.

If to Media User: _____

_____

If to Agency: _____

_____

15. Headings in this Agreement.

The headings in this Agreement are for convenience only, confirm no rights or obligations in either party, and do not alter any terms of this Agreement.

16. Entirety of Agreement.

The terms and conditions set forth herein constitute the entire agreement between the parties and supersede any communications or previous agreements with respect to the subject matter of this Agreement. There are no written or oral understandings directly or indirectly related to this Agreement that are not set forth herein. No change can be made to this Agreement other than in writing and signed by both parties.

17. Governing Law.

This Agreement shall be construed and enforced according to the laws of the State of _____ and any dispute under this Agreement must be brought in this venue and in no other.

In Witness whereof, the parties have executed this Agreement as of the date first written above.

_____ _____
Agency   Media User

Ad or other Media Agency Agreement

This Agency Agreement ("Agreement") is made and effective this _____ (Date), by and between ("Agency") and _____ (Your Firm) ("Media User").

Agency is in the business of providing media agency services for a fee.

Media User desires to engage Agency to render, and Agency desires to render to Media User, certain Agency services, all as set forth.

NOW, THEREFORE, in consideration of the mutual agreements and covenants herein contained, the parties hereto agree as follows:

1. <u>Engagement</u>.

Media User engages Agency to render, and Agency agrees to render to Media User, services in connection with Media User's planning, preparing and placing of advertising and other media services for certain of Media User's products as follows:

_____

A. Analyze Media User's current and proposed products and services and presentations and potential markets.

B. Create, prepare and submit to Media User for its prior approval advertising ideas, media suggestions, and other such related programs.

C. Prepare and submit to Media User for its prior approval estimates of costs and expenses associated with proposed advertising ideas and programs prior to any such implementation or financial commitment.

D. Design and prepare, or arrange for the design and preparation of advertisements, public relations, and other such materials.

E. Perform such other services as Media User may request from time to time such as, but not limited to, direct mail ad preparations, speech writing, publicity and public relations work, market research and analysis, and other similar and related activities.

F. Order advertising space, time or other means to be used for publication of Media User's advertisements, at all times endeavoring to secure the most efficient and advantageous rates available. All such activities to be approved in advance by the Media User unless otherwise written and stipulated.

G. Proof for accuracy and completeness of insertions, displays, broadcasts, or other forms of advertisements.

H. Audit invoices for proper and agreed upon space, time, material preparation and charges.

2. <u>Products</u>.

Agency's engagement shall relate to the following products and services of Media User:

_____.

3. Exclusivity.

Agency shall be the Agency in the United States and worldwide for Media User with respect to the products described in Section 2 above, unless otherwise specified in this section:

_____.

4.   Compensation.

A.   Agency shall receive an amount equal to ___ percentage of the gross charges levied by media for advertising placed by Agency pursuant to this Agreement; and   after volume discount, of the charges of suppliers of services or properties, such as finished art, comprehensive layouts, type composition, photostats, engravings, printing, radio and television programs, talent, literary, dramatic and musical works, records and exhibits, purchased by Agency on Media User's authorization during the term of this Agreement; provided that: No percentage will be added to Agency charges for packing, shipping, express, postage, telephone, telex, fax, travel expenses and other out of pocket expenses of Agency personnel.

B.   For those items where Agency is not compensated on a commission basis, Media User shall pay Agency on an hourly basis for services provided hereunder. The rate will be determined by the type of services provided and the person or persons providing such services, but in no event shall the rate exceed _____ per hour. Media User may elect in advance to be charged on this hourly rate basis. If Media User fails to notify Agency of its choice, it shall be presumed that Media User elected to be charged on a percentage basis.

C.   In the event that Agency undertakes, at Media User's request subject to Media User's prior approval, special projects such as those described in Section I.F above, Agency shall prepare an estimate of total charges for any such special project in advance, including any charges for materials or services purchased from outside vendors. In the event that Media User elects to proceed with the special project based upon Agency's estimated cost, Agency shall perform the services with respect to such special project at its estimated cost, subject to modification as mutually agreed by the parties.

D. For any special project or other services provided by Agency pursuant to this Agreement upon which the parties have not agreed as to charges, Media User shall pay
Agency at its regular percentage rates, as stated in Section 4.A above.

E.   Media User shall not be obligated to reimburse Agency for any travel or other out-of-pocket expenses incurred in the performance of services pursuant to this Agreement unless expressly agreed by Media User in advance.

5. Billing.

A.   Agency shall invoice Media User for all media costs where possible in advance of Agency's payment date to allow for prepayment by the Media User so that Media User may receive the benefit of any available prepayment or similar discount. For any media purchase or service for which Agency is not entitled to a commission, Agency shall ensure that the charges to Media User are net of all agency commissions and discounts.

B.   Charges for production materials and services shall be billed by Agency upon completion of the production job or, if cash discounts are available, upon receipt of the supplier's invoice.

C. On all outside purchases other than for media, Agency shall attach to the invoice evidence of the supplier's charges.

D.   All cash discounts on Agency's purchases including, but not limited to, media, art, printing and mechanical work, shall be available to Media User, provided that Media User meets Agency's requisite billing terms and there is no outstanding undisputed indebtedness of Media User to Agency at the time of the payment to the supplier.

E. Rate or billing adjustments shall be credited or charged to Media User on the next regular invoice date or as soon thereafter as otherwise practical.

F. Invoices shall be submitted in an itemized format and shall be paid by Media User within sixty (60) days of the invoice date.

6. Competitors.

During the term of this Agreement, Agency shall not accept employment from, render services to, represent or otherwise be affiliated with any person, firm, corporation or entity in connection with any product or service directly or indirectly competitive with or similar to any product or service of Media User with respect to which the Agency is providing any service pursuant to this Agreement, without the advance approval of the Media User. Media User shall not unreasonably withhold this approval.

7. Cost Estimates.

Agency shall not initiate billable work on any project pursuant to this Agreement without first estimating costs for preparation, including copy, service, layout, art, engraving, typography, processing, paste up and production. After determining the estimated cost, completion of the work shall be subject to Media User's prior approval.

8. Audit Rights.

Agency agrees that following reasonable prior notice any and all contracts, agreements, correspondence, books, accounts and other information relating to Media User's business or this Agreement shall be available for inspection by Media User and Media User's outside accountants, at Media User's expense and during the normal business hours of the Agency.

9. Ownership and Use.

A.   Agency shall insure, to the fullest extent possible under law, that Media User shall own all right, title and interest in and to, including copyrights, trade secret, patent and other intellectual property rights, with respect to any copy, photograph, advertisement, music, lyrics, video, or other work or thing created by Agency or at Agency's direction for Media User pursuant to this Agreement and utilized by Media User.

B.   Upon termination, Media User agrees that any advertising, merchandising, package, plan or idea prepared by Agency and submitted to Media User (whether submitted separately or in conjunction with or as a part of other material) which Media User has elected not to utilize, shall remain the property of Agency, unless Media User has paid Agency for its services in preparing such item. Media User agrees to return to Agency any copy, artwork, plates or other physical embodiment of such creative work relating to any such idea or plan which may be in Media User's possession at termination or expiration of this Agreement. Notwithstanding this, Media User has the unconditional right to pay for any of these materials or activities at the rate agreed upon in this Agreement and thereby these materials and activities would fall under the Section 9.A ownership and use rights accruing to Media User.

C.   Materials and advertisements created by Agency pursuant to this Agreement may be used by Media User outside the United States without additional compensation, provided that Media User shall

be responsible for any additional expense associated with such use, such as charges for translation and amounts due talent.

10. Indemnification and Insurance.

A.   Agency shall indemnify and hold Media User harmless with respect to any claims, loss, suit, liability or judgment suffered by Media User, including reasonable attorney's fees and costs, based upon or related to any item prepared by Agency or at Agency's direction, including, but not limited to, any claim of libel, slander, piracy, plagiarism, invasion of privacy, or infringement of copyright or other intellectual property interest, except where any such claim arises out of material supplied by Media User and incorporated into any materials or advertisement prepared by Agency. Agency agrees to procure and maintain in force during the term of this Agreement, at Agency's expense, an Agency liability policy or policies having a minimum limit of at least _____, naming Media User as an additional insured and loss payee under such policy or policies.

B.   Media User agrees to indemnify and hold Agency harmless with respect to any claims, loss, liability, damage or judgment suffered by Agency, including reasonable attorney's fees and court costs, which results from the use by Agency of any material furnished by Media User or where material created by Agency or at the direction of Agency subject to the indemnification in subsection A. above is materially changed by Media User. Information or data obtained by Agency from Media User to substantiate claims made in advertising shall be deemed to be "material furnished by Media User to Agency."

C.   In the event of any proceeding, litigation or suit against Media User by any regulatory agency or in the event of any court action or other proceeding challenging any advertising prepared by Agency, Agency shall assist in the preparation of the defense of such action or proceeding and cooperate with Media User and Media User's attorneys.

11. Term.

The term of this Agreement shall commence on _____ and shall continue in full force and effect until terminated by either party upon at least sixty (60) days prior written notice, provided that in no event (except breach) may this Agreement be terminated prior to _____. The rights, duties and obligations of the parties shall continue in full force during or following the period of the termination notice until termination, including the ordering and billing of advertising in media whose closing dates follow then such period.

12. Rights Upon Termination.

A.   Upon termination of the Agreement, Agency shall transfer, assign and make available to Media User all property and materials in Agency's possession or subject to Agency's control that are the property of Media User, subject to payment in full of amounts due pursuant to this Agreement.

B.   Upon termination, Agency agrees to provide reasonable cooperation in arranging for the transfer or approval of third party's interest in all contracts, agreements and other arrangements with advertising media, suppliers, talent and others not then utilized, and all rights and claims thereto and therein, following appropriate release from the obligations therein.

13. Default.

In the event of any default of any material obligation by or owed by a party pursuant to this Agreement, then the other party may provide written notice of such default and if such default is not cured within ten (10) days of the written notice, then the nondefaulting party may terminate this Agreement. In addition, the only damages collectible by Agency shall be the exact amounts due; no other damages,

for any reason whatsoever, may be assessed against Media User including, but limited to, punitive damages and unreasonable termination charges, and any other such claim. This provision shall be broadly interpreted in the favor of the Media User by any Court of competent jurisdiction.

14. Notices.

Any notice required by this Agreement or given in connection with it, shall be in writing and shall be given to the appropriate party by personal delivery or by postage prepaid, or recognized overnight delivery services such as Federal Express.

If to Media User: _____

                         _____

If to Agency: _____

                         _____

15. Headings in this Agreement.

The headings in this Agreement are for convenience only, confirm no rights or obligations in either party, and do not alter any terms of this Agreement.

16. Entirety of Agreement.

The terms and conditions set forth herein constitute the entire agreement between the parties and supersede any communications or previous agreements with respect to the subject matter of this Agreement. There are no written or oral understandings directly or indirectly related to this Agreement that are not set forth herein. No change can be made to this Agreement other than in writing and signed by both parties.

17. Governing Law.

This Agreement shall be construed and enforced according to the laws of the State of _____ and any dispute under this Agreement must be brought in this venue and in no other.

In Witness whereof, the parties have executed this Agreement as of the date first written above.

_____   _____
Agency   Media User

Ad or other Media Agency Agreement

This Agency Agreement ("Agreement") is made and effective this _____ (Date), by and between ("Agency") and _____ (Your Firm) ("Media User").

Agency is in the business of providing media agency services for a fee.

Media User desires to engage Agency to render, and Agency desires to render to Media User, certain Agency services, all as set forth.

NOW, THEREFORE, in consideration of the mutual agreements and covenants herein contained, the parties hereto agree as follows:

1. <u>Engagement</u>.

Media User engages Agency to render, and Agency agrees to render to Media User, services in connection with Media User's planning, preparing and placing of advertising and other media services for certain of Media User's products as follows:

_____

A. Analyze Media User's current and proposed products and services and presentations and potential markets.

B. Create, prepare and submit to Media User for its prior approval advertising ideas, media suggestions, and other such related programs.

C. Prepare and submit to Media User for its prior approval estimates of costs and expenses associated with proposed advertising ideas and programs prior to any such implementation or financial commitment.

D. Design and prepare, or arrange for the design and preparation of advertisements, public relations, and other such materials.

E. Perform such other services as Media User may request from time to time such as, but not limited to, direct mail ad preparations, speech writing, publicity and public relations work, market research and analysis, and other similar and related activities.

F. Order advertising space, time or other means to be used for publication of Media User's advertisements, at all times endeavoring to secure the most efficient and advantageous rates available. All such activities to be approved in advance by the Media User unless otherwise written and stipulated.

G. Proof for accuracy and completeness of insertions, displays, broadcasts, or other forms of advertisements.

H. Audit invoices for proper and agreed upon space, time, material preparation and charges.

2. <u>Products</u>.

Agency's engagement shall relate to the following products and services of Media User:

_____.

3. Exclusivity.

Agency shall be the Agency in the United States and worldwide for Media User with respect to the products described in Section 2 above, unless otherwise specified in this section:

_____.

4.   Compensation.

A.   Agency shall receive an amount equal to ___ percentage of the gross charges levied by media for advertising placed by Agency pursuant to this Agreement; and   after volume discount, of the charges of suppliers of services or properties, such as finished art, comprehensive layouts, type composition, photostats, engravings, printing, radio and television programs, talent, literary, dramatic and musical works, records and exhibits, purchased by Agency on Media User's authorization during the term of this Agreement; provided that: No percentage will be added to Agency charges for packing, shipping, express, postage, telephone, telex, fax, travel expenses and other out of pocket expenses of Agency personnel.

B.   For those items where Agency is not compensated on a commission basis, Media User shall pay Agency on an hourly basis for services provided hereunder. The rate will be determined by the type of services provided and the person or persons providing such services, but in no event shall the rate exceed _____ per hour. Media User may elect in advance to be charged on this hourly rate basis. If Media User fails to notify Agency of its choice, it shall be presumed that Media User elected to be charged on a percentage basis.

C.   In the event that Agency undertakes, at Media User's request subject to Media User's prior approval, special projects such as those described in Section I.F above, Agency shall prepare an estimate of total charges for any such special project in advance, including any charges for materials or services purchased from outside vendors. In the event that Media User elects to proceed with the special project based upon Agency's estimated cost, Agency shall perform the services with respect to such special project at its estimated cost, subject to modification as mutually agreed by the parties.

D. For any special project or other services provided by Agency pursuant to this Agreement upon which the parties have not agreed as to charges, Media User shall pay
Agency at its regular percentage rates, as stated in Section 4.A above.

E.   Media User shall not be obligated to reimburse Agency for any travel or other out-of-pocket expenses incurred in the performance of services pursuant to this Agreement unless expressly agreed by Media User in advance.

5. Billing.

A.   Agency shall invoice Media User for all media costs where possible in advance of Agency's payment date to allow for prepayment by the Media User so that Media User may receive the benefit of any available prepayment or similar discount. For any media purchase or service for which Agency is not entitled to a commission, Agency shall ensure that the charges to Media User are net of all agency commissions and discounts.

B.   Charges for production materials and services shall be billed by Agency upon completion of the production job or, if cash discounts are available, upon receipt of the supplier's invoice.

C. On all outside purchases other than for media, Agency shall attach to the invoice evidence of the supplier's charges.

D.   All cash discounts on Agency's purchases including, but not limited to, media, art, printing and mechanical work, shall be available to Media User, provided that Media User meets Agency's requisite billing terms and there is no outstanding undisputed indebtedness of Media User to Agency at the time of the payment to the supplier.

E. Rate or billing adjustments shall be credited or charged to Media User on the next regular invoice date or as soon thereafter as otherwise practical.

F. Invoices shall be submitted in an itemized format and shall be paid by Media User within sixty (60) days of the invoice date.

6. Competitors.

During the term of this Agreement, Agency shall not accept employment from, render services to, represent or otherwise be affiliated with any person, firm, corporation or entity in connection with any product or service directly or indirectly competitive with or similar to any product or service of Media User with respect to which the Agency is providing any service pursuant to this Agreement, without the advance approval of the Media User. Media User shall not unreasonably withhold this approval.

7. Cost Estimates.

Agency shall not initiate billable work on any project pursuant to this Agreement without first estimating costs for preparation, including copy, service, layout, art, engraving, typography, processing, paste up and production. After determining the estimated cost, completion of the work shall be subject to Media User's prior approval.

8. Audit Rights.

Agency agrees that following reasonable prior notice any and all contracts, agreements, correspondence, books, accounts and other information relating to Media User's business or this Agreement shall be available for inspection by Media User and Media User's outside accountants, at Media User's expense and during the normal business hours of the Agency.

9. Ownership and Use.

A.   Agency shall insure, to the fullest extent possible under law, that Media User shall own all right, title and interest in and to, including copyrights, trade secret, patent and other intellectual property rights, with respect to any copy, photograph, advertisement, music, lyrics, video, or other work or thing created by Agency or at Agency's direction for Media User pursuant to this Agreement and utilized by Media User.

B.   Upon termination, Media User agrees that any advertising, merchandising, package, plan or idea prepared by Agency and submitted to Media User (whether submitted separately or in conjunction with or as a part of other material) which Media User has elected not to utilize, shall remain the property of Agency, unless Media User has paid Agency for its services in preparing such item. Media User agrees to return to Agency any copy, artwork, plates or other physical embodiment of such creative work relating to any such idea or plan which may be in Media User's possession at termination or expiration of this Agreement. Notwithstanding this, Media User has the unconditional right to pay for any of these materials or activities at the rate agreed upon in this Agreement and thereby these materials and activities would fall under the Section 9.A ownership and use rights accruing to Media User.

C.   Materials and advertisements created by Agency pursuant to this Agreement may be used by Media User outside the United States without additional compensation, provided that Media User shall

be responsible for any additional expense associated with such use, such as charges for translation and amounts due talent.

10. <u>Indemnification and Insurance</u>.

A. Agency shall indemnify and hold Media User harmless with respect to any claims, loss, suit, liability or judgment suffered by Media User, including reasonable attorney's fees and costs, based upon or related to any item prepared by Agency or at Agency's direction, including, but not limited to, any claim of libel, slander, piracy, plagiarism, invasion of privacy, or infringement of copyright or other intellectual property interest, except where any such claim arises out of material supplied by Media User and incorporated into any materials or advertisement prepared by Agency. Agency agrees to procure and maintain in force during the term of this Agreement, at Agency's expense, an Agency liability policy or policies having a minimum limit of at least _____, naming Media User as an additional insured and loss payee under such policy or policies.

B. Media User agrees to indemnify and hold Agency harmless with respect to any claims, loss, liability, damage or judgment suffered by Agency, including reasonable attorney's fees and court costs, which results from the use by Agency of any material furnished by Media User or where material created by Agency or at the direction of Agency subject to the indemnification in subsection A. above is materially changed by Media User. Information or data obtained by Agency from Media User to substantiate claims made in advertising shall be deemed to be "material furnished by Media User to Agency."

C. In the event of any proceeding, litigation or suit against Media User by any regulatory agency or in the event of any court action or other proceeding challenging any advertising prepared by Agency, Agency shall assist in the preparation of the defense of such action or proceeding and cooperate with Media User and Media User's attorneys.

11. <u>Term</u>.

The term of this Agreement shall commence on _____ and shall continue in full force and effect until terminated by either party upon at least sixty (60) days prior written notice, provided that in no event (except breach) may this Agreement be terminated prior to _____. The rights, duties and obligations of the parties shall continue in full force during or following the period of the termination notice until termination, including the ordering and billing of advertising in media whose closing dates follow then such period.

12. <u>Rights Upon Termination</u>.

A. Upon termination of the Agreement, Agency shall transfer, assign and make available to Media User all property and materials in Agency's possession or subject to Agency's control that are the property of Media User, subject to payment in full of amounts due pursuant to this Agreement.

B. Upon termination, Agency agrees to provide reasonable cooperation in arranging for the transfer or approval of third party's interest in all contracts, agreements and other arrangements with advertising media, suppliers, talent and others not then utilized, and all rights and claims thereto and therein, following appropriate release from the obligations therein.

13. <u>Default</u>.

In the event of any default of any material obligation by or owed by a party pursuant to this Agreement, then the other party may provide written notice of such default and if such default is not cured within ten (10) days of the written notice, then the nondefaulting party may terminate this Agreement. In addition, the only damages collectible by Agency shall be the exact amounts due; no other damages,

for any reason whatsoever, may be assessed against Media User including, but limited to, punitive damages and unreasonable termination charges, and any other such claim. This provision shall be broadly interpreted in the favor of the Media User by any Court of competent jurisdiction.

14. <u>Notices</u>.

Any notice required by this Agreement or given in connection with it, shall be in writing and shall be given to the appropriate party by personal delivery or by postage prepaid, or recognized overnight delivery services such as Federal Express.

If to Media User: _____

                     _____

If to Agency: _____

                     _____

15. <u>Headings in this Agreement</u>.

The headings in this Agreement are for convenience only, confirm no rights or obligations in either party, and do not alter any terms of this Agreement.

16. <u>Entirety of Agreement</u>.

The terms and conditions set forth herein constitute the entire agreement between the parties and supersede any communications or previous agreements with respect to the subject matter of this Agreement. There are no written or oral understandings directly or indirectly related to this Agreement that are not set forth herein. No change can be made to this Agreement other than in writing and signed by both parties.

17. <u>Governing Law</u>.

This Agreement shall be construed and enforced according to the laws of the State of _____ and any dispute under this Agreement must be brought in this venue and in no other.

In Witness whereof, the parties have executed this Agreement as of the date first written above.

_____   _____
Agency   Media User

Ad or other Media Agency Agreement

This Agency Agreement ("Agreement") is made and effective this _____ (Date), by and between ("Agency") and _____ (Your Firm) ("Media User").

Agency is in the business of providing media agency services for a fee.

Media User desires to engage Agency to render, and Agency desires to render to Media User, certain Agency services, all as set forth.

NOW, THEREFORE, in consideration of the mutual agreements and covenants herein contained, the parties hereto agree as follows:

1. <u>Engagement</u>.

Media User engages Agency to render, and Agency agrees to render to Media User, services in connection with Media User's planning, preparing and placing of advertising and other media services for certain of Media User's products as follows:

_____

A. Analyze Media User's current and proposed products and services and presentations and potential markets.

B. Create, prepare and submit to Media User for its prior approval advertising ideas, media suggestions, and other such related programs.

C. Prepare and submit to Media User for its prior approval estimates of costs and expenses associated with proposed advertising ideas and programs prior to any such implementation or financial commitment.

D. Design and prepare, or arrange for the design and preparation of advertisements, public relations, and other such materials.

E. Perform such other services as Media User may request from time to time such as, but not limited to, direct mail ad preparations, speech writing, publicity and public relations work, market research and analysis, and other similar and related activities.

F. Order advertising space, time or other means to be used for publication of Media User's advertisements, at all times endeavoring to secure the most efficient and advantageous rates available. All such activities to be approved in advance by the Media User unless otherwise written and stipulated.

G. Proof for accuracy and completeness of insertions, displays, broadcasts, or other forms of advertisements.

H. Audit invoices for proper and agreed upon space, time, material preparation and charges.

2. <u>Products</u>.

Agency's engagement shall relate to the following products and services of Media User:

_____.

3. Exclusivity.

Agency shall be the Agency in the United States and worldwide for Media User with respect to the products described in Section 2 above, unless otherwise specified in this section:

_____.

4.   Compensation.

A.   Agency shall receive an amount equal to ___ percentage of the gross charges levied by media for advertising placed by Agency pursuant to this Agreement; and   after volume discount, of the charges of suppliers of services or properties, such as finished art, comprehensive layouts, type composition, photostats, engravings, printing, radio and television programs, talent, literary, dramatic and musical works, records and exhibits, purchased by Agency on Media User's authorization during the term of this Agreement; provided that: No percentage will be added to Agency charges for packing, shipping, express, postage, telephone, telex, fax, travel expenses and other out of pocket expenses of Agency personnel.

B.   For those items where Agency is not compensated on a commission basis, Media User shall pay Agency on an hourly basis for services provided hereunder. The rate will be determined by the type of services provided and the person or persons providing such services, but in no event shall the rate exceed _____ per hour. Media User may elect in advance to be charged on this hourly rate basis. If Media User fails to notify Agency of its choice, it shall be presumed that Media User elected to be charged on a percentage basis.

C.   In the event that Agency undertakes, at Media User's request subject to Media User's prior approval, special projects such as those described in Section I.F above, Agency shall prepare an estimate of total charges for any such special project in advance, including any charges for materials or services purchased from outside vendors. In the event that Media User elects to proceed with the special project based upon Agency's estimated cost, Agency shall perform the services with respect to such special project at its estimated cost, subject to modification as mutually agreed by the parties.

D. For any special project or other services provided by Agency pursuant to this Agreement upon which the parties have not agreed as to charges, Media User shall pay
Agency at its regular percentage rates, as stated in Section 4.A above.

E.   Media User shall not be obligated to reimburse Agency for any travel or other out-of-pocket expenses incurred in the performance of services pursuant to this Agreement unless expressly agreed by Media User in advance.

5. Billing.

A.   Agency shall invoice Media User for all media costs where possible in advance of Agency's payment date to allow for prepayment by the Media User so that Media User may receive the benefit of any available prepayment or similar discount. For any media purchase or service for which Agency is not entitled to a commission, Agency shall ensure that the charges to Media User are net of all agency commissions and discounts.

B.   Charges for production materials and services shall be billed by Agency upon completion of the production job or, if cash discounts are available, upon receipt of the supplier's invoice.

C. On all outside purchases other than for media, Agency shall attach to the invoice evidence of the supplier's charges.

D. All cash discounts on Agency's purchases including, but not limited to, media, art, printing and mechanical work, shall be available to Media User, provided that Media User meets Agency's requisite billing terms and there is no outstanding undisputed indebtedness of Media User to Agency at the time of the payment to the supplier.

E. Rate or billing adjustments shall be credited or charged to Media User on the next regular invoice date or as soon thereafter as otherwise practical.

F. Invoices shall be submitted in an itemized format and shall be paid by Media User within sixty (60) days of the invoice date.

6. Competitors.

During the term of this Agreement, Agency shall not accept employment from, render services to, represent or otherwise be affiliated with any person, firm, corporation or entity in connection with any product or service directly or indirectly competitive with or similar to any product or service of Media User with respect to which the Agency is providing any service pursuant to this Agreement, without the advance approval of the Media User. Media User shall not unreasonably withhold this approval.

7. Cost Estimates.

Agency shall not initiate billable work on any project pursuant to this Agreement without first estimating costs for preparation, including copy, service, layout, art, engraving, typography, processing, paste up and production. After determining the estimated cost, completion of the work shall be subject to Media User's prior approval.

8. Audit Rights.

Agency agrees that following reasonable prior notice any and all contracts, agreements, correspondence, books, accounts and other information relating to Media User's business or this Agreement shall be available for inspection by Media User and Media User's outside accountants, at Media User's expense and during the normal business hours of the Agency.

9. Ownership and Use.

A. Agency shall insure, to the fullest extent possible under law, that Media User shall own all right, title and interest in and to, including copyrights, trade secret, patent and other intellectual property rights, with respect to any copy, photograph, advertisement, music, lyrics, video, or other work or thing created by Agency or at Agency's direction for Media User pursuant to this Agreement and utilized by Media User.

B. Upon termination, Media User agrees that any advertising, merchandising, package, plan or idea prepared by Agency and submitted to Media User (whether submitted separately or in conjunction with or as a part of other material) which Media User has elected not to utilize, shall remain the property of Agency, unless Media User has paid Agency for its services in preparing such item. Media User agrees to return to Agency any copy, artwork, plates or other physical embodiment of such creative work relating to any such idea or plan which may be in Media User's possession at termination or expiration of this Agreement. Notwithstanding this, Media User has the unconditional right to pay for any of these materials or activities at the rate agreed upon in this Agreement and thereby these materials and activities would fall under the Section 9.A ownership and use rights accruing to Media User.

C. Materials and advertisements created by Agency pursuant to this Agreement may be used by Media User outside the United States without additional compensation, provided that Media User shall

be responsible for any additional expense associated with such use, such as charges for translation and amounts due talent.

10. Indemnification and Insurance.

A. Agency shall indemnify and hold Media User harmless with respect to any claims, loss, suit, liability or judgment suffered by Media User, including reasonable attorney's fees and costs, based upon or related to any item prepared by Agency or at Agency's direction, including, but not limited to, any claim of libel, slander, piracy, plagiarism, invasion of privacy, or infringement of copyright or other intellectual property interest, except where any such claim arises out of material supplied by Media User and incorporated into any materials or advertisement prepared by Agency. Agency agrees to procure and maintain in force during the term of this Agreement, at Agency's expense, an Agency liability policy or policies having a minimum limit of at least _____, naming Media User as an additional insured and loss payee under such policy or policies.

B. Media User agrees to indemnify and hold Agency harmless with respect to any claims, loss, liability, damage or judgment suffered by Agency, including reasonable attorney's fees and court costs, which results from the use by Agency of any material furnished by Media User or where material created by Agency or at the direction of Agency subject to the indemnification in subsection A. above is materially changed by Media User. Information or data obtained by Agency from Media User to substantiate claims made in advertising shall be deemed to be "material furnished by Media User to Agency."

C. In the event of any proceeding, litigation or suit against Media User by any regulatory agency or in the event of any court action or other proceeding challenging any advertising prepared by Agency, Agency shall assist in the preparation of the defense of such action or proceeding and cooperate with Media User and Media User's attorneys.

11. Term.

The term of this Agreement shall commence on _____ and shall continue in full force and effect until terminated by either party upon at least sixty (60) days prior written notice, provided that in no event (except breach) may this Agreement be terminated prior to _____. The rights, duties and obligations of the parties shall continue in full force during or following the period of the termination notice until termination, including the ordering and billing of advertising in media whose closing dates follow then such period.

12. Rights Upon Termination.

A. Upon termination of the Agreement, Agency shall transfer, assign and make available to Media User all property and materials in Agency's possession or subject to Agency's control that are the property of Media User, subject to payment in full of amounts due pursuant to this Agreement.

B. Upon termination, Agency agrees to provide reasonable cooperation in arranging for the transfer or approval of third party's interest in all contracts, agreements and other arrangements with advertising media, suppliers, talent and others not then utilized, and all rights and claims thereto and therein, following appropriate release from the obligations therein.

13. Default.

In the event of any default of any material obligation by or owed by a party pursuant to this Agreement, then the other party may provide written notice of such default and if such default is not cured within ten (10) days of the written notice, then the nondefaulting party may terminate this Agreement. In addition, the only damages collectible by Agency shall be the exact amounts due; no other damages,

for any reason whatsoever, may be assessed against Media User including, but limited to, punitive damages and unreasonable termination charges, and any other such claim. This provision shall be broadly interpreted in the favor of the Media User by any Court of competent jurisdiction.

14. Notices.

Any notice required by this Agreement or given in connection with it, shall be in writing and shall be given to the appropriate party by personal delivery or by postage prepaid, or recognized overnight delivery services such as Federal Express.

If to Media User: _____

_____

If to Agency: _____

_____

15. Headings in this Agreement.

The headings in this Agreement are for convenience only, confirm no rights or obligations in either party, and do not alter any terms of this Agreement.

16. Entirety of Agreement.

The terms and conditions set forth herein constitute the entire agreement between the parties and supersede any communications or previous agreements with respect to the subject matter of this Agreement. There are no written or oral understandings directly or indirectly related to this Agreement that are not set forth herein. No change can be made to this Agreement other than in writing and signed by both parties.

17. Governing Law.

This Agreement shall be construed and enforced according to the laws of the State of _____ and any dispute under this Agreement must be brought in this venue and in no other.

In Witness whereof, the parties have executed this Agreement as of the date first written above.

_____ _____
Agency   Media User

Printed in Great Britain
by Amazon